THE ELEMENTS

of

REASONING

Fifth Edition

Ronald Munson
University of Missouri—St. Louis

Andrew Black
University of Missouri—St. Louis

THOMSON
WADSWORTH

Australia • Brazil • Canada • Mexico • Singapore
Spain • United Kingdom • United States

THOMSON
™
WADSWORTH

Publisher: Holly J. Allen
Acquisition Editor: Steve Wainwright
Assistant Editors: Lee McCracken,
  Barbara Hillaker
Editorial Assistant: Gina Kessler
Technology Project Manager:
  Julie Aguilar
Marketing Manager: Worth Hawes
Marketing Assistant: Alexandra Tran
Marketing Communications Manager:
  Stacey Purviance
Creative Director: Rob Hugel

Executive Art Director: Maria Epes
Print Buyer: Nora Massuda
Permissions Editor: Roberta Broyer
Production Service: International
  Typesetting and Composition
Copy Editor: Peggy Tropp
Cover Designer: Bill Stanton
Cover Pattern: Jason Reed/Getty Images
Cover Printer: Phoenix Color
Compositor: International Typesetting
  and Composition
Text Printer: Courier, Westford

Library of Congress Control Number:
2005938046

ISBN 049500698X

Thomson Higher Education
10 Davis Drive
Belmont, CA 94002-3098
USA

For more information about our
products, contact us at:
**Thomson Learning Academic
Resource Center
1-800-423-0563**

For permission to use material from
this text or product, submit a request
online at
http://www.thomsonrights.com.
Any additional questions about permissions can be submitted by e-mail to
thomsonrights@thomson.com.

R.M.
To the memory of my father Callen Lemuel Munson

A.B.
To the memory of my grandmother, Anne Duggan

We dedicate this edition to the memory of our colleague and collaborator David Conway

Modest and good humored, he would find such ostentation as this both embarrassing and amusing. That's some of what we miss about him.

CONTENTS

Acknowledgments

We would like to thank the following reviewers for their input:

Bryan Baird, University of Georgia
Christina Benac, Ball State University
Paul Newberry, California State University, Bakersfield
Eugene Thomas Rice, Fort Hays State University

ORIENTATION

Reasoning is an ancient subject but an everyday practice.

We are all able to reason. Someone totally unable to assess claims and arrive at conclusions would believe anything and act in wild and arbitrary ways. That we usually don't behave in such a fashion shows how we rely on reasoning to guide our actions and ground our beliefs.

This book aims to improve reasoning skills and to enhance effective thinking. Although everyone is able to reason, this doesn't mean we always reason well. The skills of reasoning can be improved by experience, but they can also be improved by example and instruction. (Even a talented and experienced tennis player can become better through coaching.) We're concerned here with what we do when we reason well and with some of the ways we can go wrong. We're also concerned with what to look for when trying to understand and evaluate the reasoning of others. (How do we recognize an argument? How do we assess its worth?)

This book offers a set of intellectual tools to employ in the process of understanding, supporting, and testing claims. These tools are the principles, distinctions, and methods that have been developed by generations of philosophers, logicians, essayists, scientists, critics, and thinkers of all kinds.

Little here is new, but much is useful.

Basic Assumptions

Five basic assumptions have guided and shaped this book:

1. Everyone is already skilled to a degree in the rational process of analyzing, defending, and evaluating claims.

2. Everyone can improve such skills by becoming aware of the principles behind them and by doing deliberately what is usually done unreflectively.

3. The principles are not imposed from the outside but are implicit in the ordinary practices of defending and evaluating claims. We are rational creatures, even though we do not always act

rationally. We have found that these principles, when followed, produce the best overall results.

4. It is good to have some general guidelines in defending, analyzing, and evaluating claims—even if the guidelines are not always strictly accurate and reliable.

5. These guidelines can be presented in a brief but still useful way.

Organization

In this new edition, the changes are not numerous, but they are important. We corrected various infelicities, rewrote potentially confusing passages, and corrected several small errors. We also added some new explanatory material. We expanded our treatment of the differences between argument and explanation and extended the discussion of the importance of context in recognizing and analyzing arguments.

We added a large number of fresh, focused, and relevant exercises. We avoided contrived cases in favor of actual or realistic examples. A book like this, we believe, should offer no less. We also prepared a large number of supplemental exercises that will be available on the instructor's resource website.

Using This Book

The book may be read straight through, but each chapter can also be read by itself. Those not interested in technical matters may want to skip the chapters on valid argument forms, while those concerned mostly with rational arguments may wish to ignore the chapters on definition and on vagueness and ambiguity. The book does not presuppose any specialized knowledge. Each topic should be accessible to anyone, although some topics are inherently difficult and require more effort to understand than others. Technical terms are kept to a minimum and explained as they are introduced. References to additional discussions of a topic are scattered throughout the book.

The book's compact size should make it possible for someone to gain a quick grasp of a wide range of topics connected with rational analysis and argument. The book aims to be accurate as well as brief. Yet keep in mind that each topic discussed has been the sole subject of more than one book, and many important distinctions and qualifications have been passed over silently.

The justification for this approach is simple and powerful: This book is intended to be useful in an immediate and practical way. It is more of a handbook than an encyclopedia.

Chapter 1

RECOGNIZING ARGUMENTS

Arguments are the instruments we use in rational persuasion. Whenever we want to persuade someone of the reasonableness of a position we consider correct, we present arguments in its favor. We also use arguments to express our reasoning even when we have no concern with persuading others. In this chapter, we define the concept of an argument, explain how to recognize an argument, and introduce some standard terms for discussing arguments.

I. What Is an Argument?

To give an argument is to make a claim and to offer other claims as reasons for its acceptance. Thus, an **argument** is a set of claims, one of which is meant to be supported by the others.

This is not an argument:

> By the end of September in New England, the leaves are already changing to beautiful browns and reds. The nights are cooler, and the days are noticeably shorter. Some inhabitants begin to feel a sense of dread as they think of the long winter to come.

Several claims are made in this passage, but as no one of them is offered as a reason for any other, we have no argument.

This, however, is an argument:

> The only possible superpower in the world other than the United States is a unified Europe. But divisions and jealousies that date back centuries ensure that Europe will never present a truly unified front. Obviously, then, the United States will continue to be the world's only superpower.

This, too, is an argument:

> She's armed, so she's dangerous.

In both passages, some claims are offered as support for another claim. That means both contain arguments.

A **conclusion** is a claim meant to be supported by reasons offered in the argument. A **premise** is a claim put forth as a reason for a conclusion. Using these terms, we can say that an argument is a set of claims that can be divided into a conclusion and one or more premises. (Argument = conclusion + premises.)

The two arguments above are made up of premises and conclusions in the following ways:

PREMISE 1:   The only possible superpower in the world other than the United States is a united Europe.

PREMISE 2:   Divisions and jealousies that date back centuries ensure that Europe will never present a truly unified front.

CONCLUSION: The United States will continue to be the world's only superpower.

PREMISE: She's armed.

CONCLUSION: She's dangerous.

These two arguments are presented here in a form that makes it quite clear which claims are the premises and which the conclusion in each case. In Chapter 2, we will be examining procedures for presenting arguments in this kind of clear pattern, which we will call "standard form." Each time we move from a premise or set of premises to a conclusion, we **infer** or make an **inference**. (The *move from* the premise(s) to the conclusion is the inference.) In the last example, an inference (a move) is made to "She's dangerous." In the first, we infer from

---

Implying is different from *inferring,* though their meanings are often confused. Implication is a relation between statements. "This is a leap year" *implies* "this is an even-numbered year." Knowing it to be a leap year, a person may correctly *infer* that it is an even-numbered year. (Or she might incorrectly infer something mistaken, such as that it is an odd-numbered year.)

We do sometimes talk of a person implying something: the boss calls Bill into her office and tells him that his chronic tardiness has left him on thin ice at the firm. At home, Bill sadly reports, "The boss wasn't very explicit, but she implied that I would be fired if I kept arriving late for work." This is a way of saying that the boss's words implied (had the implication) that Bill is in danger of being fired. Bill infers that he is in danger of having his job terminated. *Statements imply; people infer.*

premises 1 and 2 that "The United States will continue to be the world's only superpower." Each of these arguments involves a single inference.

II. Three General Considerations

A. Length of Arguments

Our examples of arguments have been brief, but an argument may be any length. Some books are best regarded as giving one elaborate argument for a single conclusion. For instance, the whole point of some books is to make a case that the earth was visited by creatures from outer space thousands of years ago; others argue that capitalism is an evil economic system or that eating meat is immoral. Yet, despite its brevity, "She's armed, so she's dangerous" is no less an argument than these.

Arguments may occur in any context and involve any subject matter. We find arguments in mathematical treatises, newspaper editorials, and sociological, philosophical, and literary journals, as well as in barroom conversations, exchanges between sports fans, familial discussions about how to budget a limited income, and other everyday situations. Further, the subject matter can be trivial ("You better get your feet off the coffee table. Mother's coming.") or profound ("Innocent children suffer and die every day in this world. That shows life has no meaning.").

B. Arguments and Disputes

An argument in our sense is not a dispute. ("Neighbors called the police because the newlyweds were having a terrible argument.") People disputing might use arguments in an attempt to bring about agreement (or they might just yell), but the *arguments* they might offer would not be the same thing as the *dispute* they are having.

C. Arguments and Bad Arguments

An argument can fail for any number of reasons. Its premises may be false, or irrelevant, or provide inadequate support for the conclusion. For example, the premises in this argument give little or no support for its conclusion:

It hasn't rained in weeks. That means it is sure to rain tomorrow.

In later chapters we discuss ways in which arguments can be flawed. For now we want to emphasize only that whenever a set of claims is given, one of which is meant to be supported by the others, then an argument is given. If the claims offered as support are false or if they do not support the intended conclusion very well, the argument is a bad one. The argument may be so bad that we are led to exclaim, "That's not an argument at all!" Nevertheless, a bad argument is just as much an argument as a bad egg is an egg.

III. Recognizing Arguments

We first consider in this section some useful markers for identifying premises and conclusions. These help us both in recognizing arguments and in analyzing them. We then show how parts of arguments may be implicit—intended even though not explicitly stated. Finally, we consider the role that questions, commands, and other nondeclarative sentences can play in arguments.

A. Inference Indicators

Our definition of "argument" tells us that the claims that constitute premises are *meant* to support the conclusion. This means that an argument is a matter of intention. Taking the claims by themselves, it is not necessarily clear when this intention is present. Consider this example:

> Today is the 5th. Yesterday was the 4th.

Is this an argument? If it is, what is the premise and what is the conclusion? No straightforward answers are possible because the passage can be understood in three different ways.

1. The first sentence might be meant as a premise and the second as a conclusion:

   PREMISE: Today is the 5th.

   CONCLUSION: Yesterday was the 4th.

2. The first sentence might be meant as a conclusion and the second as a premise:

   PREMISE: Yesterday was the 4th.

   CONCLUSION: Today is the 5th.

3. The sentences might be meant as just two related observations with no inference intended:

   > Today is the 5th, and yesterday was the 4th.

Many cases are of this sort. Here is a more serious one: "All people are corrupt by nature. Everyone around me is corrupt." Is the first claim meant as a reason for the second or the second as a reason for the first? Or perhaps there is not any argument here and neither claim is intended as a reason for the other.

In both these examples, unless we are given more to go on, we have no grounds for choosing among the different interpretations. All we can do is note the possible interpretations and leave matters at that.

Suppose the first example said: "Today is the 5th. *So* yesterday was the 4th." Or this: "*Since* today is the 5th, yesterday was the 4th." Either of these additions makes clear that an argument is being offered and that "Yesterday was the 4th" is its conclusion.

Similarly, the second passage would not be puzzling if it said "All people are corrupt by nature. *Thus*, everyone around me is corrupt." Nor would there be a problem if it said "*Because* all people are corrupt by nature, everyone around me is corrupt." Here too the added words remove the ambiguity. We do have an argument, the first sentence being the premise, the second the conclusion.

The words we added help by "flagging" premises or conclusions. Words or phrases that do this are called **inference indicators**. There are two sorts of inference indicators. **Conclusion indicators** are words

---

Some other common CONCLUSION indicators are:

Therefore	Hence
Consequently	We may conclude
It follows that	This entails that
Which shows that	Here are some of the reasons why

Other PREMISE indicators include:

Since	Because
For	For the reason that
Seeing as	As is implied by
The reason is that	On account of the fact that

Many words and phrases just join sentences and should not be mistaken for inference indicators. Examples are:

And	But
Also	Nevertheless
Besides	In addition

These words can equally introduce claims that are premises, conclusions, or not any part of an argument at all.

These lists are not exhaustive, and generally we must rely on our knowledge of language to recognize when other inference indicators are present.

used to indicate that a conclusion is about to be drawn. In the examples in the last three paragraphs, the italicized words *so* and *thus* play this role. **Premise indicators** are words used to indicate that a premise is about to be given. In our examples, *since* and *because* are premise indicators.

Note that the occurrence of a listed word is not an infallible indication that an inference is being drawn. For example:

> *Since* lightning struck his bedroom, he has been acting peculiarly.

> Starting with the ace, she played next the king, then the queen. *Thus*, she played the entire suit until the deuce was reached and the game was won.

Since and *thus* do not serve as inference indicators in these cases. *Since* as used here means "ever since" and tells us about a temporal relationship. The *thus* in the second case means something like "in this way," rather than "therefore." Indicator words help, but sensitivity to language and context is always necessary for recognizing when an argument is intended.

B. Unstated (Implicit) Premises and Conclusions

In the absence of indicator words, the context in which an argument is presented often serves to make it clear what is intended as premise and what as conclusion, or indeed whether an argument is intended at all. For example, consider the following:

> The victim's car was last seen driving down Green Street at 10 P.M.; Smith left the pool hall at about that time; the murder took place after that time.

A journalist might state these facts simply as a matter of report, without intending to establish any conclusion. On the other hand, a detective convinced of Smith's guilt might use the first two claims as support for the third. Finally, a lawyer might use all three claims as evidence for the further conclusion that Smith is the murderer.

That last possibility also shows that context and our knowledge of language can help with another problem in recognizing arguments. Arguments can have premises or conclusions that are implicit—that is, not openly or explicitly stated. An implicit premise or conclusion is a genuine part of an argument if it is clear that the person giving the argument *meant* it to be understood this way. Arguments that have implicit premises or conclusions are called **enthymemes**.

Realizing when a sentence is implicit is seldom difficult. Consider this advertisement:

> The bigger the burger the better the burger.
> The burgers are bigger at Burger King.

The intended but unstated conclusion is obvious:

> The burgers are better at Burger King.

Advertising copywriters count on our being able to see the unstated conclusion, and they are right to do so.

Similarly, suppose someone argues that

> Herman cannot be the person who robbed the lingerie emporium, because Herman does not have a snake tattoo on his left arm.

We can be sure the unstated premise is

> The robber of the emporium has a snake tattoo on his left arm.

At times we cannot be sure if there is an unstated premise or conclusion. At other times we are sure *something* is intended, but we cannot be sure what that something is. In either case, we simply consider the argument as it is explicitly stated. The job of the author of the argument is to make it tolerably clear what her intentions are.

C. Questions, Commands, Exclamations, and Exhortations

Arguments are sets of *claims,* so questions, commands, exclamations, and exhortations cannot be parts of arguments because they make no claims. A claim is an assertion of fact, and ordinarily we express claims by uttering declarative sentences—the kinds of sentences that can be true or false. "It is now 2 o'clock" is a declarative sentence expressing a claim. You can easily check whether this sentence is true or false. However, the sentence "What time is it?" expresses a question and is neither true nor false. Nevertheless, we need to be aware that in everyday language grammatical questions, commands, and so on may have the force of making claims. You ask a friend to meet you at the beach at 3 A.M. to watch the underwater submarine races and the friend indignantly replies, "What kind of a fool do you think I am?" This is not really a question. (*You* would look the fool if you tried to give a serious answer.) It is a statement denying being a fool or being the sort of fool who would fall for such a suggestion. When a football player makes one incredible play after another and a fan shouts out, "What a great quarterback!" the fan is saying that the player *is* a great quarterback.

This means that passages like the following may be recognized as giving arguments:

> Clouds are rolling in, and the wind is picking up. Go check the boat *now*!

> Don't you know that no decent poetry has been written since T. S. Eliot died, and even he wasn't in the same class as Yeats? How can you possibly say that poetry is getting better?

In any ordinary situation, each of these cases would be understood as offering reasons for a claim. It would be natural and correct to represent them this way:

PREMISE 1:	Clouds are rolling in.
PREMISE 2:	The wind is picking up.
CONCLUSION:	You should go check the boat *now*.

PREMISE 1:	No decent poetry has been written since T. S. Eliot died.
PREMISE 2:	Eliot was not in the same class as Yeats.
Conclusion:	Poetry is not getting better.

At times we must look beyond the literal forms of sentences. If the real point of what is said is to make claims meant to be understood as premises and conclusion, then what is said should be regarded as an argument.

IV. Multiple Conclusions and Complex Arguments

Arguments sometimes appear to have more than one conclusion. In addition, some long arguments seem to have small arguments as components. How can we reconcile these features with our characterization of an argument as consisting of a single conclusion and one or more premises? We begin by considering the matter of multiple conclusions, then look at the distinction between simple and complex arguments.

A. Single or Multiple Conclusions?

We said earlier that an argument can be book length. Do these book-length arguments really have just one conclusion? Also, length aside, aren't there cases where we would want to say a single argument is offered even though more than one conclusion seems present?

Here is one sort of case where it may seem we have a single argument but more than one conclusion:

> Erlich forgot to pay his gas bill again. It looks like the poor guy is obsessed with finishing the novel he has been writing. Anyway, he sure will be cold this winter.

We might take this to be a single argument with two conclusions:

PREMISE: Erlich forgot to pay his gas bill again.

CONCLUSION 1:   Erlich is obsessed with finishing the novel
                 he is writing.

CONCLUSION 2:   Erlich will be cold this winter.

If we understand the argument in this way, the result is not disastrous. Yet what we really have here are two essentially independent inferences (two conclusions being drawn) with the same premise. And, in terms of sense or worth, the inferences have little to do with one another. Such independence indicates that a case like this is better thought of as involving two different arguments, not a single argument with two different conclusions.

The argument is best understood in this way:

PREMISE: Erlich forgot to pay his gas bill again.

Conclusion: Erlich is obsessed with finishing the novel
              he is writing.

And separately:

PREMISE: Erlich forgot to pay his gas bill again.

CONCLUSION: Erlich will be cold this winter.

Thus, if we draw multiple conclusions from a single premise (or set of premises), we are dealing with several different arguments. We are not dealing with one argument with several conclusions.

B. Simple and Complex Arguments

Now consider a different sort of case, another one where a single argument seems to contain more than one conclusion:

> If the crippling debts of Third World nations can be eased, then the national economies of these countries can start to grow at a healthy rate. And if these economies can experience growth, then millions of people can work their way out of poverty and starvation. Fortunately, it is possible to ease the debts of these nations; thus their economies can experience growth. Therefore it is possible for millions of the world's poorest people to find their way out of the cycle of poverty.

There are two inferences here:

Premise 1:	If the debts of Third World nations can be eased, then the national economies of these countries can start to grow at a healthy rate.
PREMISE 2:	The debts of Third World nations can be eased.
CONCLUSION:	The national economies of these nations can grow at a healthy rate.

Furthermore:

PREMISE 1:	If the economies of debtor nations can start to grow at a healthy rate, then millions of people can work their way out of poverty.
PREMISE 2:	The national economies of these nations can grow at a healthy rate.
CONCLUSION:	Millions of people can work their way out of poverty.

Although two inferences are present, the intention in the original passage is clearly to present a single, uninterrupted chain of reasoning aimed at concluding that millions of people can work their way out of poverty and starvation. Thus, in considering either the sense or the worth of the reasoning, we must treat this passage as a single unit. It is one argument, not two joined together.

With such cases in mind, we can distinguish two types of conclusions. First, there are conclusions used as premises in a continuing chain of reasoning. In this case "the national economies of debtor nations can grow at a healthy rate" is such a conclusion. We will call these **intermediate conclusions.** Second, there is the conclusion that is not itself a premise for anything else but the argument's final point. "Millions of people can work their way out of poverty" is such a conclusion in this case. We will call this the **final conclusion.**

Arguments with no intermediate conclusions we call **simple arguments.** When an argument has at least one intermediate conclusion, we will call it a **complex argument.** A complex argument can have any number of intermediate conclusions, but no argument can have more than one final conclusion.

Because to draw a conclusion is to make an inference, a simple argument can also be characterized as an argument that consists of only one inference; a complex argument consists of more than one inference. In the next chapter, we will examine ways of showing the structure of simple and complex arguments, with a view to evaluating them more effectively.

A number of crucial concepts were presented in this chapter. In summary:

An **argument** is a set of claims, one of which is meant to be supported by the others.

A **conclusion** is a claim meant to be supported by reasons offered in an argument.

A **premise** is a claim put forth as a reason for a conclusion.

(Argument = conclusion + premises)

An **inference** is a move from premises in an argument to a conclusion.

Inference indicators include premise and conclusion indicators.

Conclusion indicators are words used to indicate that a conclusion is about to be drawn.

Premise indicators are words used to indicate that a premise is about to be given.

Enthymemes are arguments that have implicit (unstated) premises or conclusions.

An **intermediate conclusion** in an argument is a claim that is supported by some other claim or claims, but that itself also provides support for a further conclusion.

The **final conclusion** of an argument is the argument's final point, the conclusion that is not itself a premise for anything else in that argument.

Simple arguments are arguments that have no intermediate conclusions (that contain only one inference).

Complex arguments are arguments that have at least one intermediate conclusion (contain more than one inference).

Exercises

A. *Decide whether each passage should be thought of as containing no argument, one argument, or more than one argument.*

For each argument, determine whether it is simple or complex (whether it contains only one or more than one inference), pick out any premise or conclusion indicators, and identify each premise and conclusion.

The exercises marked with an asterisk (*) are addressed at the end of the book.

*1. The snow is making driving conditions very dangerous. But I must still go out and vote even though my candidate has no chance of winning.

2. Smallpox is no longer a threat to anyone in the United States. And the vaccination against it is unpleasant and, in rare cases, life-threatening. We were wise when we ceased the routine vaccination of our children.

*3. Herbert had the highest score on the qualifying exam, and so he will get first consideration for the job. The person who gets first consideration almost always does get the job. Thus, it is pretty sure that the job will go to Herbert.

4. The substance was dissolved in dilute hydrochloric acid. A pungent smell was given off. Finally, a milky precipitate was observed at the bottom of the beaker.

*5. It looks like a duck! It sounds like a duck! It even walks like a duck! It must be a duck.

6. It is not difficult to program computers so that they "learn" from their mistakes. Thus, computers will soon exceed the abilities of humans at complex games such as chess or bridge. That makes it obvious that computers *think*.

*7. Cheetah basketball begins again on November 1st with Midnight Madness at the Cheetahdome! Get your tickets from the box office or the Student Center bookstore starting tomorrow.

8. The Taipei study of the spread of SARS doesn't establish its conclusion at all. The sample for the study was too small and wholly unrepresentative of the total population.

*9. Charlene Brown, executive chef at the Moulin Restaurant, offers one of the most exciting new menus in town. Her poached salmon with red pepper coulis is particularly inspired, and her attention to detail in her presentation is unparalleled.

10. You should stop killing every spider you see. Spiders help keep down the insect population, and most of them pose no threat to people.

*11. Duchamp's *Urinal* is considered an important work of modern art. The thing is nothing you can't find in any men's room. Modern art is garbage.

12. Stop disagreeing with everything the boss says! I can tell she is getting angry. And you don't want to lose your promotion, do you?

*13. An Oregon man said his wife had the right to commit suicide: "It's not a matter of how long you live but the quality of life you live, and it was her life and her decision and she chose. She could not do the things she loved most anymore."

14. Bamboo can grow up to four feet a day, but only after it is well established. This can take from three to five years, depending on the type of bamboo.

*15. As much as I hate to be on the side of the liberals, we definitely should not have a constitutional amendment banning flag burning. Such an amendment would be the first ever to affect a freedom guaranteed by the First Amendment. Besides, flag burners may think they are showing disrespect by burning the flag of their country, but by being allowed to do so, they prove to the world that this country practices the freedom it preaches.

16. Blaise Pascal realized that there were certain significant consequences of Torricelli's hypothesis that the Earth is surrounded by a dense sea of air. Among these were that barometers at different altitudes would contain mercury columns of differing heights. So, being a sickly fellow, he persuaded his brother-in-law to do a spot of climbing in order to test out the hypothesis. Thus was Torricelli's hypothesis comprehensively confirmed.

*17. Recently, cultural anthropologists have disagreed over whether cannibalism was ever widespread and whether it exists at all today. "Cannibals are largely creatures of our own surmise," says one. "Ritual or habitual cannibalism is rare or nonexistent: There are no reliable, first-hand witnesses of the practice, and almost all reports are based on hearsay."—*Skeptical Inquirer* (January/February 1988)

18. "Mountains of statistics suggest that the public is far more susceptible to scientific nonsense than political nonsense. More than half of Americans are unaware that the earth orbits the sun and takes a year to do it. Many people simply do not have the tools to distinguish charlatans from honest researchers."—*New York Times* (February 22, 1999)

*19. "Copyright laws are based on an underlying social value that is at the heart of our society:

> *People have the right to compensation*
> *for their creative work.*

"Why is this considered a beneficial social value? Because compensating people encourages more creative works and our society benefits from these works.

"So what is the alternative to copyright laws? Let's imagine a world where a person's creative work automatically becomes the property of society to do with as it wishes. With no chance to sell or market their works, how would creative people pay for their food and rent? Government support? Rich patrons? What kinds of works do you think would be created by people whose only support comes from the government and the wealthy?"—Nancy E. Willard, *The CyberEthics Reader*, McGraw-Hill, 1997, p. 55

20. "It forms a strong presumption against all supernatural and miraculous relations [that is, all miracles] that they are observed chiefly to abound among ignorant and barbarous nations; or if a civilized people has ever given admission to any of them, that people will be found to have received them from ignorant and barbarous ancestors."—David Hume, *An Inquiry Concerning Human Understanding*, Section X

B. *Each passage contains an argument that can plausibly be understood as having an unstated conclusion or premise(s). Determine what the argument is and supply the unstated premise(s) or conclusion.*

*1. Duchamp's *Urinal* deliberately leads us to see an ordinary object in a new and interesting way. Thus, it is rightly regarded as a genuine work of art.

2. Today is Tuesday, so this must be the day of the test.

*3. Any public official guilty of negligent conduct ought to resign. Admittedly, Lopez has been an excellent governor of this state, but she was remiss in failing to notice the bribes being taken by her chief of staff.

4. No pit bull can be trusted around children. So we certainly can't trust Tiny with the baby.

*5. It is very sad considering all her years of practice. But Hovey has used steroids, and if a person has used steroids, there is no justification for allowing that person to compete.

6. Abortion takes a life. So it's murder.

*7. Abortion kills a living human being. So it's murder.

8. Many philosophers have tried to distinguish between what they called *just* and *unjust* wars. But all war causes the suffering of innocent people. So there can be no such thing as a just war.

*9. "I found that my senses sometimes deceive me, and it is a mark of prudence never to trust completely those who have deceived us even once." —René Descartes, *Meditations*

10. Golf is a very difficult game to play well, but it is not a sport. It does not require foot speed, stamina, or quick reflexes.

*11. If there were a god, he or she would both want to and be able to prevent evil. But the world is awash in evil.

12. We may not like Mr. Whewell's wearing the American flag as a skirt, but it is a form of expression. Thus, it is constitutionally protected.

*13. The fraternity-sponsored "Sexy Legs Contest" must be outlawed at once. It is just plain offensive to a lot of us.

14. The drunk who drove his car into little Mary Jones took her life, so he deserves to lose his own life.

*15. "If everything can not-be, then at one time there was nothing in existence. Therefore, if everything can not-be, even now there would be nothing in existence." —St. Thomas Aquinas, *The Third Way*

16. "A child who has received no religious instruction and has never heard about God, is not an atheist—for he is not denying any theistic claims." —Ernest Nagel, "A Defense of Atheism"

*17. When I look at the coffee table, what I see changes. Looking straight down on the table, it looks to be of a certain size and perfectly square. As I move farther away, the size diminishes and the angles I see are no longer 90 degrees. The color is a dark and uniform brown from one side but a washed-out shiny brown from the other side as the sun reflects from the surface. What I really see, then, is not the table itself but something else.

18. Many of us become very attached to our animal friends and come to think of them as reasoning in the way we do. But the fact remains that without language nothing can reason in the full sense, and dogs, cats, horses, and other animals do not have genuine language.

*19. Elementary, my dear Watson! Whoever killed the young man was an extraordinarily accurate shot, and, assuming the killer was from London's criminal world, the only criminal with that superb a shot in London is Colonel Sebastian Moran.

20. We should all seek happiness. For we should seek that which is desirable. And happiness is desirable since it is desired by everyone.

Chapter 2

ANALYZING ARGUMENTS

Recognizing that an argument has been presented on a given occasion is a necessary step on the way to evaluating the arguer's reasoning. In this chapter we will be exploring the next step on the way to this evaluative goal. Once we have decided a passage contains an argument, we want to identify its premises and conclusion and the relationship between them. This task is not always an easy one. Arguments may deal with difficult subject matter, be stated in obscure language, or be long and complex. Nevertheless, with practice we can become skilled at analyzing arguments. In this chapter we discuss some useful techniques for dealing with difficult arguments.

I. Showing the Structure of Arguments

For both understanding and evaluating arguments, it is important to have clear ways of exhibiting how their sentences are related to one another.

A. Simple Arguments: Standard Form

So far we have shown the structure of arguments by labeling premises and conclusions. Other ways of showing the structure of arguments are clearer and more efficient. Some are variations on what is frequently called **standard form.**

We can put simple arguments (arguments with only one inference) into standard form just by listing the premises one after another, drawing a line, then stating the conclusion:

> Strikes by public employees are illegal.
> The teachers at PS 197 are public employees.
> ―――――――――――――――――――――
> The strike by the teachers at PS 197 is illegal.

Putting our argument in this form serves the purpose of graphically representing everything we need to know in order to evaluate the argument. The whole of our evaluation will consist in answering the questions "Are the premises true?" and "Is the inference logically success-ful?" The standard form for a simple argument shows us precisely which claims are the premises and precisely what inference has been drawn.

B. Complex Arguments: Standard Form

We need a more sophisticated way to exhibit the structure of com-plex arguments. Consider this argument:

> Congress continues to support the president's goal of reducing taxes, so those with income will have more of it to spend. Furthermore, more people can afford to buy their own home since the slow economy is keeping interest rates at an all-time low. For these reasons, those Americans who are employed are enjoy-ing unusually good economic fortune.

To exhibit the structure of this complex argument in standard form:

1. Arrange the claims so the premises come before the conclusion they support. Do this for both the intermediate conclusions and the final one.
2. Number the premises and conclusions in the revised order.
3. After each conclusion, write the number of the premise (or premises) that supports it.

The structure of an argument represented in this way is immedi-ately clear. A line without a number on its right is a premise; a line with a number on its right is a conclusion; the numbers on the right tell us the premises for that conclusion. Once again, this shows us everything we need to know in order to evaluate the reasoning.

Applying this procedure to our example, we get the result:

1. Congress continues to support the president's goal of reducing taxes.
2. Those with income will have more of it to spend. 1
3. The slow economy is keeping interest rates at an all-time low.
4. More people can afford to buy their own home. 3
5. Those Americans who are employed are enjoying unusually good economic fortune. 2, 4

This shows that line 2 is an intermediate conclusion supported by line 1, and that line 4 is an intermediate conclusion supported by line 3. The final conclusion is expressed in 5, and the intermediate conclu-sions 2 and 4 support it.

C. Diagrams

How do we go about putting an argument in standard form? This is the important business of argument analysis. We started that in Chapter 1 when we marked the premises and conclusions of various arguments. As a next step, we can employ a diagram that clearly displays the connections among claims in complex arguments.

Consider this simple argument:

> Most people classified as *poor* are employed. Thus, talk of "welfare chiselers" is unjustified.

The argument has one premise for its conclusion. We can show that in this way:

> Most people classified as *poor* are employed.
>
> ↓
>
> Talk of "welfare chiselers" is unjustified.

The arrow indicates that the first statement is given as a reason for the second.

A more concise way of diagramming an argument is to bracket each claim in a passage, assign each one a number, and use the number in the diagram. Our example is represented:

> ¹[Most people classified as *poor* are employed.] Thus, ²[talk of "welfare chiselers" is unjustified.]

1
↓
2

This method also can easily show that more than one premise leads to a conclusion. An argument with two premises

> ¹[Computers do not feel pleasure or pain.] And ²[they have no sense of right and wrong.] Clearly, then, ³[it would be a serious mistake to treat computers as moral agents.]

can be diagrammed in this way:

1 + 2
―――――
↓
3

The plus and the arrow show that both [1] and [2] are premises for [3].

If an argument contains more than one inference (if it is a complex argument), its diagram has more than one arrow.

> [1][Almost all U.S. Senators, throughout the history of the Republic, have been far wealthier than the average citizen.] Thus, [2][the Senate has not been, and cannot be, representative of the needs and aspirations of the common citizen.] [3][A legislative body so out of touch should not be allowed to continue with its present power.] So, [4][the Constitution should be amended to restrict the Senate to an advisory role.]

The inference indicators *thus* and *so* make the intended structure of this argument quite clear: [1] is the premise for [2], and [2] and [3] are premises for [4]. Here is the diagram of this structure:

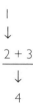

The same techniques can be used to build up a diagram of any argument, no matter how complex.

If we now wish to represent this argument in standard form, our diagram tells us what to put where. First, list the claims by number:

1. Almost all U.S. Senators have been far wealthier than the average citizen.

2. The Senate cannot be representative of the needs and aspirations of the common citizen.

3. A legislative body so out of touch should not be allowed to continue with its present power.

4. The Constitution should be amended so as to restrict the Senate to an advisory role.

Then annotate to show the inference structure. Our arrows tell us that claim 2 is inferred from claim 1 and claim 4 is inferred from claims 2 and 3:

1. Almost all U.S. Senators have been far wealthier than the average citizen.

2. The Senate cannot be representative of the needs and aspirations of the common citizen. |

3. A legislative body so out of touch should not be allowed to continue with its present power.

4. The Constitution should be amended so as to restrict the Senate to an advisory role.   2, 3

II. Strategies of Analysis

Decision procedures exist for many sorts of problems. For instance, we can give a set of rules that, if followed, will produce the right answer to any problem in long division. Unfortunately, we have no such decision procedure for analyzing arguments, no set of rules that guarantees a correct analysis. Even so, we can offer some practical advice that will increase our chances of analyzing arguments correctly. We present the advice here in the form of eight strategies to use in making an analysis. The strategies are divided into three categories.

A. Indicators and Context

1. Identify Inference Indicators
Inference indicators are the best clues to understanding an argument. So the first step in an analysis should be to go through the passage being analyzed and pick out the words indicating premises and conclusions. If the argument is a long one, drawing circles around the indicator words is useful.

2. Consider the Larger Context
In Chapter 1, we noticed that we cannot be sure which of the three possible interpretations of "Today is the 5th. Yesterday was the 4th." is appropriate unless we have additional information. Often the context in which something occurs provides the information we need to make such a decision. In a situation where someone expresses uncertainty about the day's date, and someone else utters these sentences, we can be sure the intention is to present the argument that "Today is the 5th *because* yesterday was the 4th." In a different context, a different interpretation might be justified.

The larger context in which a passage occurs is often enough to enable us to interpret it properly. However, in many cases we get no such help because we don't know the context. For instance, if we are unsure about what a newspaper editorial means, we are not likely to have access to information outside the editorial itself that will help us understand what its author intends. What we hope is that a passage containing an argument is clear enough that we can see what is meant.

B. Dealing with Claims

1. Identify Each Claim in a Passage
Each claim in a passage should be identified. (Putting each claim in brackets is helpful.) This identification is important because any claim

could turn out to be a premise or a conclusion with respect to any other. Thus, if we mistakenly take two or more claims to be a single one, then we won't notice whether a premise–conclusion relationship holds between them.

"He is destitute and utterly without hope and so will end up on the streets" is a single sentence with a single subject. Yet it contains three separate claims and is an argument:

> He is destitute.
> He is utterly without hope.
> _____
> He will end up on the streets.

No harm would be done if we treated the first two lines as making a single claim and wrote them as one premise, but failing to see that "He will end up on the streets" is a separate claim would result in missing the inference. (Notice how the conclusion indicator *so* calls attention to the claim.)

It is important to recognize when claims are separate, but it is just as important not to divide up what are really single claims. As we will see below, it is particularly important to remember that explanations, conditionals, disjunctions, and "unless" sentences make only single claims.

2. Reformulate Claims When Necessary

Sometimes we must reformulate sentences to clarify them. As we discussed in Chapter 1, questions and commands ("Don't you think you should apologize?") may need to be restated as assertions, but reformulation is necessary in other sorts of cases as well. For instance: "I don't think Stransky is competent to stand trial. She seems entirely confused even about her own identity." This case is not just a report about what someone thinks but an argument that should be understood as follows:

> Stransky seems entirely confused about her own identity.
> _____
> Stransky is not competent to stand trial.

Language is far too complex and subtle to allow a reasonable sampling of all the ways claims may be made. But if we are careful and sensitive, we can find and understand claims correctly, provided we do not expect them to come stated in just the way they should appear in an analyzed argument.

3. Discard Elements That Do Not Belong to an Argument

If we recognize that an argument is being given, we may try to fit everything said into an analysis. The following example shows how this would be a mistake:

> Come on now. Pay attention. Marriage is an institution that should be discarded. I was married for six months myself, you know. You

shouldn't listen to "Dear Abby" and those other moralists. All marriage does is make it too hard to get out of a bad relationship.

Although the comments about the speaker's marital history, "Dear Abby," and so on look at first as if they should be parts of some argument, they are not. They serve as neither premises nor conclusions. If we strip away those parts of the passage that make no claim relevant to the conclusion, we find that this is the argument:

> All marriage does is make it too hard to get out of a bad relationship.
>
> ---
>
> Marriage is an institution that should be discarded.

Statements that are not part of any argument often surround the claims making up arguments. When we analyze a passage, we must identify and discard any part of it that is neither a premise nor a conclusion. What we must discard is sometimes obvious, but deciding is often part of the further task of actually picking out premises and conclusions.

C. Structures

1. Identify the Main Argument
Every argument has exactly one final conclusion. This conclusion and the premises that directly support it can be called the **main argument.** Since the final conclusion is the point of the whole argument, it is crucial to identify it and its supporting premises as soon as possible.

2. Identify Any Subargument
The premises of the main argument may themselves be supported by other premises. Those premises may in turn be supported by yet others, and so on. That is, any premise may be an intermediate conclusion in a given argument. An intermediate conclusion together with its supporting premises constitute a **subargument.** We have to understand each subargument to understand the argument as a whole.

3. Identify Any Replies to Objections
Subarguments that counter objections to the central argument often play an important role in supporting a conclusion. For example, in the course of arguing that addictive drugs should be legalized, someone might attempt to reply to the obvious objection that legalization would increase the number of addicts. Such a reply indirectly supports the main conclusion by removing an objection that stands in the way of accepting either the main conclusion or an intermediate one.

We need follow no special order in picking out parts of an argument. In some cases, the final conclusion may be obvious, whereas the subarguments are difficult to find. In other cases, the subarguments may be clear, while the overall point of the argument is at first obscure. The only rule here is *Do what you can as you can.* In short, start with what is clear and build from there.

Analyzing an argument is something like doing a jigsaw puzzle. Looking at the collection of pieces, we may have no idea how they form a whole. But if first we put together those pieces that clearly fit, we find we can gradually join more and more pieces until the entire puzzle has come together.

III. Two Special Problems

A. Arguments and Explanations

Arguments and explanations differ in important ways. Explaining *why* she murdered her children is not the same as arguing *that* she murdered her children. Arguing that she murdered them must involve other claims that give *reasons for accepting* the claim. By contrast, an explanation of why she murdered them assumes that she did—takes it as a given fact that she did—then accounts for her doing it. In general, when the point of a passage is to explain *why* (rather than *that*) something is the case, we are dealing with an explanation, not an argument.

Arguments and explanations often resemble one another, and words that serve as inference indicators can also serve as explanation indicators. For example, despite the presence of indicator words, each of the following is far more likely to be meant as an explanation than as an argument:

> I don't love you anymore *because* you always make fun of me.

> *Since* you stayed on the beach all day, your nose is peeling in that ugly way.

> We are sitting in the dark *because* you forgot to pay the electric bill.

One way to see that these are more likely to be explanations is to construe them as single claims:

> The reason I don't love you anymore is that you always make fun of me.

> The cause of that ugly, peeling nose of yours is that you stayed out on the beach all day.

> The reason for the darkness here is that you forgot to pay the electric bill.

Put in these ways, the explanations do not resemble arguments at all and would not be mistaken for arguments. Each example contains a *single statement* about a cause or reason, not two statements, one of which is offered as a premise for the other.

To illustrate the point more clearly, consider the following passage:

> O'Leary fed the poisoned soup to the bishop because he did not know it had been tampered with. Thus, he should not be found guilty of murder.

If the first sentence is construed as an argument in itself, then we have a complex chain of argument that goes like this:

PREMISE: O'Leary did not know the soup had been tampered with.

CONCLUSION 1:   Therefore, O'Leary fed the poisoned soup to the bishop.

From which we then infer:

CONCLUSION 2:   Therefore, O'Leary should not be found guilty of murder.

The problem with this is that the second conclusion doesn't follow from the first at all. Yet we have the sense that there is a good argument here. The first sentence should be treated as an explanation, not an inference:

PREMISE: Because O'Leary did not know the soup had been tampered with, O'Leary fed the poisoned soup to the bishop.

CONCLUSION: Therefore, O'Leary should not be found guilty of murder.

Nevertheless, there is no failsafe way to tell whether something is an argument or an explanation. Consider "Teachers assign students more work than they can do because if they don't, students won't do the minimal amount." Is this an argument to the effect that teachers overassign work, or is it an explanation of *why* teachers overassign work? We need to know more about the context before we can answer this question. One of the hardest skills to develop in argument analysis is a sound sense of the function of a claim in a given context. Exercise set A at the end of the chapter is intended to help you develop this sense. Unfortunately, there is no rulebook for solving these problems.

Even though it may not be obvious whether we have an argument or an explanation, which one we have can be of the utmost importance. Whether she killed her children and we are explaining why she did it, or we are giving a reason in favor of believing that she killed them, can make all the difference in the world in a great number of ways.

To deal with cases in which an explanation forms part of an argument, we can adopt the following rule: *An explanation that occurs within an argument should be treated as a single claim.* It can be represented as, in effect, one long premise or conclusion.

B. Conditionals ("If . . . then . . . "), Disjunctives ("Either . . . or . . . "), and "Unless"

A simple sentence like "Income rose in June" makes just one claim. Compound sentences like "Income rose in June, and unemployment declined" make two claims (or more in some cases).

But how are we to treat **conditional sentences** (sentences of the form "If . . . then . . . ")? Sentences like "If the battery is charged, then the car will start" play a crucial role in many arguments, and to understand the arguments correctly, we must interpret the sentences correctly.

It may seem that a conditional sentence is an inference itself—that it makes two distinct claims, one a conclusion and the other a premise. This tempting interpretation is wrong; a conditional sentence makes only one claim. To see why this is so, reconsider the conditional sentence about the car battery. It does not assert "The battery is charged" or "The car will start." Whether the battery is charged or the car will start has nothing to do with the only claim made: *If* the battery is charged, *then* the car will start. A conditional sentence always makes a single claim (a conditional one). Thus, as a part of an argument, a conditional sentence must be treated as a single unit, as a premise or as a conclusion.

A **disjunctive sentence** presents alternatives in some version of an "Either . . . or . . . " form. The sentence "Either the roof will be patched or the documents will be damaged by the rain" is a disjunctive one. Like conditionals, disjunctive sentences contain other sentences as components, so they too may appear to be making more than one claim. Despite appearances, however, such sentences make only a single claim. Our example does not claim that "The roof will be patched," and it does not claim that "The documents will be damaged." Its only claim is that one or the other of these events will occur.

Similarly, compound sentences using "unless" make only a single claim. The sentence "There will be no tomatoes in the garden unless fertilizer is applied" claims neither that there will be no tomatoes nor that fertilizer will be applied.

We can now state another rule for analyzing arguments: *A compound sentence that is a conditional or a disjunction, or whose components are joined by "unless," makes a single claim. Thus, it is always a single unit (premise or conclusion) in an argument.*

IV. Analyzing a Complex Argument: An Example

Complex arguments may look confusing, but often they are not difficult to understand. Consider this one:

> There is a bill before Congress, S. 143, that would allow diacetylmorphine, a form of heroin, to be dispensed for the relief of intractable pain due to cancer. This bill should be passed.
>
> The case for passing the bill cannot be denied. Diacetylmorphine (DAM) is the one drug that would best relieve the agony many cancer patients suffer. And whatever drug would best prevent this agony should be available. For such agony often leads to a severe deterioration in the quality of life of the patient and heartbreak for the patient's family.
>
> There is one objection to this bill that seems especially callous. This is that a cancer patient might unexpectedly survive and turn out to be addicted. There would be time to worry about addiction if the terminally ill patient surprised his doctors.
>
> Three times I have seen loved ones die of cancer, and two of them were in such pain they could neither weep nor scream. Injections of heroin might have let them go in relative peace. It's not a great deal to ask.
>
> (Adapted from a syndicated article by James Kilpatrick, *St. Louis Post-Dispatch*, June 15, 1987)

The overall point of this passage is clear: the drug DAM should be made available to cancer patients. (Bill S. 143 should be passed.) The main argument for this claim is clearly signaled by the first sentence of the second paragraph, which all but says "Here is the main argument."

> DAM is the one drug that would best relieve the agony many cancer patients suffer.
> Whatever drug would best relieve this agony should be made available.
> _____
> DAM should be made available. (The bill should be passed.)

Furthermore, the last sentence in the second paragraph begins with "for," a premise indicator. The premise that follows *for* is clearly intended to support the second premise in the main argument. We insert this new premise, and we have

1. DAM is the one drug that would best relieve the agony many cancer patients suffer.

2. Such agony often leads to a severe deterioration in the quality of life of the patient and heartbreak for the patient's family.

3. Whatever drug would best relieve this agony should be made available. 2

4. DAM should be made available. 1, 3

5. The objection that a cancer patient might unexpectedly survive is callous.

6. There would be time to worry about addiction if a patient unexpectedly survived.

7. This is not a serious objection to the conclusion (4). 5, 6

Line 7 is not explicitly stated in the original passage. Still, it is obvious that the inference from 5 and 6 to 7 (or something like it) is intended.

Since 7 is a response to an objection to 4, we can think of it as part of the overall case being given for 4. That means we could insert 5, 6, and 7 between 3 and 4, renumbering as appropriate.

On the other hand, we can leave 5, 6, and 7 in a separate group, indicating that it gives a subargument responding to an objection to the conclusion. Either method is acceptable, so long as the structure of the overall argument is unambiguously represented.

The final paragraph of the passage contains a moving personal testimonial about the pain terminal cancer patients endure. We do not see this as a further argument. (There may be room for disagreement about this.)

The argument expressed in this passage did not prove difficult to analyze. A careful, patient reading does much to ensure that even long, complex arguments become understandable.

Exercises

A. *Determine whether each passage is most likely meant to give an argument, an explanation, or neither.*

　*1. I dislike smoking. It smells bad and makes my asthma worse.

　2. You should not smoke anywhere. It smells bad and makes other people's asthma worse.

*3. The law against spitting on the sidewalk was passed because spitting is unsightly and unsanitary.

4. Hobart was kept in solitary confinement for more than seventeen years. Then he was released and was expected to become a completely normal member of society.

*5. Jenkins walks her dog every day because the dog is getting too fat.

6. Several states have passed laws allowing citizens to carry concealed weapons. And they are entirely right to do so. Law-abiding people have to be able to defend themselves against the lawless.

*7. I hate the way you eat. You put ketchup on steak and have peanut butter for breakfast.

8. Don't move that brick! There may be a brown recluse spider underneath it, and they are quite poisonous.

*9. Jan has been sleeping in a tent ever since her house burned down in April.

10. That truck in the ditch is there because it was going too fast in the snow.

*11. Since your philosophy essay is unclear and apparently trivial, you are almost certain to flunk the course.

12. I prefer the steak to the lobster. I believe the lobster is overcooked.

*13. She has never called me since we had our only date.

14. If Fermat's Last Theorem has really been proven, many mathematicians will have to find new projects, and somehow the world will be a less interesting place.

*15. The books on this table are for sale so cheap because they are really not worth reading.

16. Since Blaylock has little education and does not get along well with people, he almost assuredly will not be successful in his new job.

*17. The fall colors are lovely, and the temperature is mild. The sun is shining, and there is just a hint of a pleasant breeze. And I am stuck in here studying for this stupid logic quiz.

18. Since an adult chimpanzee is more intelligent than a one-year-old human, the life of my chimpanzee has more value than the life of your one-year-old human.

*19. In the following, is the *first sentence* best understood as an argument or an explanation? Explain.

Allen is very ill because he was bitten by a rattlesnake. So he will survive only if snakebite antitoxin serum is made available immediately.

20. In the following, is the *first sentence* best understood as an argument or an explanation? Explain.

Since farmers are still using sixteenth-century irrigation methods, thousands are starving in the countryside. So the government should immediately begin an educational program on water management.

B. *Analyze the following arguments. Circle inference indicators, and bracket and number each statement. Then draw an arrow diagram showing the structure of the argument. Finally, represent the argument in standard form. Be sure to use the standard form for simple arguments in the case of arguments with only one inference, and for complex arguments in the case of arguments with more than one inference. You should not add any unstated premises or conclusions, but you should treat questions, commands, and so on that, in effect, make claims as making those claims.*

*1. No matter what the fast drivers think, higher speed limits will result in more needless deaths on the highway. So the speed limits should not be raised.

2. The Cat90 is the best lawn mower you can buy. Since you want the best, you should buy the Cat90.

*3. Without a tax increase there will soon be runaway inflation. But Congress refuses to raise taxes. Thus, before long there will be runaway inflation. That means that you should borrow all the money you can right now.

4. Because Henry has started on a weight-lifting program and weight lifters are very strong, it follows that Henry will soon be very strong. And anyone who is unusually strong can make the football team. So Henry will make the team this year.

*5. People who study history are wiser than those who do not. Studying history makes a person less likely to repeat the mistakes of the past, and not repeating past mistakes is a sign of wisdom. And because the primary aim of education is producing wisdom, all universities should require the study of history.

6. Never, never pass up a four-leaf clover! They are very rare because a clover normally has three leaves, and the four-leaved ones bring good luck.

*7. Anything worth recording has been entered in the ship's log, so I can be sure I've never met a mermaid. A mermaid would be worth recording, and there's nothing about meeting a mermaid in my ship's log.

8. AIDS may be the most horrible disease in the world's history. It is always lethal. There is no cure. And it is most often transmitted through pleasure.

*9. Higher education should increase our ability to think critically and to appreciate a greater variety of experiences. Thus, it is good to take courses in the humanities, science, and social science. So, students who take the advanced-level course in twentieth-century American poetry have made a wise choice.

10. We should go for a hike in the canyon this weekend. The air is crisp, and the leaves are turning to lovely reds and yellows. And the exercise will be good for us, since we haven't been out all week. So, let's take the hike.

*11. The hike has been nice, but we must be pretty far from civilization, because the only people we have seen in the last three hours have been toting big backpacks. So we better turn around before we get lost in the middle of nowhere.

12. The fate of the hikers will forever be a mystery. The *Weekly World News* said they were devoured by army ants, but not much in *WWN* is true, so probably they weren't. If they weren't, we just don't know what happened to them. So, we will always be wondering.

*13. It is obvious that the judge committed the murder, given that either the butler or the judge did it. Since the butler was passionately in love with the victim, it was not she who committed the murder.

14. The detective is unlikely to be a convincing witness because he has the reputation of being a racist. Probably, then, the defendant will be acquitted.

*15. If the detective really is a racist—which he is—then he never should have been allowed to testify at all, since white racists are especially unreliable witnesses when the accused is a person of color. So, the detective should not have been allowed to testify at all.

16. The eighteenth-century philosopher David Hume was undoubtedly a finer thinker than his even more celebrated successor Immanuel Kant. Hume was by far the more lucid writer. His contributions were more diverse than Kant's, for he was a first-rate historian as well as a philosopher. Further, Hume's ethical thought did not suffer from the rigidity of Kant's. Hume, unlike Kant, would never have said the duty not to lie is so absolute that we should answer truthfully even when a would-be murderer asks where his intended victim is hiding. Thus, there can be little doubt that, of the two, Hume was the superior thinker.

*17. Either the market has bottomed out or we're in for several more months of rocky times for investors. If this is the market's lowest point, then the Fed will not be thinking of lowering interest rates further, but the latest report from the chairman of the Fed tells us that interest rates will go down further. So clearly this isn't the bottom of the market, and consequently it's a bleak time ahead for investors.

18. Dozens of people have claimed to have seen Elvis Presley since he was supposed to have died in 1978, so he must still be alive, since that many people wouldn't be wrong. On account of the fact that Elvis is alive, "Hound Dog" will soon again be a best-selling single.

*19. The liquid is either acidic or alkaline. If it's acidic the paper will turn red, and if it's alkaline the paper will turn blue. So the paper will turn either red or blue. But since I'm color-blind, that means I won't be able to tell whether the liquid is acidic or alkaline.

20. Here are some reasons why you should stop sniffing cocaine: Cocaine is addictive; it is likely to lead to the use of even harder drugs, because the user will always be looking for an even greater high; rightly or wrongly, it is illegal; and it is actually quite bad for your nose.

Chapter 3

EVALUATING ARGUMENTS

The point of presenting arguments whether simple or complex, in standard form was to aid in their evaluation. The worth of any argument depends on two considerations: (1) the truth or falsity of its premises and (2) how much support its premises provide the conclusion. In this and the next five chapters we concentrate on the latter issue, considering how we can evaluate the degree of support the premises give the conclusion in various sorts of arguments.

Deductive arguments are meant to be valid; that is, their premises are meant to guarantee the conclusion. In **nondeductive arguments,** the premises are meant to confer some high degree of probability on the conclusion. In this chapter, we discuss deductive arguments and validity first. Then we describe common types of nondeductive arguments, discuss in some detail the types most common in ordinary life, and consider ways to evaluate their worth.

I. Deductive Arguments

Deductive arguments are characterized as valid or invalid. We begin with a discussion of validity, then consider an informal way of testing for it.

A. The Concept of Validity

The word *valid* has a technical use in logic. We speak of "valid criticisms" and "valid results," but in logic, only an *argument* can be valid or invalid. A **valid argument** is one in which there is no possible way for the premises to be true and the conclusion false at the same time. *If* all of its premises are true, the conclusion would *have* to be true. Thus, the truth of the premises of a valid argument *completely guarantees* the truth of the conclusion.

Each of these arguments is valid:

> If whales are mammals, they have lungs. Whales are mammals. Therefore, whales have lungs.

> Everyone in the ward yesterday was exposed to the virus, and you were there then. That means that you were exposed.

> James I was monarch before Charles I. And Charles I was monarch before Charles II. Thus, James I was monarch before Charles II.

> Harold is Matilda's son. So Matilda is Harold's mother.

This argument is *invalid*:

> Crombie was stoned, stabbed, shot, and scalped. So Crombie is dead.

It is possible, no matter how unlikely, that Crombie was treated in these horrible ways and yet survived. The truth of these premises does not guarantee the truth of the conclusion. That makes the argument invalid.

B. Validity, Truth, and Soundness

Validity is a matter of the support that a set of premises lends to a conclusion. It is a question of whether a certain relationship holds between premises and conclusion. (*If* we grant the premises, *must* we grant the conclusion?) Hence, validity does not require the premises of an argument to be true. Yet if they are true and the argument is valid, the conclusion must be true also.

Given what it means for an argument to be valid, a valid argument can have (1) false premises and a true conclusion; (2) false premises and a false conclusion; or (3) true premises and a true conclusion. The only combination incompatible with validity is true premises and a false conclusion.

This argument is valid despite the false premises:

> The moon is made of green cheese, and everything made of green cheese orbits the earth. Therefore, the moon orbits the earth.

This conclusion is true even though both premises are false. With respect to the premises, the truth of the conclusion is obviously just a matter of luck. If an argument has false starting points, we cannot expect to arrive at a true conclusion, although sometimes it may happen. This is made obvious by the fact that a very similar (and similarly valid argument) with false premises has a *false* conclusion:

> Neptune is made of green cheese, and everything made of green cheese orbits the earth. Therefore, Neptune orbits the earth.

Consider a more serious example:

The last person to see the victim alive must have been the murderer, and Wainsworth was the last person to see the victim alive.
Thus, Wainsworth must have been the murderer.

This form of reasoning, quite unexceptionable in its logic, might occur
in the course of a criminal investigation. But if there's any reason to
doubt either that Wainsworth *was* the last person to see the victim alive
or that the last person to see the victim alive was the murderer, then we
should not put too much confidence in the conclusion of the argument.

By contrast, we can place the greatest reliance on valid arguments
with true premises. Because the truth of the premises in a valid argument guarantees the truth of the conclusion, we do not have to count
on any lucky coincidences. Valid arguments, all of whose premises
are true, are called **sound arguments.** These are the valid arguments
we are most interested in establishing.

Since the most virtuous argument is a **sound** one, why do we place so
much emphasis in our study on validity rather than on truth of premises?
The answer is quite simple. Arguments arise in every imaginable context
of discourse. There are scientific arguments, legal arguments, medical
arguments, arguments in sports, aesthetic arguments, practical arguments,
and so on and on. The premises of these arguments are very often matters of specialized technical interest. The best person to judge the truth
of a premise in chemistry is a chemist; of a judicial argument, a lawyer or
jurist. As students of critical thinking, we can't be expected to be experts
on every subject. But the principles that govern the validity of arguments
are the same across the disciplines. It is these principles that we seek to
understand in this book.

C. Validity and Added Premises

A surprising characteristic of valid arguments is that if an argument is
valid, it remains valid no matter what other premises are added. Here
is a simple valid argument:

All platypuses are mammals.
Nadine is a platypus.
_____
Nadine is a mammal.

Suppose we add new premises, getting this result:

> All platypuses are mammals.
> Nadine is a platypus.
> *Almost no mammals lay eggs.*
> *Nadine lays eggs.*
> _____
> Nadine is a mammal.

We now have premises within the argument that give strong reason for rejecting the conclusion, and the argument no longer has a valid look. Nonetheless, it is still valid. If Nadine is a platypus, and *every* platypus is a mammal, we *must* conclude that Nadine is a mammal, regardless of what the other premises might be.

This principle, that valid arguments remain valid no matter what other premises are added, is important. As we often find valid arguments nested in a context of additional premises, it tells us that we need not be concerned about these premises if our concern is with validity. It also explains why, when we start from true premises in geometry and give a valid proof of some property of triangles (e.g., that in a right triangle the sum of two angles is equal to the third angle), it is not only unnecessary but even foolish to then "check" the result by going out and measuring some triangles. No result of such measurements could overturn the validity of the demonstration or the truth of its conclusion.

Clever students of logic often try another way to make a valid argument invalid by adding premises:

> All platypuses are mammals.
> Nadine is a platypus.
> *Nadine is a duck, not a platypus.*
> _____
> Nadine is a mammal.

Surely *this* argument is not valid.

But as incoherent as it appears to be (and is), nonetheless it is technically valid. Remember that an argument is valid if it is not possible for the premises to be true *and* the conclusion false. But for it to be possible that the premises are true *and* the conclusion false, it must first be possible for the premises to be true. And it is not possible for these premises to be true because they contradict one another: Nadine cannot be *both* a platypus and *not* a platypus. In short, since we cannot have all true premises, we cannot have all true premises *and* a false conclusion.

That means that the argument is technically valid. Even the clever way of adding premises does not succeed in making a valid argument invalid.

The reasoning that shows that the Nadine argument is valid can be generalized: Any argument that has a contradiction in its premises is valid. The content of the conclusion is actually irrelevant. Since such arguments are valid just because the premises cannot be true, it does not matter what is concluded. "Contradictions imply everything" is the way this is often put.

Should we be disturbed by these apparently absurd cases of validity? Not at all. In conceding that these arguments are valid, we are not saying that they are good or convincing arguments. The very factor that makes the arguments valid—the contradiction in the premises—means that the premises are known not to be all true, and so the arguments are *not* good or convincing or *sound*.

D. Checking Validity

In Chapters 4 and 5 we will present formal ways of determining whether some arguments are valid. Here we will consider a useful, informal way of thinking about whether any particular argument is valid.

Since an argument is valid if there is no possible way its premises can be true and its conclusion false, one way we can check validity is by conducting thought experiments to try to determine whether there are any possible circumstances in which the combination "true premises and false conclusion" would occur. If we discover a possible case, then the argument is not valid. We can think of this as trying to "tell a story" in which the premises are true and the conclusion is false.

To see how this procedure works, consider this simple example:

Ninety-nine percent of students in the course will pass.
Patrick is a student in the course.

Patrick will pass the course.

Obviously, these premises would be true and the conclusion false if, for instance, there were 100 students in the course; ninety-nine pass; one fails; the one who fails is Patrick. So the truth of the premises does not guarantee the truth of the conclusion, and the argument is not valid.

Consider a slightly more difficult example:

All the relatives of the deceased were at the funeral. So there's no denying everyone at the funeral was a relative of the deceased.

Suppose the deceased had exactly five relatives, and they were all at the funeral. Suppose, too, that several unrelated friends of the deceased were also present. Under these circumstances, the premises are true and the conclusion false, and so this argument is also invalid.

Here is one more invalid argument:

> The thimbleful of water has been in the 10° Fahrenheit freezer for twenty-eight hours. Thus, it is frozen.

Clearly, there are *possible* circumstances under which these premises are true but the conclusion false. For instance, the thimbleful of water is placed in the 10° freezer; it remains there for twenty-eight hours; *water has no freezing point—no water ever freezes;* the thimbleful of water (of course!) is unfrozen; it is as liquid as ever.

In evaluating the validity of this or any other argument, we must be careful to distinguish what is true from what is possible. It is not *true* that the water would not be frozen, because the freezing point of water is in fact 32°. But the given premises do not include this fact; they do not rule out the possibility that water never freezes. And since the premises of a valid argument must rule out any possibility that the conclusion is false, this argument as it stands is invalid. (If we add premises about the freezing point of water and how long it takes certain quantities to freeze, we will get a valid argument. But that does not mean this argument as stated is valid.)

Is it *really* possible that a thimbleful of water would be liquid at 10°? Given the law of nature that the freezing point of water is 32°, it is not *physically* possible. Similarly, laws of nature make it physically impossible for dogs to fly, for the dead to walk, and for anything to move faster than the speed of light.

Even though all of these are physically impossible, none is *logically* impossible or contradictory—that is, literally inconceivable. We can coherently imagine that laws of nature are different than they in fact are. And so, even though we know in fact there cannot be any such thing, we can coherently conceive of flying dogs, of walking dead, and of water being unfrozen at 10°. Thus, the argument about water freezing is not valid. It is conceivable (though not physically possible) that the premises are true and the conclusion false.

By contrast, look again at "Harold is Matilda's son. So Matilda is Harold's mother." Given the meanings of "son" and "mother," it is literally inconceivable, logically impossible, contradictory, for her to be his mother and he not her son. So the argument is valid.

In contrast, consider this valid argument:

Some vegetarians are malnourished.
All malnourished people need vitamin supplements.

Some vegetarians need vitamin supplements.

We can assure ourselves that there are no circumstances in which the premises are true and the conclusion false by imagining certain possibilities. Suppose the first premise is true because there are three malnourished vegetarians. For the second premise to be true, each of these three, being malnourished, must need vitamin supplements. Thus, we have three vegetarians who need vitamin supplements, and the conclusion is true. Since the reasoning would be the same no matter how many malnourished vegetarians there might be (as long as there are *some*), we can be confident that it is not possible for the premises to be true and the conclusion false.

This informal method has limitations. If we can imagine a situation in which the premises are true and the conclusion false, we know the argument is not valid. But failing to imagine such a situation does not rule out the possibility that one exists. We may just lack the imagination to think of it. (It is unlikely we have missed any possibilities in the vegetarian argument, but not all cases are so simple.) The rigorous methods for assessing validity given in the next two chapters are helpful in dealing with some arguments that are hard to handle using the thought experiment procedure.

Exercises

A. *Decide whether each argument is valid. Explain your decision in each case.*

* 1. If a dog bites the mailman, it must be punished. Our dog Genevieve didn't bite the mailman, so she mustn't be punished.

   2. My friends and I all seem to need more sleep than we did as children. So I guess it follows that adults need more sleep than children.

* 3. Halliwell cuts himself shaving every morning. So Halliwell cuts himself every morning.

   4. If Green had mastered calculus, she would have no difficulty with the math in first-year physics. But she's having difficulty with the math in first-year physics, so she didn't master calculus.

*5. All bats are mammals, and most mammals do not have wings. Clearly, then, bats do not have wings.

6. Ten minutes ago Henrietta ingested a dose of arsenic that is unfailingly lethal within five minutes. Henrietta is quite dead.

*7. The moon is bigger than the earth, and the earth is bigger than the sun. So the moon is bigger than the sun.

8. The earth is bigger than the sun, and the moon is bigger than the earth. So the sun is bigger than the moon.

*9. In an experiment performed by the Viking lander on Mars, dust from the surface of the planet was mixed with water. If there had been organic matter in the dust, methane gas would have been given off. But since no methane was given off, there was no organic matter in the dust.

10. He hit the ground at 500 mph. At minimum, then, he must have severe bruises and a multitude of broken bones.

*11. There is no water at all in the desert. Palm Springs is in the desert. That means that there is not a drop of water in Palm Springs.

12. All those who guide their lives by the horoscope column in the newspaper are superstitious. And some people who are superstitious will not stay on the thirteenth floor of a hotel. That means that no one who reads the horoscope column in the newspaper will stay on the thirteenth floor of your new hotel.

*13. Because it is one of the most fundamental principles of physics that it is not possible for any object to move faster than the speed of light, a spacecraft cannot go faster than the speed of light if physics is right.

14. Tennessee needs 4 yards for a first down. If the penalty on the other team is for roughing the kicker, Tennessee gets 15 yards. If the penalty is for running into the kicker, Tennessee gets 5 yards. So either way Tennessee gets a first down.

*15. All flying squirrels are mammals. No birds are mammals. So, no flying squirrels are birds even if they can soar like an eagle and dive like a hawk.

16. Some students are hard workers, and some students get very good grades. That shows that at least some hard workers get very good grades.

*17. If the medicine is the correct one, then if you take it according to directions, you will recover. The medicine is correct. Thus, you are sure to recover.

18. All vegetarians are undernourished. Some undernourished people need vitamin supplements. You can't deny then that some vegetarians need vitamin supplements.

*19. Since Randy has squash and beans in his refrigerator, he has some vegetables there.

20. I am going to hand out twenty pieces of candy to the students in the class. Because there are exactly nineteen students, at least one will get more than one piece of candy.

II. Nondeductive Arguments

As we said at the start of this chapter, a nondeductive argument is any argument that is not meant to be valid but is meant to confer some high degree of probability on the conclusion. In this section, we begin by discussing general features of such arguments and criteria appropriate for evaluating them. Then we characterize several types of these arguments. (Here is an odd possibility. Suppose an argument is stated in such a way that clearly the conclusion is meant to be made likely. But in fact the argument is valid. This rarely happens, but if it should, we would just note that the argument is valid and go on to ask if the premises are true. The discussion that follows applies to the more normal nondeductive arguments that are not unintentionally valid.)

We use "nondeductive" for the broad class of arguments that are *not* deductive. Sometimes the word "inductive" is used in this same broad way. But "inductive" has often also been used more narrowly just for arguments that reason *from the specific to the general,* as in inductive generalizations.

> Swan A is white. Swan B is white. Swan C is white. . . . Swan N is white. And so, *all* swans are white.

Sometimes the broad and narrow meanings of "inductive" have been confusedly run together, as if *all* arguments that are not deductive reason from the specific to the general (essentially that all arguments are like math or are like the swan example).

The simplest and clearest way out of this muddle is to reserve "inductive" for inductive generalizations and use the descriptive "nondeductive" for the broad class of arguments that aim for the likelihood of the conclusion.

A. Characteristics of Nondeductive Arguments

Nondeductive arguments share some basic characteristics. We illustrate three of these with the following nondeductive statistical arguments. (Note, however, that not all nondeductive arguments are statistical.)

Ninety-six percent of Americans belong to some religious group or other.
Xiu is an American.

Therefore, Xiu belongs to some religious group or other.

Seventy-eight percent of Americans are Christians.
Wallace is an American.

Therefore, Wallace is a Christian.

Fifty-five percent of Americans do not regularly attend religious services.
Mujtaba is an American.

Therefore, Mujtaba does not regularly attend religious services.

These arguments are not valid, even though their premises provide some support for their conclusions. The first general characteristic of nondeductive arguments is that they are not meant to be valid, but they are meant to make their conclusions *probable* or *likely*.

Next, notice that in the first argument the premises make the conclusion very probable (96 percent likely); the premises of the second do not support its conclusion nearly as well (making it only 78 percent likely); and in the third case it is barely more probable than not that Mujtaba does not attend religious services.

This illustrates the second general characteristic of nondeductive arguments. Whereas validity is not a matter of degree (an argument is either valid or it is not), nondeductive support for a conclusion *is* a matter of degree. We will say that an argument is *nondeductively successful* if it is nondeductive and its premises make its conclusion more likely than not. Of course, this is a minimal criterion for success. We prefer that premises make conclusions more than just "more likely than not."

The third general characteristic of nondeductive arguments is that, whereas valid arguments remain valid no matter what new premises are added, the addition of new information in the premises of a nondeductive argument may radically alter the overall amount of support we have for the conclusion. Suppose we add some new premises to the last argument:

> Fifty-five percent of Americans do not regularly attend religious services.
> Mujtaba is an American.
> Eighty-three percent of Americans of Pakistani heritage regularly attend religious services.
> Mujtaba is of Pakistani heritage.
> _____
> Therefore, Mujtaba does not regularly attend religious services.

The added premises make it much more likely that Mujtaba *does* regularly attend religious services, thus significantly decreasing the probability of the conclusion. That additional premises can make this sort of difference is important in evaluating the conclusion of a piece of nondeductive reasoning. (See "Overall Argument Evaluation" later in this chapter.)

B. Some Varieties of Nondeductive Arguments

Nondeductive arguments come in a variety of types. We will distinguish some of these here and briefly consider how to evaluate the degree of support the premises give to the conclusions.

1. Statistical Syllogism

A **syllogism** is a three-line argument. In a **statistical syllogism,** the reasoning is from some proportion of a population having (or not having) a certain attribute to some individual within the population having (or not having) that attribute. Each of the three original "religion arguments" above is a statistical syllogism. Here is one that is slightly different in that it argues that an individual does not have a certain attribute:

> Only 3 percent of college students know the capital of South Dakota.
> Morris is a college student.
> _____
> Morris does not know the capital of South Dakota.

Evaluating statistical syllogisms is usually simple and straightforward. The conclusion of the last argument is 97 percent probable given the premises. In general, a premise that x percent of a population has a certain attribute makes it likely to degree x that a given individual in the population has that attribute. Let's remind ourselves, however, of the effect that adding premises will have on the strength of this argument. Consider, for example, the impact of the premise

"Morris is from South Dakota" on the argument. For the most part, our best evaluations of nondeductive arguments are *relative*—this argument is strong*er* than that one; this premise makes the argument weak*er*—rather than absolute evaluations of strength or weakness.

In most nontechnical discourse, arguments are not put in precise statistical terms.

> Most people who read *The New Republic* are liberals.
> Freedman reads *The New Republic*.
> _____
> Freedman is a liberal.

Phrases such as "almost all of," "the great majority of," or "well over half of" frequently occupy the place of "most" in syllogisms such as the last example.

The lack of precision in phrases such as "most," "almost all of," and the like may make it difficult to evaluate these arguments. "Most," for instance, could mean anything from 51 percent to 99 percent. When such differences are important, we should try to obtain more information so we have, if not some specific percentage, at least a sufficiently precise estimate for whatever the purpose at hand may be.

2. Inductive Generalization

In an **inductive generalization,** the inference is from some sample of a population to all or some percentage of its members.

> Every wolverine so far encountered by humans has been unfriendly and aggressive.
> _____
> All wolverines are unfriendly and aggressive.

> In the phone survey, 58 percent of the registered voters intending to vote in the election said they planned to vote for Larson.
> _____
> Larson will receive about 58 percent of the votes in the election.

When is evidence adequate to support a generalization? The question has no simple answer, but we can use statistical techniques and standards to avoid gross errors. The aim is to generalize from cases representative of the population being studied (wolverines, voters in the next election). The sample is more likely to be representative if the number of cases is large and if they are selected in a random way to avoid bias. Consider a conclusion about the public attitude toward federal economic policy based on a survey of twenty delegates to the Republican National Convention who arrived by private jet. Such a sample would be neither large nor random, and we would have little reason to accept the conclusion.

3. Causal Arguments

Causal arguments are crucially important in everyday reasoning as well as in specialized fields such as medicine and the natural and social sciences. We care a great deal about reasoning correctly to the causes of our automobile not starting, of lung cancer, or of persistent poverty in our society. Because of the importance and complexity of causal analysis, we will devote Chapter 6 to this topic.

4. Arguments by Analogy

If one reasons that hamsters make good housepets, that gerbils are *like* hamsters in various respects, and so gerbils will make good housepets, then one is reasoning by analogy. Arguments of this form are common in everyday life, particularly in moral reasoning, and in many specialized areas of study. The use of models in science is a form of reasoning by analogy. In Chapter 7, we will discuss analogies in more detail.

5. Plausibility Arguments

Many nondeductive arguments, called plausibility or case-building arguments, do not neatly fit any particular pattern.

> The First Federated Bank was robbed yesterday.
> Kelly bought a gun two days ago.
> Kelly needed money to pay his bookmaker.
> Kelly was seen near the First Federated Bank earlier in the day.
> The bookmaker's enforcers stopped looking for Kelly today.
> _____
> It was Kelly who robbed the First Federated Bank yesterday.

> Lawrence was widely praised for her acting in two films last year.
> Both of these films were huge box-office hits.
> Lawrence has never won a major award for her work.
> _____
> Lawrence will win this year's "Hollywood Woman of the Year Award."

> "Howl" is superficial and dated.
> "The Second Coming" has profound social significance.
> _____
> "The Second Coming" is a finer poem than "Howl."

The premises of such arguments are meant to work together to build a case for the conclusions, to make the conclusions *plausible*. And we would all agree that they often are successful in doing so. However, it is very difficult to formulate criteria for evaluating the degree to which the premises support the conclusion in such arguments.

One straightforward requirement for the success of any argument is that *at least some of the premises of the argument must be positively relevant to the conclusion;* that is, some premises must count in favor of the conclusion. The argument "Congressman Smith would be an excellent senator because he was born on Independence Day" fails because of its irrelevant premise. (See Chapter 8 for fallacies of relevance.)

The requirement of positive relevance aside, there are no straightforward criteria for evaluating how well the given premises support the conclusion in a plausibility argument. We can, however, adopt a variant of an evaluative strategy we employed for assessing the validity of deductive arguments. This is the method of thought experiments.

A plausibility argument, like any other nondeductive argument, is meant to make its conclusion at least more likely than not, given the premises. ("His jacket was covered with blood, and he can't explain why. It is a better than fifty-fifty chance he killed her.") It is meant to show that the conclusion is true in the majority of circumstances in which the premises are true. This informal check for likelihood, then, requires one to imagine a variety of circumstances in which the premises of an argument are true and consider whether the conclusion would be true in the majority of these situations.

To see how this procedure works, consider the example of Lawrence and the "Hollywood Woman of the Year Award." Because we do not know what the criteria for the award are, we cannot be sure the premises are even relevant to the conclusion. But even if they are, we can easily imagine that another actress performed better in more films; that other films with another actress made more money; and that other actresses had been more overlooked for many years. We can also imagine other criteria for the award that Lawrence does not fulfill but others do. On the whole, then, we must judge the argument to be unsuccessful because there are so many circumstances under which the premises could be true but the conclusion false.

The argument about the relative merits of "Howl" and "The Second Coming" fares somewhat better when we evaluate it in this way. Surely some circumstances occur in which one poem possesses profound social significance, the other is superficial and dated, but the former is not the finer poem. The superficial one, for instance, could have technical merits entirely independent of its superficial content. But in most cases, a poem receiving high marks for profundity will on the whole be better than one that is rated superficial and dated. These premises do, then, give good nondeductive support for the conclusion.

The procedure of thought experiments is not rigorous or foolproof. Nevertheless, it is very useful in evaluating the degree to which the premises of an argument support the conclusion. And that is an important part of an overall evaluation of any argument. We will come back to overall evaluation in the last section of this chapter.

III. Complex Arguments

To estimate the degree to which the premises of an argument support its conclusion when they do so through two or more inferences, we first assess the strength of each individual inference and then use these assessments to arrive at an evaluation of the support the premises give for the final conclusion. We assess individual inferences just as we would assess a simple argument: consider whether deductive inferences are valid, whether analogies are good enough, and so on.

We evaluate the support for the final conclusion according to the following principles:

a. *If each inference in a complex argument is valid, the whole argument is valid.*

Consider the simplest form of a complex argument:

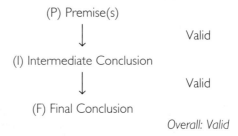

If the truth of *P* would guarantee the truth of *I*, and the truth of *I* would guarantee *F*, then obviously the truth of *P* would guarantee *F*. And that is what this principle tells us.

b. *If any inference in a complex argument is unsuccessful, the whole argument is unsuccessful.*

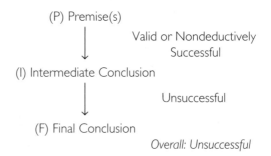

No matter how strong any other inferences are, since the reasoning from *I* to *F* is unsuccessful, the overall reasoning from *P* to *F*, because it includes step *I* to *F*, must be unsuccessful.

c. *If a complex argument is made up of one or more valid inferences and exactly one nondeductively successful inference, the whole argument is nondeductively successful.*

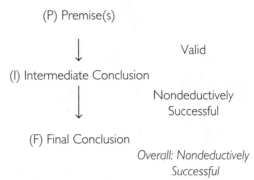

If the truth of *P* would guarantee the truth of *I*, and *I* makes *F* likely to be true, then the truth of *P* would make *F* likely to be true.

d. *If a complex argument is made up of two or more nondeductively successful inferences or of two or more nondeductively successful and some valid inferences, the whole argument may be either nondeductively successful or unsuccessful.*

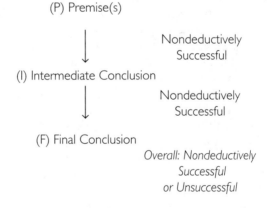

Because the presence of valid inferences can never weaken an argument, what we need to understand is why the combination of two or more nondeductively successful inferences may not result in a nondeductively successful argument. Consider this example:

1. Sixty percent of the volunteers in the arthritis study were given placebos rather than ibuprofen.

2. Cohen was a volunteer in this study.

3. Cohen was given a placebo. 1, 2

4. Seventy percent of those given placebos experienced increased stiffening of the joints.

5. Cohen experienced increased stiffening of the joints. 3, 4

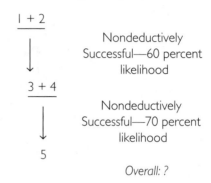

Determining the overall likelihood that Cohen experienced increased stiffening of the joints is easy enough. Suppose that there were exactly 100 volunteers. By premise 1, sixty of them would have received placebos. By premise 4, 70 percent *of those sixty*—that is, forty-two (of the 100 volunteers)—will have experienced increased stiffening of the joints. Thus, it is just 42 percent likely that Cohen will have experienced increased stiffening of the joints, so overall the argument is unsuccessful.

The general point here is that in any nonvalid inference, even those that are nondeductively successful, some loss of certainty occurs, and the loss of certainty accumulates with each additional step in a series of inferences. The result may be an argument that is, overall, unsuccessful. (Of course, it need not be. If the number in premise 1 above were 90 percent, the conclusion would be 63 percent likely, and the argument overall would be nondeductively successful.)

As we have noted before, most everyday arguments are not given in such precise numerical terms, and that makes it difficult to estimate the overall degree of loss of certainty through several inferences. Nonetheless, we often have to carry out these estimations. And we can do it with enough accuracy for practical purposes if we are thoughtful and careful.

Exercises

B. *Analyze the arguments and determine whether they are valid, nondeductively successful (the premises make the conclusion more likely than not), or nondeductively unsuccessful. For those that are nondeductively successful, consider whether the premises make the conclusions barely more likely than not, a great deal more likely than not, or close to certain. (We are concerned here with the degree to which the premises support the conclusions. Assume the premises are true for this exercise.)*

*1. If the child tax credit is properly applied, then it will not be given to those who already pay no taxes. Families with a joint income of under $29,000 pay no taxes, so if they receive the credit it has been improperly applied.

2. Five hundred of the two thousand Cactus County Public Library cardholders were randomly selected and asked whether they prefer fiction or nonfiction. Three hundred thirty-eight said they prefer fiction. Thus, you can bet that most of the Cactus County cardholders prefer fiction.

*3. Since Xaviera has a proven IQ of 153 and is an experienced test-taker, she will do very well on the law school admissions exams next week.

4. Fewer than 2 percent of people who work in New York City live in Connecticut, so you should infer that Allen, who works in a Times Square bookstore, doesn't live in Connecticut.

*5. In almost all recent presidential campaigns, no candidate has been willing to challenge an incumbent on his conduct of military campaigns overseas. Thus, in the next election, no candidate will challenge the current president on his approach to the recent war in the Middle East.

6. Since most birds can fly, the bird over there can fly. And all flying creatures can elude any mammal. So that bird can elude the bear that is sneaking up on it.

*7. I asked several other students in my Advanced Algebra class what they thought of Professor Crator's Intro to English Literature last semester. Most of them were really bored with the lit class. So, Professor Crator must be a boring teacher. I'm sure not going to take her course.

8. Dumwaith is an expert on the eighteenth century, and he is a well-regarded teacher. Therefore, he is the person best qualified for the opening in the English department.

*9. The great majority of children of Republicans are Republicans. I know Teasdale's parents are devoted Republicans. So surely Teasdale is one too.

10. Usually freshmen do better work than seniors in Professor Cohen's course on English literature. Thus, because Harold is a freshman and his brother is a senior, we should expect Harold's work in the course to be better than his brother's.

*11. Studies of the lowland gorilla in zoos have revealed virtually no cases of aggressive behavior. We can conclude that the gorilla is generally a nonaggressive beast.

12. An animal has been gnawing at my sleeping bag. Some of my trail mix has been eaten. I was awakened by something scurrying across my face last night. There are no signs of bears or other large mammals around. So, there must be giant rats in our campground.

*13. No former First Lady who subsequently became a U.S. Senator has ever gone on to be President of the United States. So none will ever be President.

14. A popular television "newsmagazine" surveyed viewers on the question "Should citizens who do not have criminal records be allowed to carry concealed handguns?" Callers dialed one 900 telephone number to vote "yes," another to vote "no." Each call cost 50 cents. Sixty-five percent of the callers voted "yes."

Conclusion 1: "The survey shows that the American people approve of the concealed weapons proposal by a margin of nearly 2 to 1."

Conclusion 2: "The survey shows that viewers of this newsmagazine approve of the concealed weapons proposal by a margin of nearly 2 to 1."

Conclusion 3: "The survey shows that people who chose to call at the cost of 50 cents/call approve of the concealed weapons proposal by a margin of nearly 2 to 1."

*15. A *New York Times*/CBS News poll conducted March 31 to April 2, 1996, concluded that if the presidential election were held at that time, 49 percent of registered voters would back President Clinton and 39 percent would support Republican nominee Robert Dole. The poll was based on telephone interviews with 1,257 adults throughout the United States. The margin of sampling error of the poll is plus or minus three percentage points.—*The New York Times* (April 7, 1996)

We can, then, be quite sure that if the election had been held at that time, Mr. Clinton would have won fairly handily.

16. A large majority of persons who die of lung cancer have been heavy smokers. So, if you smoke, the odds are that you will die of lung cancer.

*17. A large majority of heavy smokers develop lung cancer, and most people with lung cancer die within five years. So, since most smokers eventually die of lung cancer, you should never begin smoking.

18. Prosecutor: "This poor, mutilated man was sleeping peacefully at the time of the attack. The DNA evidence makes it overwhelmingly likely that the blood on this woman's knife is the victim's blood. No one saw her drinking at the bar where she says she was at the time of the attack. Everyone had heard her threaten that if she couldn't have him, no other woman would either. Clearly she is guilty."

*19. Any cat normally found in the wild is classified as a nondomesticated animal, and cheetahs are normally found in the wild. So cheetahs are classified as nondomesticated animals. Since a permit is required to keep a nondomesticated animal in one's home, Alexander needs a permit to keep his cheetah at home. I know that Alexander does not have a permit. Anyone who needs a permit but does not have one is subject to arrest, so Alexander is subject to arrest. In this town, most people who are subject to arrest for animal violations do get arrested pretty quickly. Chances are, then, that Alexander will be arrested before long.

20. Mary is probably the one who sent you those roses without including a card. She's a romantic, after all, and besides that she's shy. Also, I saw her walking toward the florist shop that morning, and there's no other reason for her to be on that block. Sarah told me that Mary has a crush on you, and I know you're not dating anyone right now. Add to all this that it's not your birthday! You can bet the flowers came from Mary.

IV. Overall Argument Evaluation

A. Evaluating Deductive Arguments

Evaluating deductive arguments is fairly straightforward. They aim at validity. If an argument meets this aim and its premises are true, then its conclusion will be true. And, as we have seen (pp. 36–38), additional information will not alter this. Thus, we need ask only whether the premises are true and the argument valid. (In some cases, if a deductive argument fails to be valid, we might want to consider whether its premises supply any support at all for its conclusion. If they do, we could go on to evaluate it as if it were a nondeductive argument.)

We evaluate validity by using the thought experiment method described above or, in some cases, by the formal methods discussed in the next two chapters. The truth of the premises might be established by some further arguments, based on experience, self-evidence, or the word of others. Chapter 11, "Reasonable Beliefs," looks at nonargumentative ways of establishing premises.

B. Evaluating Nondeductive Arguments

Nondeductive arguments are not meant to demonstrate their conclusions, but to make a case for them, to make them likely. Thus, we must ask whether the given premises do, in themselves, make a case for the conclusion and whether the premises are true.

Evaluating nondeductive arguments is generally more difficult than evaluating deductive ones, for two reasons. First, determining how well the given premises support a conclusion is (except in statistical syllogisms) far less "rule-governed" than is determining validity. This is particularly true for the nondeductive arguments we have called plausibility arguments. We have offered useful ways of thinking about degrees of nondeductive support (conducting thought experiments, adding premises), and we will resume discussion of the evaluation of causal and analogical arguments in Chapters 6 and 7. But no one would pretend that these methods have the precision of a demonstration of validity.

Second, we have seen that the introduction of new information in the premises can affect the degree to which nondeductive arguments support their conclusions. And so, when we are dealing with a nondeductive argument, we must consider whether known information that would have an important effect on the acceptability of the conclusion is left out of the premises. We saw that we would reach a false conclusion about whether Mujtaba attends religious services if we did not take other information into account.

Here is a case in which we would ignore relevant information at our peril:

> Almost all snakes found in the United States are nonpoisonous. So, the little snake in my path ahead is nonpoisonous.

Suppose it is also true that

> The little snake in my path ahead has rattles on its tail.

Given this information, together with what we all know about rattlesnakes, our assessment of the conclusion that the little snake is nonpoisonous is radically altered.

Ideally, of course, we should take *all* relevant information into account in evaluating a nondeductive argument. But we do not know all the relevant information, and we can take into account only what we know. And there are practical constraints on what we can find out in a timely manner. Still, when the issue in question is of great importance, it may be necessary to do all we can to learn more of the relevant information. As always, our safest evaluations of nondeductive arguments are going to be of the strength or weakness of one argument *relative to* another.

We want to make rational decisions about a myriad of difficult matters: Is Kelly really guilty? Should the death penalty be abolished? Is there a god? Could everyone around me actually be a robot? Was Faulkner a better novelist than Hemingway? Will I make more money if I go to business school or law school? To answer such hard questions in a rational way, we must consider arguments and counterarguments, taking into account evaluations, practical results, and plain facts. No magic formulas exist for reaching the truth about such questions, but knowledge of the critical tools discussed in this book can help us think clearly and effectively about them.

Some main concepts of argument evaluation:

A **deductive** argument is one in which the premises are meant to guarantee the conclusion.

A deductive argument is **valid** if and only if in every possible case that the premises are true, the conclusion is also true.

A deductive argument is sound just in case it is valid and each of its premises is true.

A **nondeductive argument** is one in which the premises are meant to confer some high degree of probability on the conclusion.

A nondeductive argument is **successful** to the degree that its premises confer probability on its conclusion.

Adding premises to a *deductively valid* argument always yields an argument that is also valid.

Adding premises to a *nondeductively successful* argument may yield an argument that is unsuccessful.

Exercises

C. *An argument may be unconvincing overall because its premises are not true, because the premises are not relevant to the conclusion or (even if relevant) do not give adequate support to the conclusion, or (in the case of nondeductive arguments) because known, relevant information is not taken into account. Explain exactly why each of the following arguments is unconvincing overall.*

*1.   Millikan's novel can't be counted as good literature because it focuses on plot at the expense of character. All good literature depends on the development of the characters.

2.   There are times when any of us may need to protect himself or herself from intruders. Thus, we should all keep hand grenades on our bedside tables.

*3.   Most intellectuals cannot explain the mathematical supposition called "Goldbach's Conjecture." My calculus professor is an intellectual, so he wouldn't know about the Goldbach thing.

4.   King has just received a scholarship to play basketball at a major Division I college. This leads us to believe that King must be a very athletic young man.

*5.   Pierce is the best person to be put in charge of the arrangements for our club's trip to the International Debate Meet next year. After all, he does hold the number-one position on our team.

6.   Jameson is strong and quick and tall. We should recruit her for our basketball team.

*7.   It is all right to shoplift that necklace. You like it, and there is almost no chance you will be caught.

8.   I was kept up all night by something barking. It must have been a big terrier.

*9.   All American automobiles are much better than any Japanese one. So buy a Buick, not a Toyota.

10.   Vermont is hardly a breeding ground for national politicians. Don't expect there to be a U.S. president from Vermont in our lifetimes.

*11.   If you believe in God, you will be happier. That shows that God really does exist.

12.   Since Alma Schindler inspired Gustav Mahler, Oskar Kokoschka, and Walter Gropius in turn to do some of their greatest work, she must have been a great artistic genius herself.

*13.   One way of being healthier is to work out at a gym every day. So, since you want to be healthier, you should go to Bailey's Gym every day.

14.   Most undergraduate students never take organic chemistry. So, the chances are that Claude, a graduating premed student, did not take it.

*15. Giving tax breaks to the poor completely defeats the object of sound tax policy. Thus, we should not give tax breaks to the poor.

16. Two of the most recent holders of the office of Secretary of State have been women and two have been minority groups. It's quite clear from this that recent presidents have been using this office to make up their quota of cabinet members from underrepresented groups.

*17. Either there are still large caches of weapons of mass destruction lying undiscovered in Iraq despite an enormous presence of our troops and officials, or the administration was lying about the existence of such weapons. Either way, this administration is not competent to govern our nation.

18. The days when natural disasters such as earthquakes, hurricanes, or volcanoes had the power to bring death to thousands are fortunately behind us. Unlike the times of such catastrophes as the 1906 San Francisco earthquake or the hurricane of 1900 in Galveston, these days modern construction methods for buildings, sophisticated advanced warning systems, mass communication, and modern healthcare developments mean that we are able to keep the toll from even the worst natural events to tens or at most one or two hundred.

*19. The U.S. national soccer team has its best ever chance to win the World Cup next year. The team won its qualifying group with ease and features a very talented collection of players, many of whom play with the best professional clubs in Europe. So, the U.S. team has as good a chance of winning as anyone.

20. Widespread logging in the rainforests of the Amazon basis is not the natural disaster that many ecologists claim. After all, the logging companies bring jobs, housing, and healthcare to an impoverished and backward part of the world.

Chapter 4

SOME VALID ARGUMENT FORMS

In the last chapter, we explained an informal thought experiment method for determining whether arguments are valid. In this chapter and the next, we'll show how the validity of some arguments can be demonstrated by rigorous methods.

The methods make use of the idea of argument *forms*. The methods we will explain let us recognize immediately the validity of many practical, simple inferences and construct demonstrations showing the validity of certain longer, more complex arguments. Acquaintance with valid forms often has the added benefit of helping us analyze arguments, because the forms are likely to be important clues as to how the parts of an argument are meant to fit together.

In this chapter, we will be concerned with arguments that are valid because of their *sentential forms*.

I. Sentential Form

A. Form and Variables

Consider these arguments:

> If the presence of the anthropologist changed the normal lifestyle of the islanders, then her conclusions are not reliable. Her presence did cause such a change. So her conclusions are not reliable.

> If the spider is a brown recluse, then it is dangerous. The spider is a brown recluse. Therefore, it is dangerous.

The subject matter of these arguments is entirely different, but the arguments have similarities. In each case,

> The argument contains two premises and a conclusion.

> One premise is a conditional ("If..., then...") sentence.

> The other premise is the same as the clause that comes immediately after the "if" in the conditional.

The conclusion is the same as the clause that follows "then" in the conditional.

The arguments, then, have the same form.

If we use letters to replace the component sentences in either argument, we represent the form in this way:

$$\text{If } P, \text{ then } Q$$
$$P$$
$$\text{Therefore, } Q$$

Since the letters replace the simple sentences that make up the compound sentences of the argument, this is called the **sentential form** of the argument, and the letters (*P*, *Q*, and so on) are called **sentential variables** (*variables* because they stand for any sentence that might be substituted for them). We can use any letters for variables. Logicians often start with *P* and move on to *Q*, *R*, *S*, and so on. We usually choose letters that remind us of the sentences in the original argument. Also, it is customary in sentential form to use either the three-dot pattern ∴ or the line before the conclusion instead of the word *therefore*.

B. Connectives

In addition to using sentential variables, we can simplify the representation of argument forms by using symbols to replace ordinary connective words like "and," "or," and "if . . . , then . . . " that are used to join simple sentences. We should regard these symbols as representing the logical function performed by a number of phrases that have a common role, rather than as the translation of one specific English phrase.

Ordinary Words	Symbol	Name
either . . . or	∨	Disjunction
. . . or . . .		
Either it is a cat or it is a dog. $C \vee D$		
and, but, yet	•	Conjunction
It is a dog, and it bites. $D \cdot B$		
if . . . , then . . .	→	Implication
If it bites, then you should be wary. $B \rightarrow W$		

Sentences of the form "if . . . , then . . . " are called **conditionals** or **hypotheticals.** In a conditional, the component immediately following *if* is called the **antecedent;** the component sentence following *then* is the **consequent.** That is, in $P \rightarrow Q$, P is the antecedent, and Q is the consequent. In our example, "it bites" is the antecedent, and "you should be wary" is the consequent.

C. Negation

There is also a useful symbol for expressions that serve the purpose of *denying* or *negating* a claim.

not (and other ways of denying)   ~   Negation
It is not a dog.   ~D

Putting the negation symbol ~ before a variable forms its **denial.** It is like putting "It is not the case that" before a sentence. When denied (negated), the sentence "Cats like cream" becomes "It is not the case that cats like cream," or, more idiomatically, "Cats do not like cream." In formalizing arguments, use the negation of a variable for a negative sentence. (For instance, use ~C for "Cats do not like cream.")

Note that a *negative* sentence such as "Cats do not like cream" can also be denied by adding the prefix, "It is not the case that." Similarly, we can deny a negative variable, ~C, by adding another ~. But the resulting double negatives ("It is not the case that cats do not like cream" and ~~C) are clumsy and sometimes hard to understand. In ordinary speech, we recognize that we can deny that cats do *not* like cream by saying, "Cats do like cream." Instead of adding another "not," we remove the one we already have. This commonsense practice is entirely legitimate. We will treat the denial of negative variables in the same way, generally using C (rather than ~~C) to deny ~C. (The formal equivalence of C and ~~C will be discussed under "Equivalent Forms" later in this chapter.)

D. An Example of Symbolizing

This sentence may at first seem difficult to symbolize:

> If cigarette advertising leads teenagers to smoke and advertisers lie about their aims, then either cigarette advertising should not be allowed or it should be strictly regulated.

Actually, such sentences are easy to deal with if we consider their constituent parts one at a time. First, identify the main connective phrase in the whole complex sentence—the claim that holds the whole sentence together. It's "If..., then..." The antecedent in this case is

> Cigarette advertising leads teenagers to smoke, and advertisers lie about their aims.

$$C \cdot L$$

And the consequent is

> Either cigarette advertising should not be allowed or it should be strictly regulated.

$$\sim A \lor R$$

Once we have analyzed the form of the antecedent and the consequent, we see that the form of the whole conditional must be

$$(C \bullet L) \to (\sim A \lor R)$$

Generally, symbolizing complex sentences and even lengthy arguments presents little difficulty if we take them one part at a time.

Before leaving this example, notice how parentheses are used to group simple sentences into units to prevent ambiguity. In the same way that $2 + 5 \times 3$ is ambiguous without parentheses, so too is a formula such as $A \bullet B \to C$. Does this mean "If A and B, then C" or "A and if B, then C"? Parentheses can resolve the doubt: $(A \bullet B) \to C$ gives the first reading; $A \bullet (B \to C)$ gives the second. (Very long sentences might require brackets, braces, and large parentheses to keep the reading straight.)

Hints on Symbolizing Complex Sentences:

1. Identify the simple component sentences—those that are not made up of further sentences and connective phrases.

2. Identify the *main connective*. This is the connective phrase that holds the whole together.

3. Try to symbolize the components that are connected by the main connective as separate sentences. This involves applying Steps 1 and 2 again to these subcomponents of the sentence.

Think about this procedure as applied to the example already given.

Exercises

A. *Using sentential variables and symbols for negation, disjunction ("or"), conjunction ("and"), and implication ("if . . . , then . . ."), show the form of each of the following. Be sure to use negative variables to represent negative statements. (We suggest letters that would be convenient to use in each case.)*

   *1. If the quarterback is healthy and the referees are honest, then either the team will win or the coach will be fired. (Q, R, W, F)

2. Either animals are capable of feeling pain and they should not be used in surgical experiments without anesthesia, or they are incapable of feeling pain. (*P, E*)

*3. If the book is exciting, then if it is well advertised, it will be a best-seller.

   The book is being well advertised, and it is exciting.

   The book will be a best-seller. (*E, A, B*)

4. Either Bono wrote an excellent new song or the song was an old reggae tune and the arrangement was new. The song was not an old reggae tune.

   Bono wrote an excellent new song. (*N, O, A*)

*5. If there is anything to the story of the *Matrix* and contemporary science is further advanced than people think, then we could be brains controlled by a supercomputer.
   We could not be brains controlled by a supercomputer.

   Therefore, either there's nothing to the story of the *Matrix* or contemporary science is no further advanced than people think. (*M, C, B*)

II. Valid Argument Forms

The eight argument forms given below are valid forms; that is, any inference having one of these forms will be valid. (There is no possible way for its premises to be true and its conclusion false.) As we have said, acquaintance with the forms is of significant practical value, helping us to analyze, evaluate, and construct convincing arguments in everyday life and specialized disciplines.

We give each form twice. On the left we express it in variables and ordinary connective words; on the right we put it in its most succinct form, using variables and connective symbols. We then give an example of an argument having the form. We also give the standard name attached to each form and its abbreviation.

1. *Modus Ponens* (MP)

$$
\begin{array}{ll}
\text{If } P, \text{ then } Q & P \rightarrow Q \\
P & P \\
\hline
\text{Therefore, } Q & Q
\end{array}
$$

The anthropologist and spider examples (given at the beginning of this chapter) are both instances of *modus ponens*. Here is another:

If Manning is healthy, then the Colts will win.
Manning is healthy.
_____

The Colts will win.

Four observations may help avoid some possible confusions. First, complex as well as simple sentences can occupy the places of *P* and *Q*. An argument whose form would be fully expressed as

$$(P \bullet Q) \rightarrow (R \lor S)$$
$$P \bullet Q$$
$$\overline{}$$
$$R \lor S$$

is also a case of *modus ponens* because there is a conditional, a premise that asserts the antecedent of the conditional, and a conclusion that asserts the consequent of the conditional.

Second, the components can be negative sentences. These are also cases of *modus ponens*:

$$\sim P \rightarrow \sim Q \qquad \sim P \rightarrow Q \qquad P \rightarrow \sim Q$$
$$\underline{\sim P} \qquad\qquad \underline{\sim P} \qquad\qquad \underline{P}$$
$$\sim Q \qquad\qquad Q \qquad\qquad \sim Q$$

Thirdly, the order in which the premises are given does not matter. This is also *modus ponens*:

$$P$$
$$P \rightarrow Q$$
$$\overline{}$$
$$Q$$

Finally, however, the following form is not an instance of *modus ponens*:

$$\sim(P \rightarrow Q)$$
$$\sim P$$
$$Q$$

The first premise, although it contains an arrow, is not a conditional. The overall type of a sentence (whether it is a conditional, conjunction, negation, etc.) is determined by its main connective. In this case, the main connective is the tilde ($\sim$), so this is a negation.

The foregoing observations apply equally to any of the following argument forms.

2. *Modus Tollens* (MT)

If P, then Q	$P \rightarrow Q$
Not Q	$\sim Q$
Therefore, not P	$\sim P$

If Putnam is guilty, she is lying now.
She is not lying now.

Putnam is not guilty.

Since the second premise in *modus tollens* denies the consequent of the conditional, and P and Q are ways of denying ~P and ~Q, the following and other obvious variations are also *modus tollens*:

$$\sim P \rightarrow \sim Q$$
$$\underline{Q}$$
$$P$$

3. Hypothetical Syllogism (HS)

If P, then Q	$P \rightarrow Q$
If Q, then R	$Q \rightarrow R$
Therefore, if P, then R	$P \rightarrow R$

If taxes go up, inflation goes down.
If inflation goes down, most people are better off.

If taxes go up, most people are better off.

The forbidding name of this argument is easy to remember if we bear in mind that a syllogism is a three-line argument and that this argument form is made up entirely of hypotheticals (conditionals).

As we have seen, the presence of extraneous premises does not make a valid argument invalid. Nor do such premises change the fact that a valid form is present. Thus, the following argument is valid by hypothetical syllogism, even though the second premise does not contribute:

If recent census figures are accurate, Malthus was right.
If Malthus was wrong, there will not be famine.
If Malthus was right, there will soon be world famine.

If recent census figures are accurate, there will soon be world famine.

4. Disjunctive Syllogism (DS)

Either P or Q	$P \vee Q$
Not Q	$\sim Q$
Therefore, P	P

or

Either P or Q	$P \vee Q$
Not P	$\sim P$
Therefore, Q	Q

Either Picasso was the twentieth century's greatest artist or Matisse was. Matisse was not the twentieth century's greatest artist.

Picasso was the twentieth century's greatest artist.

The name of this argument form derives from its being a three-line argument whose crucial premise is a disjunction, an either/or sentence.

5. Constructive Dilemma (CD)

Either P or Q	$P \vee Q$
If P, then R	$P \rightarrow R$
If Q, then S	$Q \rightarrow S$
Therefore, R or S	$R \vee S$

Either astrology is a science or it is superstition.
If it is a science, then newspapers shouldn't print horoscopes on the comics page.
If it is superstition, horoscopes shouldn't appear in newspapers at all.

Either newspapers shouldn't print horoscopes on the comics page or horoscopes shouldn't appear in newspapers at all.

A **dilemma** is a set of alternatives. This argument form uses a set of alternatives and a disjunction to allow the inference to another set of alternatives.

6. Conjunction (Conj)

P	P		P
Q	Q	or	Q
Therefore, P and Q	$P \cdot Q$		$Q \cdot P$

The tomato plants are dying.
The squash have rotted.

The tomato plants are dying, and the squash have rotted.

This form just makes explicit the obvious fact that it is valid to join two separate sentences to form a single conjunctive sentence. The following form is equally obvious.

7. Simplification (Simp)

$$P \text{ and } Q \qquad\qquad \frac{P \bullet Q}{P} \quad \text{or} \quad \frac{P \bullet Q}{Q}$$

Therefore, P

I am a sick man, and I am a spiteful man.

I am a sick man.

8. Addition (Add)

$$P \qquad\qquad\qquad \frac{P}{P \vee Q}$$

Therefore, P or Q

Harpo was one of the Marx brothers.

Harpo was one of the Marx brothers or Karl was one of the Marx brothers.

This form may look peculiar, but it is valid. For if P is true, then of course P *or* anything else whatsoever will be true.

III. Two Invalid Argument Forms

Two invalid argument forms are easily confused with *modus ponens* (in which the antecedent of the conditional is affirmed) or *modus tollens* (in which the consequent of the conditional is denied).

1. Denying the Antecedent—NOT VALID

$$\frac{\begin{array}{l} P \rightarrow Q \\ \sim P \end{array}}{\sim Q}$$

If Haley shares drug needles with strangers, he is at considerable risk of contracting the AIDS virus.
Haley does not share drug needles with strangers.

Haley is not at considerable risk of contracting the AIDS virus.

This argument is clearly not valid. (Perhaps Haley does not share drug needles, but for other reasons, such as his sexual practices, he is at considerable risk.) So, the argument form it exemplifies cannot be valid.

2. Affirming the Consequent—NOT VALID

$$P \rightarrow Q$$
$$\frac{Q}{P}$$

If Petrie is an atheist, she opposes compulsory prayer in public schools.
She does oppose such compulsory prayer.

Petrie is an atheist.

Again, it should be clear that this argument form is not a valid one. (Many who are not atheists oppose compulsory school prayer.)

At least partially because of their similarities to *modus ponens* and *modus tollens,* it is easy to fall into thinking particular cases of these invalid forms are valid. And often, mistaken reasoning taking these forms has important or even dangerous consequences. (The examples just given may be cases in point.) This is just one reason why we should be acquainted with valid and invalid argument forms and be able to tell the difference.

(Denying the antecedent and affirming the consequent are often called **formal fallacies.** We will discuss fallacies in Chapter 8.)

Exercises

B. *Identify the inference form (modus ponens, disjunctive syllogism, denying the antecedent, and so on) in each case, and note whether or not it is valid.*

*1. $P \rightarrow Q$
  $\dfrac{P}{Q}$

2. $P \rightarrow Q$
  $\dfrac{\sim Q}{\sim P}$

*3. $P \rightarrow \sim Q$
  $\dfrac{\sim P}{Q}$

4. $\sim P \rightarrow \sim Q$
  $\dfrac{\sim P}{\sim Q}$

*5. $P \rightarrow Q$
  $\dfrac{Q}{P}$

6. $\sim P \rightarrow \sim Q$
  $\dfrac{Q}{P}$

*7. $(P \bullet Q) \rightarrow R$
  $\dfrac{\sim R}{\sim (P \bullet Q)}$

8. $P \rightarrow \sim Q$
  $\dfrac{\sim Q}{P}$

*9. $(P \bullet Q) \rightarrow R$
  $\dfrac{P \bullet Q}{R}$

10. $\sim P \rightarrow Q$
    P
    _____
    $\sim Q$

16. $\sim Q \rightarrow R$
    $P \rightarrow \sim Q$
    _____
    $P \rightarrow R$

*23. $\sim P \vee \sim Q$
    $\sim Q \rightarrow R$
    $\sim P \rightarrow \sim S$
    _____
    $R \vee \sim S$

*11. $(P \bullet Q) \rightarrow R$
    R
    _____
    $P \bullet Q$

*17. $R \rightarrow \sim(P \bullet Q)$
    $\sim(P \bullet Q) \rightarrow S$
    _____
    $R \rightarrow S$

24. $(P \bullet Q) \rightarrow (R \vee S)$
    $\sim(R \vee S)$
    _____
    $\sim(P \bullet Q)$

12. $(P \bullet Q) \rightarrow R$
    $\sim(P \bullet Q)$
    _____
    $\sim R$

18. $(P \bullet Q) \vee (R \vee S)$
    $\sim(R \vee S)$
    _____
    $P \bullet Q$

*25. $(P \bullet Q) \rightarrow (R \vee S)$
    $(R \vee S)$
    _____
    $(P \bullet Q)$

*13. $P \rightarrow Q$
    $Q \rightarrow R$
    _____
    $P \rightarrow R$

*19. P
    _____
    $P \vee Q$

14. $\sim P \vee \sim Q$
    P
    _____
    $\sim Q$

20. $P \vee Q$
    $P \rightarrow R$
    $Q \rightarrow S$
    _____
    $R \vee S$

*15. $P \rightarrow (R \vee S)$

    P
    _____
    $R \vee S$

*21. P
    $\sim Q$
    _____
    $P \bullet \sim Q$

22. $\sim P \bullet Q$
    _____
    $\sim P$

C. *Using sentential variables and symbols, show the form of each of the following. Also identify the inference form (modus ponens, disjunctive syllogism, denying the antecedent, and so on) in each case, and note whether or not it is valid.*

*1. If sharks are not fish, then they do not have gills.
   Sharks do have gills.
   _____
   Sharks are fish. (*F, G*)

2. If Serena Williams continues her current form, she will win at least half of the Grand Slam tennis titles for the rest of her career.
   If she wins at least half of the Grand Slam tennis

titles for the rest of her career, then she will be the most successful tennis player of all time.

If Serena Williams continues her current form, she will be the most successful tennis player of all time. (*S, G, T*)

*3. I am a sick man.

I am a sick man or I am a spiteful man. (*S, P*)

4. If Hoyle's theory of why the universe is expanding was correct, then the universe had no beginning in time.
Hoyle's theory turned out not to be correct.

The universe did have a beginning in time. (*H, B*)

*5. Either Artemisia Gentileschi's talent has been over-hyped, or she should be counted among the great artists.
Her talent has not been overhyped.

She should be counted among the great artists. (*G, C*)

6. Mix either killed all the people he said he killed or he is totally out of touch with reality.
If he killed them all, he should be locked up in the state penitentiary at Raiford.
If he is totally out of touch with reality, he should be locked up in the state hospital at Macclenny.

Mix should be locked up in the state facility at Raiford or he should be locked up in the facility at Macclenny. (*K, O, R, M*)

*7. If Aristotle was a more profound thinker than Wittgenstein, then there has not been progress in philosophy.
Aristotle was the more profound thinker.

There has not been progress in philosophy. (*A, P*)

8. There are clouds.
It is very cold.

There are clouds and it is very cold. (*C, V*)

*9. The senior U.S. Senator for Maine is either Olympia Snowe or Olympia Dukakis.
She's not Olympia Dukakis.

She's Olympia Snowe. (*S, D*)

10. If capital punishment deters murder, then the murder rate should increase when capital punishment is abolished.

> The murder rate does not increase when capital punishment is abolished.
> ───────────────────────────────
> Capital punishment does not deter murder. (*D, I*)

IV. Using the Forms to Show Validity

We may quickly discover that many seemingly valid arguments do not have one of these eight forms. Yet, it is possible to use the forms to show their validity.

Here is an argument made up of two inferences, each of which is an instance of a valid argument form. We have identified and numbered each claim in the example, and after each claim we have given its sentential form in brackets. (Notice that each different sentence is represented by a different variable, each repetition of a sentence by the same variable, and the negation of any sentence by a negated variable.)

> (1) If life imprisonment is as effective as capital punishment in deterring murder, then capital punishment is not necessary. [*E* → ~*N*] (2) If it is not necessary, then it should be abolished altogether. [~*N* → *A*] So (3) if life imprisonment is as effective as capital punishment in deterring murder, capital punishment should be abolished altogether. [*E* → *A*] And all the evidence indicates that (4) life imprisonment is just as effective in deterring murder. [*E*] Thus, (5) capital punishment should be abolished altogether. [*A*]

To show the argument is valid, we arrange the sentential forms into *standard form*. (We will again give two versions, one without and one with the symbolic connectives.)

1.	If *E*, then not *N*		1.	*E* → ~*N*		
2.	If not *N*, then *A*		2.	~*N* → *A*		
3.	If *E*, then *A*	1, 2 HS	3.	*E* → *A*	1, 2 HS	
4.	*E*		4.	*E*		
5.	*A*	3, 4 MP	5.	*A*	3, 4 MP	

As when we used standard form before, to the right of each conclusion we write the line(s) from which it follows. We also give the *justification* for each valid inference; that is, we give the name of the form of the inference, a form we know to be valid. It is natural, now, to think of the valid forms, *modus ponens* and so on, as **inference rules**—rules that enable us to move from one step to another in a valid way. When we have justified each inference in an argument, we have **demonstrated** that the argument as a whole is valid.

Each inference in the previous argument was explicitly given to begin with. Often that is not the case. Consider this argument that might be given in reaction to rising college grades:

> (1) Either students are learning more than in the past or professors are becoming more lax in their grading standards. [S ∨ P] But (2) if students are actually learning more, their scores on standardized tests would be higher than they used to be. [S → H] The sad fact is that (3) scores on standardized tests are not higher than they were in the past. [~H] The conclusion is inescapable: (4) Professors are becoming more lax in their grading standards. [P]

The argument, as given, has this form:

1.	Either S or P		1.	S ∨ P	
2.	If S, then H		2.	S → H	
3.	Not H		3.	~H	
4.	P	1, 2, 3 ?	4.	P	1, 2, 3 ?

As it stands, this is a simple argument, and its premises 1, 2, 3, and conclusion 4 do not conform to any of our valid argument patterns. But if we are careful, we can *deduce* 4 from the premises; that is, we can devise a set of valid inferences leading from the premises to the conclusion. And if the conclusion follows from the premises by valid inferences, then the argument is valid, whether or not those inferences are explicit in the argument to begin with.

Here is the complete deduction for the grading argument. (The conclusion, *P*, of course, has a different number because there are now more lines before it.)

1.	Either S or P		1.	S ∨ P	
2.	If S, then H		2.	S → H	
3.	Not H		3.	~H	
4.	~S	2, 3 MT	4.	~S	2, 3 MT
5.	P	1, 4 DS	5.	P	1, 4 DS

How do we know which inferences will get us to the desired conclusion? If it isn't obvious to begin with—which it probably won't be if the argument is at all long or complicated—the best strategy is to *try something* and see if it is promising. In the grading argument, the only valid form we can use at the outset is MT with 2 and 3, and so we try it. Then the valid step to the conclusion should be obvious. (Failing to find a valid deduction does not necessarily mean there is not one; it may be we just failed to find it.)

Exercises

D. *Using sentential variables and symbols, put the following arguments into standard form. Be sure to cite the lines from which each conclusion follows and give its justification. (The preceding capital punishment argument can serve as a model for the form in which these arguments should be expressed.)*

> *1. (1) If Harvey did not win the croquet tournament, then either his mallet was broken or Mary has been taking lessons. (2) Harvey did not win the competition. So, (3) either Harvey's mallet was broken or Mary has been taking lessons. But (4) Mary has not taken any lessons. Thus, (5) Harvey's mallet was broken. (*H, B, L*)

> 2. (1) If the private industrial sector had been willing and able to install effective scrubbers in smokestacks, harmful emissions would not now be a problem. Further, (2) if these emissions were not now a problem, there would not be ongoing damage to the environment. And so, (3) if the private sector had been willing and able to install the scrubbers, there would not be ongoing damage to the environment. But it is entirely clear that (4) there is ongoing damage to the environment. (5) The private sector, then, has just not been willing and able to install effective scrubbers. (6) If it has not been willing and able to install these devices up until now, it will not change its ways in the future regarding the control of pollution. Thus, (7) it will not change its ways in this regard. But there are really only two possibilities: (8) Either the private industrial sector will change its ways in the future or there must be strict governmental regulation of industry when the environment is at issue. As regrettable as some may find it, (9) there must be strict governmental regulation of industry when the environment is at issue. (*P, E, D, C, G*)

E. *Using sentential variables and symbols, show that the conclusions follow from the premises by a series of valid inferences. Be sure to cite the lines from which each conclusion follows and give its justification. (The preceding grading argument can serve as a model for these exercises.)*

Find two different ways of reaching the conclusions in #3, #5, #6, and #13.

We will start with two arguments you have already symbolized.

*1. If the book is exciting, then if it is well advertised, it will be a best-seller.
The book is being well advertised, and it is exciting.

The book will be a best-seller. (*E, A, B*)

2. If there is anything to the story of the *Matrix*, then contemporary science is further advanced than we think.
If contemporary science is further advanced than we think, then we could all be brains controlled by a supercomputer.
We could not all be brains controlled by a supercomputer.

There is nothing to the story of the *Matrix*. (M, C, B)

*3. If studying logic helps with reasoning skills, it will help you prepare for standardized tests.
If logic helps you prepare for standardized tests, you should study logic before you take the LSAT.
Studying logic does help with reasoning skills.

You should study logic before you take the LSAT. (*S, P, L*)

4. If my grass won't grow, either the soil contains too much acid or I am using the wrong fertilizer.
The soil tests out OK, but the grass doesn't grow.

I am using the wrong fertilizer. (*G, S, F*)

*5. If killing is always wrong, then war is always wrong.
If war is always wrong, then we should have allowed Hitler to rule the world.
We should not have allowed Hitler to rule the world.

Killing is not always wrong. (*K, W, H*)

6. Either we have been put here for some special purpose or life has no meaning.
If we have been put here for a special purpose, we know what the purpose is.
If life has no meaning, most of us live in quiet despair.
We do not know what the purpose of life is.

Most of us live in quiet despair. (*P, M, K, D*)

*7. Either there will soon be a vaccine to prevent AIDS or a massive "safe sex" educational campaign is required. If the medical establishment is correct, there will not be a vaccine in the immediate future. Unfortunately, there is little doubt that the doctors are correct this time. But if a large-scale educational campaign is required, the prospects are not bright because of the costs involved. The prospects, then, are not at all bright. (V, E, M, P)

8. $\sim P \rightarrow \sim Q$
    Q
    $\underline{P \rightarrow S}$
    S

10. $P \rightarrow Q$
    $\sim Q \vee R$
    $\underline{\sim R}$
    $\sim P$

12. $P \rightarrow \sim Q$
    $P \vee S$
    $\sim Q \rightarrow R$
    $\underline{S \rightarrow T}$
    $R \vee T$

*9. $P \rightarrow Q$
    $P \vee R$
    S
    $\underline{S \rightarrow \sim Q}$
    R

11. $P \rightarrow (Q \vee R)$
    $\underline{\sim Q \bullet P}$
    R

13. Q
    $Q \rightarrow \sim R$
    P
    $\underline{\sim R \rightarrow S}$
    $P \bullet S$

V. Conditionals

Since several of the valid argument forms involve the use of conditionals, we must be able to recognize and deal with conditional sentences when they're stated in any of the many different ways in which conditionals can be expressed. Clearly,

Q if P is symbolizable as $P \rightarrow Q$

More surprising, in the "only if" locution, the word *if* immediately precedes the *consequent* of the conditional.

P only if Q is symbolizable as $P \rightarrow Q$

For instance, in

Tom is a cat only if Tom is a mammal.

"Tom is a mammal" is the consequent, and the meaning of the sentence is the same as the meaning of "If Tom is a cat, then Tom is a mammal." This equivalence makes sense. Since being a mammal is a *requirement* for being a cat, then Tom is a cat *only if* Tom is a mammal. And, *if* Tom is a cat, he *must* be a mammal.

It is easy to become confused when dealing with sentences using "only if," but we can avoid the confusion by remembering that

P only if Q is symbolizable as $P \rightarrow Q$

Ordinary English contains yet other ways of expressing conditionals.

P provided that Q is symbolizable as $Q \rightarrow P$

She will win the election provided that she debates well.

    means

If she debates well, then she will win the election.

P unless Q is symbolizable as $\sim Q \rightarrow P$

The grass will die unless there is rain soon.

    means

If there is not rain soon, the grass will die.

VI. Equivalent Forms

We observed before that it is seldom necessary in arguments to use clumsy sentences such as "It is not the case that cats do not like cream," because the clearer "Cats like cream" conveys the same claim. We can rephrase this idea now by saying that the sentences are *equivalent,* for neither one can be true unless the other is. That is,

    $C \rightarrow \sim\sim C$ and $\sim\sim C \rightarrow C$

If we take it that the arrow can go either way, we can express the equivalence relationship most succinctly as

    $C \leftrightarrow \sim\sim C$

(The double arrow is usually read as "if and only if," often abbreviated as "iff.")

When two forms are equivalent, we can infer either one from the other. Thus, knowing equivalent forms puts another supply of valid inferences at our disposal and increases our ability to evaluate and construct arguments. Like *modus ponens* and the other valid forms discussed previously, equivalences can be thought of as inference *rules* because they justify valid argument steps. Here are six equivalent forms. (Symbols should be familiar enough now so that we can dispense with ordinary language connectives and negations.)

1. Double Negation (DN)

    $P \leftrightarrow \sim\sim P$

This just makes explicit the equivalence discussed before.

2. Commutation (Com)

$(P \cdot Q) \leftrightarrow (Q \cdot P)$

The chairman is a convicted felon, and he is a moral pervert.

is equivalent to

The chairman is a moral pervert, and he is a convicted felon.

Also, $(P \vee Q) \leftrightarrow (Q \vee P)$

Either April is the cruelest month or December is.

is equivalent to

Either December is the cruelest month or April is.

3. Contraposition (Contra)

$(P \rightarrow Q) \leftrightarrow (\sim Q \rightarrow \sim P)$

If the biblical account of creation is correct, then the scientific account is wrong.

is equivalent to

If the scientific account of creation is *not* wrong, then the biblical account is *incorrect*.

Both contraposition and *modus tollens* involve a conditional and the negation of its consequent. To avoid confusing them, remember that in *modus tollens* we infer to the negation of the antecedent. In contraposition, we *contrapose* the component sentences of a conditional and end with another conditional.

4. Definition of Implication (Imp)

$(P \vee Q) \leftrightarrow (\sim P \rightarrow Q)$

Either judges are being too lenient in their sentencing or parole boards are behaving irresponsibly.

is equivalent to

If judges are not being too lenient in their sentencing, then parole boards are behaving irresponsibly.

To see that these forms are equivalent, consider that $(P \vee Q)$ says that either P is true or Q is true. So, if P is not true, then Q is. And that is what $(\sim P \rightarrow Q)$ says.

5. Exportation (Exp)

$[(P \bullet Q) \to R] \leftrightarrow [P \to (Q \to R)]$

If the tire is flat, and the spare is missing, then you must walk.

is equivalent to

If the tire is flat, then if the spare is missing, then you must walk.

To export something is to send it out. This rule tells us we can send out one of the sentences in a conjunction that appears in the antecedent of a conditional.

6. De Morgan's Rules (DM)

There are two of them. The first is:

$\sim(P \bullet Q) \leftrightarrow (\sim P \vee \sim Q)$

Oh, come now. It can't be *both* that Darwell works for the CIA *and* that he is employed by the FBI.

is equivalent to

Either Darwell does not work for the CIA or he does not work for the FBI.

This form is not nearly as mysterious as it may first appear. It says that *not both P and Q are true* is equivalent to *either P is not true or Q is not true.*

The second De Morgan equivalence is

$\sim(P \vee Q) \leftrightarrow (\sim P \bullet \sim Q)$

It just isn't true either that Ellis will have a competent attorney appointed by the court or that he will be able to defend himself.

is equivalent to

Ellis will not have a competent attorney appointed by the court, and Ellis will not be able to defend himself.

This form says that *it is not the case that either P or Q is true* (neither is true) is equivalent to *both P and Q are false.*

If we should become confused about a De Morgan equivalence, there is a simple mechanical way to proceed. Change everything! For instance, starting with $\sim(P \vee \sim Q)$, drop the negation sign outside the parentheses, getting $(P \vee \sim Q)$. Change the signs of the component sentences, getting $(\sim P \vee Q)$. And change the disjunction to a conjunction, getting $(\sim P \bullet Q)$. Thus, we see that $\sim(P \vee \sim Q)$ is equivalent to $(\sim P \bullet Q)$.

Following these simple steps will infallibly result in producing a De Morgan equivalent of any conjunctive or disjunctive sentence.

Exercises

F. *Identify alternate ways of expressing the conditionals.*

   1. Which of the following are ways of expressing the conditional "If she is telling the truth, then she is innocent"?

     a. She is innocent if she is telling the truth.

     b. If she is innocent, then she is telling the truth.

     c. She is innocent only if she is telling the truth.

     d. She is telling the truth only if she is innocent.

     e. Only if she is innocent is she telling the truth.

  *2. Which of the following are ways of expressing the conditional "If the knots are secure, escape is impossible"?

     a. The knots are secure, and escape is impossible.

     b. Escape is impossible provided that the knots are secure.

     c. The knots are secure unless escape is impossible.

     d. Escape is impossible unless the knots are not secure.

     e. The knots are secure provided that escape is impossible.

G. *Using sentential variables and symbols, show the form of each of the following. Also identify the inference form* (modus ponens, contraposition, definition of implication, and so on) *in each case and note whether or not it is valid.*

   1. There will be peace in the Middle East only if the Israelis and the Palestinians conclude that peace is in their self-interests. They will reach this conclusion only if they sit down and talk to one another. So there will be peace in the Middle East only if the Israelis and the Palestinians sit down and talk to one another. (*P, T, C*)

  *2. If the earthquake was not severe, life will go on as usual.

     ―――――――――――――――――――――――――

     If life will not go on as usual, the earthquake was severe. (*E, L*)

   3. If we have to know what an artist was thinking in order to understand the work of art, then its meaning cannot be known. Thus, if the meaning of the work can be known, we do not have to know what the artist was thinking in order to understand it. (*T, K*)

*4. It just isn't true that capital punishment will be abolished and also the murder rate will go down. So, either capital punishment will not be abolished or the murder rate will not go down. (*A, D*)

5. If you have no cash then if your credit card has expired, you will have to sleep in the park.

   If you have no cash and your credit card has expired, you will have to sleep in the park. (*C, E, S*)

*6. If you don't shape up, you will ship out.

   You will either shape up or ship out. (*S, O*)

7. Watson: I tried to tell them that it is a vampire or it is a werewolf. But they deny that.

   Holmes: They deny that it is either a vampire or a werewolf? Interesting. So, they think it is not a vampire and not a werewolf. I wonder what they think it is. (*V, W*)

*8. If Clara develops her talents as a composer, she does not spend all her time attending to the needs of her husband.

   It's not true that she does not spend all her time attending to the needs of her husband.

   Clara does not develop her talents as a composer. (*C, H*)

9. What she used in the casino was either a $1000 bill or an incredibly good imitation. So, if it wasn't a $1000 bill, it must have been an incredibly good imitation. (*B, I*)

*10. Many people have looked at the suffering in the world and have concluded that either God is not good or God is not powerful. So, they think, God is not both powerful and good. (*G, P*)

VII. Using Inference and Equivalence Rules

Finally, consider this argument:

(1) If women are paid less than men, and sexism is not the reason, it must be that women are not as good at their jobs as men are. [(L • ~S) Æ ~G] (2) Women are paid less, but there is not a shred of truth to the charge that they are not as good at their jobs as men. [L • ~~G] So, (3) there is clearly sexism at work here. [S]

That is,

1. $(L \cdot {\sim}S) \rightarrow {\sim}G$
2. $L \cdot {\sim}{\sim}G$
   ───────────────
3. S

Let's see if we can deduce the conclusion from these premises.

Looking for a starting point, we see we can easily develop a step of *modus tollens*. We will try this and see if it proves useful. (If it doesn't work out, at worst we will have wasted a little time.)

1. $(L \cdot {\sim}S) \rightarrow {\sim}G$
2. $L \cdot {\sim}{\sim}G$
3. ${\sim}{\sim}G$ 2 Simp
4. ${\sim}(L \cdot {\sim}S)$ 1, 3 MT

What might we do now? Since the first negation sign in line 4 goes with everything inside the parentheses *as a unit*, we cannot deal with L or ${\sim}S$ as individual variables as long as they appear within the parentheses. It would be a promising strategy then to change line 4 in such a way that we could deal independently with the individual variables. Fortunately, we now have a way to make a change of this sort.

5. ${\sim}L \vee S$ 4 DM

Since L was part of premise 2, another step of simplification leads to L, and L combined with 5 gives the conclusion we were after.

The entire deduction, then, is as follows:

1. $(L \cdot {\sim}S) \rightarrow {\sim}G$
2. $L \cdot {\sim}{\sim}G$
3. ${\sim}{\sim}G$ 2 Simp
4. ${\sim}(L \cdot {\sim}S)$ 1, 3 MT
5. ${\sim}L \vee S$ 4 DM
6. L 2 Simp
7. S 5, 6 DS

As we have said, being able to construct and recognize valid arguments is a skill, and developing it requires practice. Honing the skill and applying it in the everyday world also requires a certain turn of mind, a habit of looking at arguments with a constantly careful and critical eye. The more we do this, the better we will be able to construct our own valid arguments, to recognize whether the arguments of others are valid, and to avoid being taken in by arguments that appear to be valid but are not.

Quick Reference

Valid Argument Forms

Modus Ponens (MP)

$P \rightarrow Q$
P
_____
Q

Modus Tollens (MT)

$P \rightarrow Q$
$\sim Q$
_____
$\sim P$

Hypothetical Syllogism (HS)

$P \rightarrow Q$
$Q \rightarrow R$
_____
$P \rightarrow R$

Disjunctive Syllogism (DS)

$P \vee Q$ $P \vee Q$
$\sim P$ $\sim Q$
_____   _____
Q P

Constructive Dilemma (CD)

$P \vee Q$
$P \rightarrow R$
$Q \rightarrow S$
_____
$R \vee S$

Conjunction (Conj)

P P
Q Q
_____   _____
$P \cdot Q$ $Q \cdot P$

Simplification (Simp)

$P \cdot Q$ $P \cdot Q$
_____   _____
P Q

Addition (Add)

P
_____
$P \vee Q$

Invalid (Fallacious) Argument Forms

Denying the Antecedent

$P \rightarrow Q$
$\sim P$
_____
$\sim Q$

Affirming the Consequent

$P \rightarrow Q$
Q
_____
P

Equivalent Forms

Double Negation (DN)

$P \leftrightarrow \sim\sim P$

Commutation (Com)

$(P \cdot Q) \leftrightarrow (Q \cdot P)$

Contraposition (Contra)

$(P \rightarrow Q) \leftrightarrow (\sim Q \rightarrow \sim P)$

Definition of Implication (Imp)

$(P \vee Q) \leftrightarrow (\sim P \rightarrow Q)$

Exportation (Exp)

$[(P \cdot Q) \rightarrow R] \leftrightarrow [P \rightarrow (Q \rightarrow R)]$

De Morgan's Rules (DM)

$\sim(P \cdot Q) \leftrightarrow (\sim P \vee \sim Q)$

$\sim(P \vee Q) \leftrightarrow (\sim P \cdot \sim Q)$

Exercises

H. *Using sentential variables and symbols, show that the conclusions follow from the premises by a series of valid inferences. Be sure to cite the lines from which each conclusion follows and give its justification.*

Find two different ways of reaching the conclusions in #5, #6, and #7.

*1. The AIDS panel will be perceived as balanced only if it includes leaders of the gay community. And it will include leaders of the gay community only if pressure is brought to bear on politicians. Thus, the panel will be perceived as balanced only if the pressure is brought to bear. Because no one will be able to bring about pressure on politicians, the panel will not be perceived as balanced. Clearly, the AIDS panic will continue to increase if this panel is not perceived as balanced. And so, sadly, the AIDS panic will continue to increase. (B, L, P, I)

2. If Chowdhury will rise to the top level of executives in the company, it will be by ruining some careers or by a change in boardroom attitudes. She will not rise to the top by ruining careers, and there will be no change in boardroom attitudes. So, she will not rise to the top level of executives. *(C, R, B)*

*3. If today is Friday, then if it is the thirteenth, it is not a lucky day.
Actually, it is a lucky day.

Either today is not Friday or it is not the thirteenth.
(F, T, L)

4. If it is not true that a strike by the teachers will both harm their image among the local members of the Steelworkers' Union and cause them to lose the support of white-collar workers in the community, then the teachers should strike. But either a strike by the teachers will not harm their image among the steelworkers or it will not cause them to lose the support of the local white-collar workers. Therefore, the teachers should strike. (H, L, S)

*5. If Lee succeeds in climbing Everest solo, then she will not be able to afford to pay her bills unless there is publicity for the event. She does succeed, but there is no publicity for the event. Thus, Lee will not be able to pay her bills. (L, B, P)

6. If the prosecution did a good job of presenting the evidence, and the jury gave due deliberation, the defendant would have been found guilty of murder. The prosecution did do a good job, but the defendant was acquitted on all counts. Thus, the jury did not give due deliberation. (P, J, D)

*7. If the governor is going to wear a monkey costume when he objects to the teaching of evolution in schools, then if the legislators listen to him, they are all manifest fools. He is going to wear the monkey suit, but many of the legislators aren't fools at all. So, the legislators will not listen to the governor. (*G, L, F*)

8. If we should seek only the good, and happiness is the only good, then we should seek only happiness. It is surely not true that we should seek only happiness. So, if we should seek only the good, then it is false that happiness is the only good. (*G, H, S*)

*9. $(\sim P \vee Q) \rightarrow \sim (R \bullet \rightarrow S)$
   R
   $\underline{\sim P \qquad\qquad\qquad}$
   S

12. $\sim(P \bullet Q) \rightarrow \sim R$
    $\sim S$
    $\underline{\sim R \rightarrow S \qquad}$
    $Q \vee T$

10. $\sim(P \bullet Q) \rightarrow \sim (R \rightarrow S)$
    $\sim P \vee \sim Q$
    $\underline{\sim S \qquad\qquad\qquad}$
    $\sim R$

*13. $\sim(\sim P \bullet \sim Q) \rightarrow R$
    $\underline{P \qquad\qquad\qquad}$
    R

*11. $Q \vee (R \bullet S)$
    $\sim Q$
    $\underline{S \rightarrow (T \vee U)}$
    $\sim T \rightarrow U$

Chapter 5

MORE VALID ARGUMENT FORMS: CATEGORICAL REASONING AND VENN DIAGRAMS

In the previous chapter, we saw that some arguments are valid because of their sentential form—that is, because of formal relationships between whole sentences. For instance, *modus ponens,*

If *P*, then *Q*

P

Q

is valid because the complete sentences represented by *P* and *Q* occur in the way they do in the premises and the conclusion. Now we will show that arguments can be valid because of the relationships between the terms *within* the sentences of arguments.

> The first person on record who systematically studied formal methods of reasoning was Aristotle (384–322 BCE). Aristotle developed a complete system of logic based on the principles that we will examine in this chapter. This system is sometimes referred to as *categorical logic* or as *syllogistic.* The reason behind each of these names will become evident as we go along.

I. Categorical Statements

Many everyday sorts of statements put things into **categories** or **classes.** "All trout are fish" says that anything included in the category (class) *trout* is also included in the category (class) *fish.* "Some numbers are even" says that some of the members of the category *numbers* are also members of the category *even numbers.* "Moby Dick is a whale" says that this individual is a member of the class *whales.* Other familiar sorts of statements *exclude* things from classes or categories. "No dogs are reptiles" excludes every member of the class *dogs* from the class *reptiles.* **Categorical statements** such as these enter into some reasoning patterns whose validity or invalidity we can conclusively demonstrate. (Often we use adjectives just as a sort of shorthand to put things into categories. "All dogs are lovable" can mean "All dogs are lovable animals.")

The easiest and perhaps most commonsensical way of showing validity or invalidity in categorical reasoning is to construct intersecting circles to form Venn diagrams. Let's begin with a diagram of the single statement "All trout are fish." We need one circle to represent the category *trout*

John Venn (1824–1923) was a distinguished British church minister and theologian. As a result of reading such logicians as De Morgan (see Chapter 4), and Mill (see Chapter 6), his major interest changed from theology to logic. He then ingeniously devised the diagram method of evaluating validity that bears his name.

Although other related methods can be used, Venn diagrams remain the standard method of evaluating the validity of categorical syllogisms.

Trout

and another circle to represent the category *fish*.

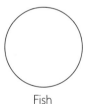

Fish

Anything within the first circle is a trout, and anything within the second circle is a fish.

Since we want to represent the relationship between the trout and the fish categories, we must connect the circles so that they overlap.

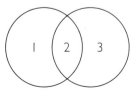

Trout   Fish

The section called "1" here (Venn diagrams do not really contain such numbers) is within the trout circle but not within the fish circle, so it contains everything that is a trout but not a fish. Section 3, being within the fish circle only, includes all things that are fish but not trout. The intersection, "2," is within both circles, so it contains all and only things that are *both* trout and fish.

Now it is easy to use the diagram to represent "All trout are fish." Since section 1 would contain things that are trout but not fish, section 1 is *empty;* it has no members. We show that a section of a diagram is empty by shading it. So, we shade out section 1 and have:

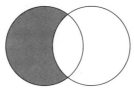

Trout   Fish

This shows that all the trout there are within the fish circle—that is, "All trout are fish."

To this point, all we have is a picture. It is not a particularly pretty picture, but it is a very useful one. Suppose we wonder whether "All trout are fish" means the same thing as (in logic terms, *is equivalent to*) "No trout are not fish." A quick look back at the last diagram shows that it does mean just that. Since in that diagram of "All trout are fish" we have shaded out just the trout-not-fish area, "All trout are fish" must mean just what "No trout are not fish" means.

Suppose instead that somehow we are not sure if

All trout are fish.
_____
All fish are trout.

is valid. Inspecting the "All trout are fish" Venn diagram again shows clearly that it is not. Section 3, the fish-not-trout section of the diagram, is not shaded out. So, given the premises, there can be fish that are not trout. The premises can be true while the conclusion is false, which means the inference is not valid.

No one is likely to make the "Trout are fish so fish are trout" mistake, but mistakes like it are too frequent. We often hear "All users of hard drugs started with marijuana" cited to show that all users of marijuana become users of hard drugs. Or that "All sex criminals use pornography" proves that all users of pornography become sex criminals. The Venn diagrams for the premises in these cases are exactly like the diagram for "All trout are fish," and the inferences are not valid for the same reason: section 3, the one on the right, is not shaded out. The diagram for "All sex criminals use pornography" is

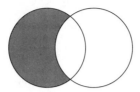

Sex Criminals   Pornography Users

which clearly does not validly imply "All pornography users are sex criminals," since there is an unshaded portion of pornography users who are not sex criminals. And the Venn diagram for "All hard drug users use marijuana" does not show "All users of marijuana are hard drug users."

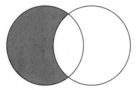

Hard Drug Users   Marijuana Users

The popular inferences about drugs and pornography may be appealing, but the most basic use of Venn diagrams shows that they are just *wrong*.

Categorical statements that *exclude* members of one class from another class are easily understood. Statements like "No snakes are mammals" say that anything that is a snake is *not* a mammal. This means that in the Venn diagram the part of the snake circle that intersects the mammal circle must be shaded out. (From now on we will label the circles with convenient letters rather than whole words.)

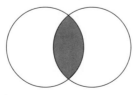

S   M

What would the Venn diagram for "No mammals are snakes" look like? We shade out any part of the mammal circle that intersects the snake circle.

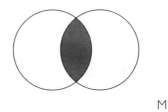

S   M

Since the diagrams are identical, "No snakes are mammals" and "No mammals are snakes" are saying the same thing (are *equivalent*).

Categorical statements may not be about *all* Xs or *no* Xs but rather about *some* Xs. "Some students are females" and "Some politicians are not honest" are examples. To understand statements like these, first we need to know that in logic "some" means "at least one." In everyday talk, "some" may mean "several but not all." An announcement that some students passed the test would likely not be taken to mean that just one student out of 500 passed nor that all 500 passed. But in logic, the statement is true if one student, several students, or all students passed. It is false only if no student passed. (As long as we know this, it causes no problems.)

In Venn diagrams, we show that some (at least one) *S* is or is not *F* by putting a mark (for instance, an asterisk) in the relevant section of the diagram. The diagram for "Some students are female" would be

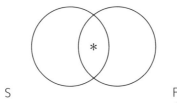

S   F

The diagram for "Some females are students" would be just the same, and so they are equivalent and we can infer either one from the other. The diagram for "Some politicians are not honest," on the other hand, would be:

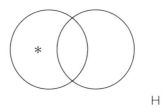

P   H

It may seem that we never need to use the asterisk, since a diagram like the one for "All trout are fish"

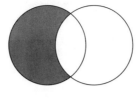

T   F

already shows that some (*all* in this case) trout are fish and some fish are trout. But according to modern logic, the diagram shows no such thing. "All trout are fish" says that anything that is a trout is a fish. It does not say that there exists anything that actually *is* either a trout or a fish. "All unicorns have one horn" says that anything that is a unicorn is a one-horned creature. It does *not* say there really are any such things as unicorns or one-horned animals. On the other hand, "*Some* trout are fish" and "*Some* unicorns have one horn" do say that *there exist* trout that are fish and unicorns that have one horn. And that is what the asterisk means in the Venn diagrams. Of course, a segment of a diagram cannot both be shaded and contain an asterisk.

Exercises

A. *Draw a Venn diagram for each of the following. Determine which of the statements are equivalent.*

*1.   All snakes are reptiles.

2.   No snakes are not reptiles.

*3.   All reptiles are snakes.

4.   Some snakes are reptiles.

*5.   Some reptiles are not snakes.

6.   A few reptiles are snakes.

*7.   No snakes are reptiles.

8.   All snakes are not reptiles.

*9.   Some reptiles are snakes.

10.   Only reptiles are snakes.

*11.   No reptiles are not snakes.

12.   Some snakes are not reptiles.

*13.   No reptiles are snakes.

14.   All reptiles are not snakes.

*15.   Some things that are not reptiles are snakes.

16.   Snakes are the only reptiles.

> *Here is an exercise that is a bit different from those discussed before. How could we deal with it?*
>
> 17. All nonsnakes are nonreptiles.

II. Categorical Syllogisms

Categorical syllogisms are syllogisms that have two premises and a conclusion, all of which are categorical statements.

All lawyers are educated people.
All educated people are clever people.
___
All lawyers are clever people.

All bankers are wealthy.
No wealthy people are happy.
___
No bankers are happy.

Some novelists are astute observers.
All astute observers are reliable witnesses.
___
Some novelists are reliable witnesses.

In order to evaluate such arguments, we diagram the premises together and then see whether the result shows the truth of the conclusion. The basics of Venn diagrams that we have already seen give us what we need to construct the diagrams.

We will take each of the above arguments in turn.

All lawyers are educated people.
All educated people are clever people.
___
All lawyers are clever people.

We must have three interlocking circles to represent the relationships between the categories in the three statements. Putting the circles for the conclusion at the bottom (this is not necessary, but it is usual and helpful), first we have:

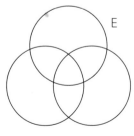

Ignore the *C* circle for the moment, and shade the lawyer-not-educated area to represent the information given in the first premise.

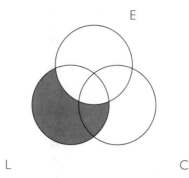

Look just at the *E* and *C* circles, and do the same for the second premise, "All educated people are clever people."

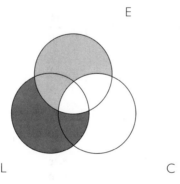

The diagram now represents all of the information given in the premises. What does this tell us about the conclusion? The *L* and *C* circles represent the conclusion, "All lawyers are clever." The only nonshaded—that is, nonempty—area of the *L* circle is within part of the *C* circle, so all lawyers are clever. We might say that, after taking into account all the information in the premises, "the only lawyers left" are the clever ones. So, the truth of the premises guarantees the truth of the conclusion. The argument is shown to be *valid*.

Turning to the second of the examples above:

All bankers are wealthy.
No wealthy people are happy.

No bankers are happy.

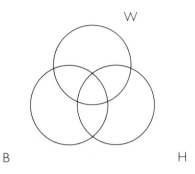

The first premise gives

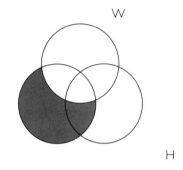

Now we shade in accordance with the second premise.

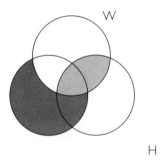

Since the entire overlap between the *B* and *H* circles is now shaded out, the premises do show that no bankers are happy, and the argument is *valid*.

The third example is:

Some novelists are astute observers.
All astute observers are reliable witnesses.

Some novelists are reliable witnesses.

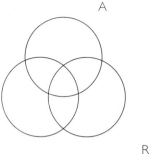

We will use the asterisk to indicate "Some novelists are astute observers." But since the overlap between *novelists* and *astute observers* is divided into two parts, we do not know just where to put the asterisk. (Look carefully at the blank diagram above to see that this is so.) This brings out the general rule that we should *begin with any premise of universal form*. Here we start with "All astute observers are reliable witnesses."

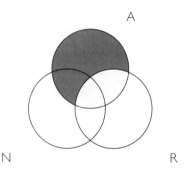

Now we have only one possible place to put the asterisk, in the one unshaded area of the *N* and *A* intersection.

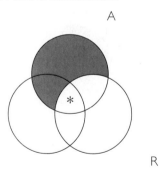

Since the asterisk is within the intersection of *N* and *R*, the premises show that at least one member of *N* is a member of *R*. So, the truth of "Some novelists are reliable witnesses" is dictated by the premises, and the argument is *valid*.

Of course, not all categorical syllogisms are valid. When they are not, Venn diagrams tell us that too.

All works of art are profound.
No cartoons are works of art.

No cartoons are profound.

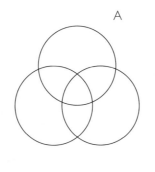

Shading each premise in turn we get:

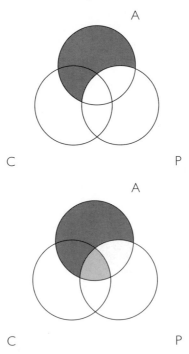

Does this show that "No cartoons are profound"? Not at all. Part of the intersection between the *C* and *P* circles is unshaded, so the argument does not rule out there being cartoons that are profound. The argument is *not valid*.

A final case:

All vegetarians are very thin.
Some very thin people are undernourished.

Some vegetarians are undernourished.

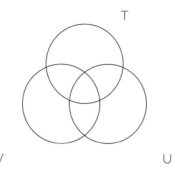

Again, we first represent the universal premise:

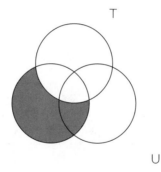

But where do we put the asterisk to represent the second premise? It has to be in the overlap of the *T* and *U* circles, but that overlap is divided into two parts, and we have no warrant for choosing one or the other of these. A convenient way of showing this is to put it on the line between the sections.

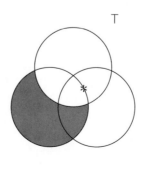

Since we do not know whether the asterisk is inside the intersection of *V* and *U* (the very center section of this diagram), the argument is *not valid*.

Exercises

B. *Draw a Venn diagram for each of the categorical syllogisms below. Using your diagram and the section numbering in the "dummy diagram," explain why each argument is or is not valid. The answers given for #1 and #3 serve as models for the sorts of explanations you can give.*

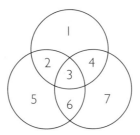

*1. All computers are machines.
   No machines can think.

   No computers can think.

2. All pro basketball players are fine athletes.
   No professor of mathematics is a pro basketball player.

   No professor of mathematics is a fine athlete.

*3. All fallacies are dangerous.
   All dangerous things are things to be avoided.

   All fallacies are things to be avoided.

4. Some snakes are poisonous.
   Anything that is poisonous should be destroyed.

   Some snakes should be destroyed.

*5. All slow learners require extra attention in school.
   Some who require extra attention in school need to be in specialized classrooms.

   Some slow learners need to be in specialized classrooms.

6. All flying squirrels are mammals.
   No birds are mammals.

   No flying squirrels are birds.

*7. All flying squirrels are mammals.
No birds are mammals.

No birds are flying squirrels.

8. All tortoises are terrestrial.
Some turtles are not terrestrial.

Some turtles are not tortoises.

*9. All tortoises are terrestrial.
Some turtles are not tortoises.

Some turtles are not terrestrial.

10. No Martians speak English.
All officers on the Starship do not speak English.

All officers on the Starship are Martians.

*11. No officers on the Starship do not speak English.
No Martians speak English.

No officers on the Starship are Martians.

12. No spiders are insects.
No insects are lizards.

No spiders are lizards.

*13. All religious fundamentalists are conservative.
All Republicans are conservative.

All religious fundamentalists are Republicans.

14. Some students are hard workers, and some students get very good grades. So, some hard workers get very good grades.

*15. No poor person who is willing to work deserves to be hungry. And every poor person who does not deserve to be hungry should get government aid. Thus, every poor person who is willing to work should get government aid.

16. Some murderers were molested as children. Everyone molested as a child deserves pity. So, some murderers deserve pity.

*17. All alligators do not enjoy cold weather. Some carnivores do not enjoy cold weather. Thus, some carnivores must be alligators.

18. Anyone who reads this book will immediately find enlightenment. Some people who find enlightenment will become rich, so anyone who reads this book will become rich.

*19. No one under 21 is allowed in the bar. Some people under 21 are allowed in the restaurant. Thus, some people who are allowed in the restaurant are not allowed in the bar.

20. No one who pays taxes will not receive a tax break, and anyone who will not receive a tax break will not be happy. Therefore, no one who pays taxes will not be happy.

Chapter 6

CAUSAL ANALYSIS

Identifying causes is important in ordinary life, as well as in criminal investigation, business, law, medicine, and the sciences. Our interest in causes reflects a variety of concerns. These four are among the most important:

1. **Explanation.** We want to explain why an event occurred, so we attempt to discover its cause. (What caused the World Trade Center buildings to collapse so quickly after the impact of the airplanes?)

2. **Responsibility.** We want to know whether we can hold anyone responsible for an event, so we ask what someone did to cause it. (Did Franklin cause Hajib's death by tampering with the brakes on his car? Did Sih's use of the Heimlich maneuver save Kitt's life?) Knowing this lets us decide if anyone deserves blame or praise.

3. **Control.** If we know the causal factors that produce an event, we may be able to manipulate them and obtain results we want. (What causes coronary artery disease? Why do some families remain on welfare for generations?)

4. **Prediction.** We want to know if we can expect an event to happen, so we attempt to discover what causes such events. (When will a major earthquake strike San Francisco? How will declining interest rates affect employment?)

I. Basic Causal Relationships

The term *cause* is used in several distinct but related ways. Hence, it is not possible to give the word a single definition without being arbitrary. Instead, we must review several prominent uses of the term.

A. Cause As Sufficient Condition

The eighteenth-century British philosopher David Hume formulated the basic analysis of a causal relationship that is still generally accepted. According to Hume, by "cause" we mean nothing more than that a "constant conjunction" holds between events. We notice that events of kind *A* are always followed by events of kind *B,* and we say "*A* causes *B.*" Thus, to claim a causal relationship between events of types *A* and *B* is to say: Whenever *A* occurs, then *B* occurs. (To say all causal relations are regular in this way is not to say all regular relations are causal. See "Testing Causal Claims" later in this chapter.)

> The Greek philosopher Aristotle distinguished four **causes:** final, efficient, material, and formal. Thus, a sculptor, wanting to create something beautiful (final cause), carves (efficient cause) a block of marble (material cause) to produce a statue (formal cause).
>
> Aristotle's analysis continues to be useful in areas like the law in which we are concerned with human action, intention, and responsibility. Consider, for example, how the actions of a counterfeiter of banknotes might be analyzed in terms of Aristotle's four causes.

Consider this example. You are driving and notice the red warning light glowing on your dashboard—the engine has overheated. You pull over, raise the hood, and see a long tear in a radiator hose. The hose has burst, and all the coolant has run out. We can say the engine overheated because there was no coolant in the radiator. The lack of coolant *caused* the engine to overheat. Hence, we are asserting that "Whenever a car engine is running and no coolant is in its radiator, the engine will overheat."

In this construal of "cause," the lack of coolant is also said to constitute a **sufficient condition** for the engine's overheating. A factor is a sufficient condition for the occurrence of an event if whenever the factor occurs, then the event occurs: Whenever *A,* then *B.* We regard factual generalizations of this form, if true, as **causal laws.**

1. Other Sufficient Conditions
We have named one factor sufficient for the occurrence of the event "overheated engine." Yet other factors can also make an engine overheat. That is, other conditions are also sufficient for overheating:

The water pump breaks, so coolant no longer circulates through the engine.

The fan belt breaks, so the fan no longer blows on the radiator and carries off the heat from the liquid circulating inside.

The small tubes inside the radiator become clogged, so coolant no longer circulates in them.

Any one of these three factors is a sufficient condition for the occurrence of the event, and it is in this sense we may say that an overheated engine can have several possible causes. If your engine overheats, even if you know the possible causes, you have no way of knowing the actual cause without investigating the matter. (This list of sufficient conditions is not complete. We might mention a faulty thermostat, a defective oil pump, an oil leak, or a number of others.)

2. Causal Chains

We may want to know more about the overheated engine than the sufficient condition responsible for it. For example, we may want to know how the coolant came to be absent; that is, we may want a sufficient condition for that event. The radiator may have rusted through, the drain valve may have broken off, or (as in our example) the radiator hose may have burst—any of these would be sufficient for a loss of coolant.

By such inquiries, we establish causal chains leading to the occurrence of an event that interests us. In principle, we can extend the chain as far into the past as we wish or are able to. (We may ask what caused the radiator to rust, the drain valve to break off, the hose to burst.) In practice, we usually end causal inquiry at the point where our actions can affect the outcome. We can do little about the chemistry of metals and their interaction with coolant and water, so we are not likely to ask what caused the metal of our radiator to become rusty. We are most likely to stop when we learn why the coolant drained out of the radiator. (Replacing a radiator or checking it for leaks is something we can do.) By contrast, a radiator designer would push the inquiry further backward and want to know why the radiator rusted. In a new design, he might use different metal alloys or coatings.

3. Cause As a Set of Conditions

The lack of coolant cannot genuinely be a sufficient condition for an overheated engine, although we have talked as if it were so. The engine is not going to overheat if it has been running for only a minute or so or if the outside temperature is very low. And of course we did not specify that we were talking about an internal combustion engine, not an electric or atomic one. We accept the lack of coolant as a sufficient condition because we have taken for granted that we are talking about an ordinary car being driven down the street under normal operating conditions for some typical period of time. If we had any reason to do so, we could specify just what additional factors should be added to the lack of coolant so that the sum of the factors would constitute a sufficient condition for an engine's overheating.

Thus, the *A* in the scheme "Whenever *A*, then *B*" must actually be understood to represent a set of conditions, not a single factor. To take another familiar example, we know room lights do not go on just because you flip the switch. Other factors must be present: The points of the switch must come into contact with the power source; electricity must be flowing through the wires; a working lightbulb has to be properly screwed into the socket; and the socket has to be connected to the power source through the switch. You may flip the switch all you wish, but if all these conditions are not satisfied, the light will not come on. Strictly, then, the whole set of conditions constitutes a sufficient condition for the event. The whole set is "the cause" of the event. To recognize this, we can elaborate our scheme:

Whenever A [= C_1, C_2, . . . C_n], then B.

We may not be able to fill in the whole set of conditions (C_1, C_2, C_3, and so on). Often we know some of them, but not all of them. If an event is important, we may try to reduce our ignorance by causal investigation. Thus, we try to determine more completely the factors that lead to suicide, cancer, and heart disease. Similarly, we try to discover what causes children to fail at school and what turns some people into serial killers.

4. Effect As a Set of Outcomes

What about effects? Just as the cause of an event is not a single factor, the effect of a cause is not a single event. The leaking radiator does more than make the car engine overheat—it leaves puddles on the ground, releases vapors into the atmosphere, and deposits chemicals in the soil. To be accurate, we should amend our causal scheme in the following way:

Whenever A [= C_1, C_2, . . . C_n], then B [= E_1, E_2, . . . E_n].

As we have seen, we often choose one factor from a set of factors and call it "the" cause of an event. The same holds for the set of outcomes. The one we call "the" effect is the one with which we are most concerned for some reason or other. An interest in highway safety might lead us to focus on the puddle of liquid left on the road as the effect, whereas a concern with the environment might lead us to focus on the chemical coolant that soaks into the soil.

B. Cause As Necessary Condition

Poliomyelitis—polio—is a disease of the central nervous system caused by a specific virus. Yet not everyone infected with the virus gets polio. Thus, infection with the polio virus is not a sufficient condition for getting the disease. But we do not know what other factors have to be present for someone to contract it.

Does this mean we don't know the cause of polio? Not according to one legitimate use of the term *cause*. What we know about the cause of polio is that anyone who has the disease has been infected by the virus. The virus, we can say, is a **necessary condition** for the disease.

A factor is a necessary condition for an event if the event does not occur in the absence of the factor. Everyone who gets polio has been infected with the polio virus, but not everyone infected with the polio virus gets polio. Thus, the polio virus is a necessary, but not sufficient, condition for the disease.

We can represent the relationship of a necessary condition to the occurrence of an event more formally. Let *A* stand for the causal factor and *B* for the event.

1. If *B*, then *A*. (If polio occurs, then the virus is present.)
2. If not-*A*, then not-*B*. (If the virus is not present, then polio does not occur.)

Both schemes express the meaning of sentences of the form "*A* is a necessary condition for *B*."

We usually do not speak of just any necessary condition as a cause. The presence of oxygen in the air was a necessary condition for World War II; yet we would consider it absurd to mention oxygen as the cause of the war. We regard such conditions as trivial with respect to explanation because they constitute relatively constant background conditions. Unusual factors or those varying from case to case (the presence of the polio virus, for example) are the necessary conditions we identify as causes.

C. Cause As Necessary and Sufficient Condition

The most rigorous interpretation of a causal relationship consists in construing "cause" as a condition both necessary and sufficient for the occurrence of an event. If factor *A* is *necessary and sufficient* for the occurrence of event *B*, then: Whenever *A* occurs, *B* occurs; and whenever *A* does not occur, then *B* does not occur. In an abstract scheme:

If *A*, then *B*; and if not-*A*, then not-*B*.

For illustration, assume diamonds are produced only when carbon is subjected to great pressure and in no other way. Carbon and great pressure are each a necessary condition for diamonds, and both together constitute a sufficient condition. Thus, if you know something is a diamond, you know great pressure acting on carbon caused it. Also, you know how to produce (cause) diamonds—subject carbon to great pressure.

This construing of cause is so rigorous that very few (if any) actual relationships in ordinary experience can satisfy it. A technique for producing diamonds without employing pressure has recently been developed, so even the standard example used here is no longer a genuine case.

Some philosophers hold that this construing of cause represents the kind of invariant relationship scientific laws ought to express. Laws of physics provide examples. For instance, according to Newton's second law, objects attract one another with a force equal to the inverse of the square of the distance between them. Thus, if we know the force of attraction between two bodies, we can calculate the distance between them; and if we know the distance between them, we can calculate the force of attraction. The values assigned to one set of factors determine the values assigned to the others, and the relationship can be understood in terms of necessary and sufficient conditions.

Causal generalizations in the social and biological sciences are rarely offered as expressions of necessary and sufficient conditions. Many consider the demand that laws be of this sort to be unrealistic and inappropriate. Further, some philosophers have denied that laws like Newton's are causal ones. This would make them inappropriate as models.

Koch's Postulates

For the field of bacteriology, the second half of the nineteenth century was a time of great excitement. Dozens of new bacteria were discovered, and familiar diseases like diphtheria and whooping cough were shown to be caused by bacteria. It was also a time of confusion, however, because investigators were often unclear about which one of several kinds of bacteria infecting a sick person was responsible for the person's disease.

Robert Koch developed a set of rules or "postulates" to determine when a particular organism is the cause of a particular disease. The organism must:

1. Be present in every case of the disease

2. Be isolated from a case of the disease and grown in a pure culture

3. Produce a case of the disease when inoculated into a susceptible animal

4. Be recovered from the diseased animal

These rules brought order to the field of bacteriology, and they remain helpful in identifying the agent responsible for newly diagnosed infectious diseases.

II. Contributing Factors As "Causes"

Each factor making up a set of factors sufficient (or necessary) for the occurrence of an event can be called a **contributing factor.** Thus, the methane gas that accumulated in the room was a contributing factor of the explosion that occurred. So, too, was the oxygen present in the room, as well as the spark that set off the mixture.

The factor we mention as the cause of an event is rarely one we consider sufficient or even necessary for such events. Rather, we frequently select one of the contributing factors and say it is the cause of the event. The factor we choose usually depends on our aims and interests. Legal, practical, medical, or moral concerns may influence our selection. Here we discuss only three considerations that may lead us to designate a single contributing factor as "the cause" of an event, but others are easily imagined.

A. Triggering Factor (Proximate Cause)

The contributing factor that triggers an event is often designated the cause of the event. This is the one that occurs last and completes the causal chain (the set of sufficient conditions) producing the event.

When the pistol is loaded and cocked, pulling the trigger causes it to fire. Similarly, we might say, "Halton caused the explosion when he turned on the light." Turning on the light (sending an arc of electricity across the poles of the switch) was the last event to occur before the explosion, but flipping the switch was a successful trigger only because the room was filled with methane. Also, oxygen was present in the room, and the switch was electrically live.

These factors are also ones that go toward making up a sufficient condition for an explosion. As contributing conditions, they constitute the **background** (or **standing** or **preexisting**) conditions that were triggered by the switch. Throwing the switch (making an electrical spark) was the factor that completed a set of sufficient conditions for the explosion. Proximate means "nearest," and the triggering factor of an event is often called the event's **proximate cause.**

B. Unusual Factor

We sometimes say "the cause" of an event is the unusual factor in a set of conditions. Thus, we might say, "The explosion was caused by an accumulation of gas." The "whole cause" of the explosion was the set of contributing factors: accumulated gas, the presence of oxygen, and the spark from the light switch. But oxygen is usually in the air, and people ordinarily turn on lights. What is unusual is the accumulation of methane.

Thus, if we are concerned with fixing moral or legal responsibility for the explosion, we are likely to focus on the person who left on the gas, not the one who turned on the light. (Brixon may have murdered Zloba in just this fashion, knowing she would turn on the light, thus triggering a deadly explosion.)

C. Controllable Factor

Sometimes we want to focus on controlling occurrences of an event by calling attention to a contributing factor known to be instrumental in producing it. We can then point out that since the factor can be controlled, so can the event.

"Cholesterol causes heart disease" may be understood as saying that eating foods high in saturated fats increases the chances of developing heart disease. Hence, anyone wanting to avoid heart disease should avoid eating such foods.

We might with equal truth say "Heredity causes heart disease," but since heredity is not a controllable factor, we rarely call it "the cause" of heart disease. When we refer to heredity as a *risk factor*, it's usually in the context of encouraging those who are at risk of heart disease to alter the contributing factors over which they have some control (such as diet and exercise).

Developing an extensive list of motives leading us to identify contributing factors as causes isn't important. What is important is realizing that when people call a factor "the cause" of an event, this doesn't necessarily mean they think it's a sufficient (or necessary) condition.

III. Causal Explanations

To explain an event is often to say what caused it to occur. Thus, we say "The explosion occurred *because* somebody left the gas on," or "The chicks ran for cover *because* the hawk-shape is a releasing mechanism." Such an explanation apparently involves no laws, and we explain the event merely by mentioning its cause. The causal sentence has the form "*A* caused *B*" and seems to be about individual events and circumstances.

Despite appearances, such explanations are really incomplete versions of explanations that rely upon causal laws. The explanatory force of sentences with the form "*A* caused *B*" (about particular events) depends upon an implicit reference to a generalization asserting an invariant or constant connection between occurrences of events of the two kinds. Thus, we can express the claim of a causal relationship between events of type *A* and type *B* by the scheme:

When *A* occurs (under conditions *C*), then *B* occurs.

Generalizations of this form, if true, are causal laws. (We will limit discussion to laws expressing a causally sufficient condition.) In terms of this analysis, a causal sentence such as "A bacterial infection is the cause of Mr. Wu's bronchitis" gains its power to explain from the implicit assumption that a bacterial infection, under the appropriate conditions, is a sufficient condition for bronchitis. That is, the sentence acquires its power to explain from a causal law.

If we make the causal law explicit and describe the circumstances Mr. Wu is in, we can see how the explanation consists of showing that this particular event is an instance of a general pattern:

Whenever a bacterial infection occurs in the lungs, bronchitis results.
Mr. Wu has a bacterial infection in his lungs.

Mr. Wu has bronchitis.

Causal explanation thus consists in bringing a case under a law—in showing that a particular case is an instance of a connection that always holds between events of two kinds.

In philosophy of science we refer to such explanations as **deductive nomological explanations.** The word *nomological* means "containing a law," and deductive refers to the fact that the explanation involves deducing a description of the event requiring explanation from the law or laws. A deductive nomological explanation has this form:

$$L_1 \ldots L_n$$
$$\underline{C_1 \ldots C_n}$$
$$E$$

The abbreviations in the first line stand for laws or generalizations. Those in the second line stand for what are called **initial conditions**—the circumstances under which an event took place. (They typically include the condition we identify as "the cause" of the event.) In the sciences, these conditions are usually called **experimental variables,** and they include such factors as temperature, years of education, coefficient of expansion, and so on. The letter E stands for a description of the event that is explained.

The following criteria are generally accepted as adequate for determining that a deductive nomological explanation is worthy of acceptance:

1. The explanation contains at least one law established by evidence and accepted as true.

2. The law (or laws) is actually employed in explaining the event. (This condition rules out pseudoscientific explanations that mention laws but do not actually use them.)

3. The sentences describing the initial conditions are true. (That is, the experimental conditions and the values assigned to the variables are correctly stated.)

4. The description of the event is true. (If the event did not occur as described, the laws are irrelevant to explaining it.)

5. The sentence describing the event is a deductive consequence of the laws and initial conditions. (This condition shows that the event fits into the pattern expressed by the laws and that, in this circumstance, the laws are properly applied.)

IV. Testing Causal Claims

Two kinds of events can be regularly related without being causally related. "Whenever the maple leaves in Canada change color, the geese fly south" may be true; yet the change in leaf color does not *cause* the geese to fly south. We recognize that the two events are independent and are related the way they are only because both are triggered by a third event—the onset of winter, with the lowering of the average daily temperature and fewer hours of daylight.

We need ways to separate causal relationships from regular but accidental relationships. That is, we need ways to identify causal factors and distinguish them from merely associated conditions.

The following four experimental methods help us make such distinctions. First formally stated in the nineteenth century by the philosopher John Stuart Mill, they are often called "Mill's methods." (Mill proposed five methods, but the fifth is essentially equivalent to one of the others and is omitted here.) Although science has now become more complicated, Mill's methods continue to express the underlying logic of many experimental investigations. The methods themselves are relatively straightforward, but often unknown or uncontrollable factors complicate actual cases. Hence, there is no automatic way of applying the methods that will guarantee a solution to any causal question.

A. Method of Difference

The **method of difference** involves comparing situations in which an event of interest occurs with similar situations in which it does not. If the presence of a particular factor is the only difference between the two kinds of situations, that factor may be said to be "the cause" of the event.

Suppose we are comparing situations S_1 and S_2, and we represent them as sets of conditions or variables. We find through inquiry that event E occurs only in S_1 and never in S_2. (That is, when the conditions of S_1 are present, E occurs, but it does not when the conditions of S_2 are present.) We draw up lists of the conditions we believe constitute S_1 and S_2 and look for any difference between them:

S_1: *p, q, r, s*

S_2: *p, q, r*

The two sets are exactly alike, except S_1 contains the condition (variable) *s* that is missing in S_2. The factor *s* marks the *difference* between S_1 and S_2. Hence, *s* is the cause of *E*.

Adams and Bardini, let's assume, have shared a dinner of poached salmon and garlic-sautéed spinach, but as they are strolling home, Adams buys (and consumes) a cup of ice cream from a sidewalk vendor. Three hours later, Adams becomes violently ill, with vomiting and stomach cramps. This looks like food poisoning, and, using the method of difference, we can identify the cause of Adams' symptoms:

Adams: Salmon, spinach, ice cream: illness

Bardini: Salmon, spinach

We can identify the (perhaps contaminated) ice cream as the cause of Adams' illness, for it is the only thing he ate that Bardini didn't.

But of course we could be completely wrong. Maybe Adams didn't get sick from food poisoning, but from something else. He just happened to get sick after eating ice cream. Even so, identifying the ice cream as the possible cause is a reasonable first step in the inquiry.

B. Method of Agreement

The **method of agreement** involves comparing situations in which the same kind of event occurs. If the presence of a certain factor is the only respect in which the situations are the same (that is, agree), then this factor may be identified as the cause of the event.

We represent two situations as two sets of conditions or variables, and we assume each set is associated with an occurrence of an event of type *E*:

S_1: *p, q, r, s*

S_2: *t, u, v, s*

Mill's Methods

1. Method of Difference

Case 1: P, Q, R, **S**   EVENT OCCURS

Case 2: P, Q, R   EVENT DOES NOT OCCUR

    The only *difference* between Case 1 and Case 2 is the condition S, so S must be/may be/probably is the cause of the event.

2. Method of Agreement

Case 1: P, Q, R, **S**   EVENT OCCURS

Case 2: T, U, V, **S**   EVENT OCCURS

    The only factors Case 1 and Case 2 have in common (the only point of *agreement*) is S, so S must be/may be/probably is the cause of the event.

3. Joint Method of Agreement and Difference

Case 1: **P**, Q, S   EVENT OCCURS

Case 2: **P**, T, U   EVENT OCCURS

Case 3: R, V, S   EVENT DOES NOT OCCUR

    The event occurs only in Case 1 and Case 2, and the only factor they have in common is P, so P must be the cause. Although Case 1 and Case 3 have factor S in common, the event does not occur in Case 3, so S cannot be the cause.

    We have found a factor that Case 1 and Case 2 have in common (agreement), but Case 3 does not (difference).

4. Method of Concomitant Variation

Case 1:   When P increases in a population, EVENT E occurs more often.

Case 2:   When P decreases in a population, EVENT E occurs less often.

    Case 1 and Case 2 indicate that changes in P and E occur concomitantly (at the same time), so this suggests that P may be the cause of E.

The two sets differ in every respect but one—S_1 and S_2 share factor *s*. Hence, *s* is the cause of the event *E*.

    Of course, the world never presents us with two situations wholly unlike except for one shared factor. When we use the method of agreement, as with the other methods, we must use our knowledge and judgment in designing experiments to fit the requirements of the method and in determining when the method may be appropriately employed in any given nonexperimental situation.

Suppose three people share a dish of moo shu pork at a Chinese restaurant. Afterwards, they have different desserts: the first has pie; the second, ice cream; the third, almond cookies. Later, all three develop headaches, mild sweating, and a feeling of tension around the temples. What is the cause of these symptoms? The method of agreement identifies the moo shu pork as the cause because it is the only factor common to all three people.

Notice that in reaching this conclusion, we rely on unstated assumptions about what is relevant to consider and what is not. We do not compare the people's age, gender, race, shampoo, politics, and so on. We assume, quite naturally, that the symptoms are the result of something the three of them ate. We might be wrong, but additional evidence would be necessary to determine if we are.

Ordinary experience (common sense) also tells us we need to look further at the circumstances in which the symptoms occurred. Did other people develop the same symptoms? What did they eat? Did they also eat moo shu pork? We might decide to test the particular dish the initial three ate from for the presence of bacteria or chemicals that might cause such symptoms; or to check the ingredients that went into all dishes associated with the symptoms. Indeed, we now know from empirical studies that the presence of monosodium glutamate (MSG), a flavor enhancer commonly used in Chinese cooking, is the cause of so-called Chinese restaurant syndrome.

C. Joint Method of Agreement and Difference

The **joint method of agreement and difference** involves the simultaneous application of the two methods discussed previously. We compare cases in which an event of interest occurs with ones in which it does not occur. The cause of the event will be the only factor *present* in each case in which the event occurs and *absent* in each case in which the event does not occur.

Suppose Sikes, Miller, and Kline have lunch at the same restaurant, and later Sikes and Miller become ill with something resembling food poisoning (nausea, vomiting, and so on). Since all three dined at the same place, it is reasonable to suspect that something Sikes and Miller ate caused their illness.

Accordingly, we interview all three, and they provide a list of what they ate:

Sikes: chicken salad, onion soup, chocolate pie

Miller: chicken salad, arugula, sliced oranges

Kline: steak tartare, arugula, chocolate pie

Since Sikes and Miller both became ill and Kline did not, we want to find a dish Sikes and Miller consumed (agreement) but Kline did not (difference). Looking at the list, it is immediately obvious that chicken salad meets this description. Thus, we can identify it as the cause of the illness.

We could not have identified the chicken salad as the causal factor had we been limited to comparing Sikes and Kline or Miller and Kline. Neither of these comparisons meets the conditions for the method of agreement or the method of difference. (Though both Sikes and Kline have chocolate pie, only Sikes gets sick. Though both Miller and Kline have arugula, only Miller gets sick.)

D. Method of Concomitant Variation

Concomitant means occurring at the same time. The **method of concomitant variation** involves varying a factor and determining whether a change in it is accompanied by variation in some other factor that interests us. If the two factors vary together, this is a reason to consider the first factor causally related to the second.

For example, if the more beer a group of people drink, the drunker they get, then it is reasonable to believe drinking the beer is causing the drunkenness. To verify this connection, we might seek more exact information. We might use criteria that allow us to determine in a more precise fashion particular states or stages of drunkenness. Too, we would want to measure the quantity of beer consumed and the time it took. We could then collect data allowing us to plot curves relating beer consumption over time to drunkenness. Presumably we could show, in a more definitive way, a connection between the amount of beer consumed and stages of drunkenness. (At a certain point, we probably could not formulate criteria to distinguish stages reliably.)

The problem with this method is that it is no more than a technique for establishing correlations, even when used in conjunction with sophisticated statistical techniques. Yet many correlations are not causal connections. Suppose that as the number of maple leaves turning brown increases, the number of geese flying south increases. The method of concomitant variation would assure us the change in leaf color is causally responsible for the departure of the geese. Once again, though, what is actually happening is that as the weather gets colder and the days shorter, the number of leaves changing color increases and the number of geese flying south increases—both for the same reason.

While establishing a correlation between two factors does not demonstrate a causal connection between them, finding a correlation is often an important step in uncovering a causal relationship. Correlations suggest what factors might be causal ones and so direct additional investigation.

Further, when correlations are expressed statistically, they may serve as a basis for prediction or as a guide to action. A statistically significant correlation between the amount of animal fats consumed and the incidence of coronary artery disease may lead the prudent person to eat less animal fat. The connection may be only fortuitous and not causal; yet that possibility might not be the one to bet on.

V. Experimental Trials

Before new drugs can be used to treat diseases, researchers must conduct studies to show that the drugs are safe and effective. The method of difference is frequently employed in testing experimental drugs. If two situations can be constructed to resemble each other in every respect, and if a drug is used in one but not the other, then any change in that situation not matched by a change in the other can be ascribed to the drug.

Suppose you are a researcher interested in determining whether the chemical compound THC is effective in lowering blood pressure. You begin with animal studies. You identify a large population of laboratory rats with blood pressures that exceed the normal range. You then divide the rats into a control group and an experimental group, taking care that the two groups resemble one another in all respects you consider relevant.

The rats must all come from the same genetic line, so the influence of potential genetic variables can be reduced, if not eliminated. Further, the distribution of blood-pressure readings should be the same for each group. (That the groups have the same average is not enough, because they might have different ranges of readings, making any results potentially misleading.) Also, the groups should be equally distributed for sex, age, physical condition, and weight. Both groups should also be treated in exactly the same way: fed the same diet, housed in the same kind of cages, kept at the same temperature, and so on. The control group and the experimental group should resemble one another as much as possible in all respects.

The only way you treat the groups differently is by administering THC to the rats in the experimental group. Of course, giving an injection may in itself cause a difference between the two groups. To keep this from affecting the results, you also inject the rats in the control group, only instead of using the drug you use an inactive substance, such as distilled water.

At the end of some predetermined course of treatment, you measure the blood pressure of the rats in each of the groups and compare the results. If the blood pressure in the experimental group is lower than it is in the control group, you have grounds for concluding that the drug you're testing was the cause. After all, the injection of the rats in the experimental group with THC is the only relevant difference between the two groups.

Such results seem unquestionable. Yet even in a relatively simple experimental setup like this one, grounds for doubting that the causal claim has been adequately established are easily discovered. For example, the possibility of **experimental bias** has not been eliminated. If the experimenters know which rats are getting THC, they might unintentionally treat them in different ways. They might spend more time with them, be more gentle in handling them, and so on. Thus, these differences, not THC, may be the factors that are causally responsible for lowering the blood pressure in that group. Or the experimenters might make unconscious errors in recording blood pressures. Without meaning to, their measurements might tend to favor the hypothesis that the drug has the power to lower blood pressure.

To prevent possibilities like these, so-called **blind** (or **masked**) **experiments** have been devised. Researchers involved in conducting the experiment are kept in ignorance (blind) about which animals are in the control group and which are in the experimental group. They may also be kept from knowing whether they are injecting distilled water or the actual drug. (This makes the trial a **double blind.**) Whatever errors the experimenters make may cancel one another, and the possibility of a systematic error will be minimized.

But notice that even this simple experiment assumes that the experimenter can identify the factors likely to affect the outcome of the test. The ability to do this is required in setting up the control and experimental groups. Because they cannot be identical, they must be made similar in relevant ways. If we are interested in testing the effects of a drug on blood pressure, we assume it does not matter if the experimental group contains more rats with black spots on their fur. So far as we know, the presence or absence of spotted fur has no connection with blood pressure. Age and weight are known to be relevant, but coat color is not.

We may be wrong in such assumptions, however. We may ignore variables that make a difference to blood pressure, either because we are ignorant of their existence or we wrongly consider them irrelevant. Thus, we may fail to keep constant in both groups a variable affecting the results. This may lead us to identify a factor as the cause of a result when it is not.

For these and similar reasons, causal inquiry is usually not a matter of conducting a single experiment. Even factors considered relevant often cannot all be controlled for at the same time, and often doubts about other factors are raised after an experiment has been performed. When possible and important, a series of experiments, in which different factors are chosen to be kept constant while others are varied, is always preferable.

Much experimental thinking in the sciences involves Mill's methods. The methods of agreement and difference express the underlying logic of the controlled experiment, and the method of concomitant variation is the basis of statistical correlation.

Exercises

A. *Match each causal concept in List 1 with the item in List 2 that seems to best illustrate or illuminate it.*

List 1

*1. Necessary condition

2. Sufficient condition

*3. Necessary and sufficient condition

4. Controllable condition

*5. Background condition

6. Proximate cause

List 2

a. Whenever *A*, then *B*.

b. If *B* occurred, *A* must have occurred.

c. The cannon fired when Thompson lighted the fuse.

d. A vitamin deficiency causes hair loss.

e. Sunlight was a factor no one thought about.

f. Eat vegetables to decrease your cancer risk.

g. Regular exercise helps prevent depression.

h. If hydrogen and oxygen are mixed in a 2:1 proportion in a sealed container and energy is introduced into the system (e.g., an electric spark), water results.

B. *Explain the apparent causal identifications asserted in the cases below. Is the cause that is mentioned or implied in each case (a) a necessary condition; (b) a sufficient condition; (c) the necessary and sufficient condition; (d) the proximate cause (or triggering condition); (e) a controllable condition; (f) a background (or standing) condition; (g) some other sort of contributing condition? (Keep in mind that these categories are merely ways of approaching an analysis. Not every case fits neatly into a category.)*

*1. The space shuttle *Columbia* disintegrated when a piece of the heat shield broke off and damaged its left wing, setting in motion a chain of destructive consequences.

2. Oscar Wilde would never have been tried on a charge of sodomy had he not filed a lawsuit against his lover's father, who had written Wilde a letter he considered libelous.

*3. Without freedom, art is impossible.

4. On June 28, 1914, a member of a Serbian secret society called the Black Hand shot and killed Archduke Ferdinand, heir to the Hapsburg throne, during a parade in Sarajevo. The assassination was the event that led to World War I.

*5. The crash of Flight 705 was due to inadequate deicing.

6. No shirt, no service.

*7. Bacterial infection is one of the causes of fever.

8. The cost of jet fuel is a significant factor in producing the financial crisis now affecting passenger airlines.

*9. Adolph Hitler's deliberate weakening of the German officer corps by replacing professional soldiers with loyal handpicked amateurs was partly responsible for the atrocities committed by the German army during the Second World War.

10. AIDS is caused by infection with HIV, the human immunodeficiency virus.

*11. Earthquakes are caused by the shifting of tectonic plates. When the margins of two plates moving in opposite directions come together, get stuck, then suddenly break loose and slide past one another, the result is an earthquake.

12. The mercury compound used as a preservative in childhood vaccines is responsible for the increase in autism.

*13. Regular exercise, a low-fat diet, and one alcoholic drink a day help prevent heart disease.

14. When the firing pin in the pistol's hammer struck the primer in the cartridge, the powder ignited.

*15. If no animals enter a reproducing population and none leaves, then if there is an increase in the frequency of a particular gene in the population, the increase is the result either of mutation or of selection.

C. *Tell how you might use the information and generalizations provided to construct deductive explanations for the following events.*

1. **Why did the snow on the sidewalk turn to slush?**

   Event: The snow on the sidewalk turned to slush.

   a. Salt was sprinkled on the snow on the sidewalk.

   b. The temperature remained the same.

   c. When the temperature remains the same, the snow in a salt-snow mixture will turn to slush.

   d. The snow on the sidewalk turned to slush.

2. **Why did some of the metal parts on Don's bike get rusty?**

   Event: Some metal parts on Don's bike are rusty.

   a. The rusty parts are made of steel.

   b. The rusty parts are not coated with paint or any other protective covering and so are exposed to rain and other weather conditions.

   c. Steel contains iron.

   d. Rust is (consists of molecules of) iron oxide.

   e. Don left the bike outside last night.

   f. It rained last night.

   g. Oxygen atoms when combined with iron atoms produce molecules of iron oxide.

   h. Rain is water.

   i. Some metal parts on Don's bike are rusty.

D. *Provide at least two explanations for the following event: Your car fails to start when you turn the key.*

E. *Discuss the use of Mill's methods in identifying the (possible) cause in the following schemes and examples.*

   1. $(A, B, C) \rightarrow$ Event
      $(A, D, F) \rightarrow$ Event

   2. $(A, B) \rightarrow$ No event
      $(A, B, C) \rightarrow$ Event

   3. $(A, B, C) \rightarrow$ Event
      $(A, D, E) \rightarrow$ Event
      $(B, D, C) \rightarrow$ No event

   4. You have two battery-operated, bulb-type flashlights. One works; the other doesn't. You switch batteries. The flashlight that worked no longer does, and the one that didn't now does. Why is this?

5. Same as above, except when you switch batteries, the flashlight that didn't work still doesn't. What else might be wrong?

6. Same as initially described, except when you switch batteries, neither flashlight works. How could this be possible?

F. *Discuss the methods of experimental investigation illustrated in the cases below. (The investigation need not have led to a conclusion we now accept as true.)*

1. Joseph Goldberger conducted the classic investigation into the cause of pellagra, a disease we now know to be caused by nutritional deficiency. Goldberger was convinced that pellagra was not, as many claimed, an infectious disease.

   To test his belief, he conducted experiments in which he and his assistants injected themselves with blood drawn from people with the disease. To rule out another source of transmission, he and his assistants also swallowed capsules filled with excrement taken from pellagra sufferers. Neither Goldberger nor anyone else developed pellagra.

   Explain the reasoning that led Goldberger to reject the hypothesis that pellagra was an infectious disease.

2. Blaise Pascal provided evidence for Toricelli's hypothesis that the earth is surrounded by a "sea of air" by sending his brother-in-law to the top of a mountain with a barometer.

   The barometer consisted of a tube of mercury upended in an open dish. Toricelli had claimed that the mercury in a full tube falls until it reaches the level at which the force it exerts balances the weight of air pressing on the surface of the dish. The brother-in-law climbed the mountain with the barometer, and the level of mercury in the tube fell.

   Explain the reasoning leading Pascal to think that this result would support Toricelli's hypothesis.

3. Pasteur tested the claim that living organisms can arise by spontaneous generation by performing an experiment in which he allowed one sample of meat broth to stand in an uncovered flask and placed another sample in a sealed flask from which the air had been evacuated. Within days, the uncovered broth was teeming with microorganisms, but the broth in the other container was sterile.

   Explain why this test was convincing. Which of Mill's methods does the experiment employ?

4. Jews of central and northern European origin form a distinct group known as the Ashkenazim. As a population, they have a disproportionate number of cases of genetic disorders resulting from mutations that affect the cell's management of certain types of lipids (sphinogolipids). The diseases include Tay-Sachs, Niemann-Pick disease, Gaucher disease, and mucolipidosis type IV.

The mutations causing these disorders apparently occurred only about 1,100 years ago, and geneticists have wondered what forces of natural selection have preserved them in the Ashkenazim.

Some argue that just as sickle-cell anemia remained in populations of African origin because the mutation responsible for it helps protect carriers against malaria, there must have been some similar adaptive advantage for carriers of the mutations responsible for the lipid diseases. With the mutations giving them a selective advantage, the carriers would reproduce and spread the mutations into the next generation. The mutations responsible for the lipid diseases would be a selective advantage.

Crities of the hypothesis argue that if the mutations provided a selective advantage, the mutation causing the lipid diseases would also be preserved in the European population. They are not. Thus, whatever is responsible for the greater frequency of the mutations in the Ashkenasim, it is not because mutations for a lipid disease provided a selective advantage.

Most likely, some geneticists argue, the preservation of the mutations is due to the founder effect. When a population is reduced for a time, as happened to European Jews, then any mutation is likely to spread in the population. The original (founder) population is small, so when the population grows, the genes of the founders are overrepresented in it.

What needs to be explained in this case? What is the hypothesis offered to explain it? What objections are presented as tests or criticisms of the hypotheses? What is the logical form of the first test? Is the second criticism an alternative explanation?

5. A 1997 academic study called "On Behalf of a Moratorium on Prison Construction" noted that crime rates tend to be high when imprisonment rates are high and concluded that crime would fall if imprisonment rates could only be lowered.—Steven D. Levitt and Stephen J. Dubner, *Freakonomics* (Morrow, 2005)

Knowing no more than this about the study, does it appear to be well conceived? If not, what error may be involved?

G. *Analyze the case below, then discuss it from the point of view of (1) the homeowner's attorney, who wants to recover damages for the homeowner; (2) the architectural engineer who designed the house's support structures; (3) the contractor who built the house; and (4) the investigator for the company that wrote the insurance policy on the house with a clause that rules out paying calims for any damages attributable to "acts of God."*

Alan Riding, an architectural engineer, spent more than a day studying the shattered remains of the house that had once belonged to Humphrey Bogart. Riding, who had no previous connection with the house, concluded that although the concrete supports intended to anchor the house to the Laguna Beach hillside extended about twenty feet into the ground under the house's foundation, they hadn't been sunk into bedrock. When five days of unusually heavy rain soaked the hillside, the water-laden soil became unstable, and the resulting mud slide carried the house down the hill and destroyed it.

Chapter 7

ARGUMENT BY ANALOGY AND MODELS

To draw an **analogy** is to call attention to specific similarities between two distinct subject matters. In an argument by analogy, the similarities are offered as a basis for the conclusion. **Models,** as employed in the sciences, are special kinds of analogies.

I. Analogical Arguments

An **analogical argument** (argument by analogy) is one to the effect that because two distinct subjects have certain features in common and one subject possesses an additional feature, then the other subject probably possesses that feature as well. Thus, analogical arguments have the form:

> A is similar to B in possessing features 1, 2, 3, . . .
>
> A also possesses feature N.
> _____
>
> B possesses feature N.

(Moral analogical arguments claim that B *ought* to possess the additional feature.) Arguments by analogy are a special kind of nondeductive argument. The premises support, but do not guarantee, the conclusion.

A. Factual Arguments

A factual analogical argument uses an analogy to establish a claim about some (nonmoral) state of affairs. The two subject matters may be different people, policies, countries, ceremonies, styles of dress, or whatever. This example compares a different historical period with the present one:

> This country is headed for an economic depression. Just compare the way things are now with the way they were before the depression of the 1930s. We've had a major stock crash, and investors are

increasingly unwilling to put their money in the market. Some of
our largest corporations have failed. The manufacturing sector is
slowing down, so unemployment is growing. It's just a matter of
time before massive unemployment puts such a strain on our social
systems that they collapse—just the way they did in the 1930s.

The premises spell out resemblances between the present economy
and that of the 1930s and offer them as evidence for the conclusion
that we are headed for economic collapse.

Not all analogical arguments deal with such ordinary matters of
fact. John Stuart Mill originally formulated an argument that
addresses the problem of other minds: How can we know whether
the subjective experiences of others are like our own? Mill reasoned
as follows about the experience of pain:

Other people have the same sensory equipment as I have—eyes,
nose, ears, and so on.
The physiological mode of operation of this equipment seems the
same for other people as for me.
When I accidentally cut myself or drop a heavy weight on my foot,
I feel pain.
In my own case, such circumstances are usually accompanied by
such behavior as jumping around, contorting my face, cursing, and
so on.

Anyone else who cuts himself or drops a heavy weight on his foot
and exhibits the same sort of behavior as I do is also feeling pain.

Arguments from analogy are often not as explicit as our examples.
"Dogs can obviously think. Haven't you ever seen a dog get excited
when his owner picks up the car keys?" is just as much an analogical
argument as the ones we've considered.

B. Moral Analogical Arguments

Analogical arguments are used in the moral context to argue that
cases similar in relevant respects should be treated in similar ways.
(Some arguments try to show the cases *may* be treated similarly, that
the treatment is permissible but not morally required.) Since fairness
demands that we apply moral rules, as well as social policies and laws,
in a uniform fashion, the arguments may be seen as arguments for
equal treatment. We can distinguish two types of arguments of this
sort.

One form of moral analogical argument is to the effect that because
two cases are similar, we should extend the treatment *already given* to
one to the other. Such arguments often have the following structure:

A and B both have characteristics 1, 2, 3, 4.
A received treatment *T*.
B did not receive treatment *T*.
―――――――――――――――――――――
B *ought* to receive treatment *T*.
(Or we ought to compensate B for not receiving *T*.)

The following argument has this form:

Because migrant farmworkers are hired on a part-time basis,
employers are legally exempt from paying them the minimum
wage they must pay workers classified as full-time. However,
during peak harvesting periods, migrants labor at least as many
hours as workers classified as full-time. Thus, migrants ought to be
paid minimum wage for work done during peak periods.

A variation on arguments like these holds that *if* a treatment is
going to be accorded to one case, then it *ought* to be accorded to a
similar case as well:

A and B both have characteristics 1, 2, 3, 4.
―――――――――――――――――――――
If A receives treatment *T*, then B should receive it too.

The treatment includes penalties as well as benefits. This example
illustrates the above form:

The evidence shows that both Ling and Hawkins worked together
to plan and execute the theft of the documents, and both profited
from their sale to a foreign government. So, if Ling receives a prison
term for his role in the crime, then Hawkins should receive a similar
sentence. It would be unfair to treat Hawkins in a different way.

A second form of moral analogical argument involves attempting
to show that an instance in which an action's legitimacy is in doubt
resembles an instance in which the action would be justified:

Action A is not obviously justified in case *C*.
A is obviously justified in case *D*.
C resembles D in respects 1, 2, 3, . . .
―――――――――――――――――――――
Action A is justified in case *C*.

Here is a sketch of this kind of reasoning in an argument for the
right of a woman to have an abortion:

It is wrong to kill an innocent person. But in some unusual circumstances, everyone agrees it can be morally legitimate.

For example, suppose a mad scientist invents an implantable device that can take over a person's brain, blanking out his consciousness and controlling his body like a robot's. The mad scientist implants the device in your neighbor Pack's brain. When you arrive home, Pack grabs you, holds a knife to your throat, and in a toneless voice says, "I'm going to kill you."

You happen to have in your pocket an autosyringe loaded with a poison that causes instant paralysis and death. Is it morally permissible to kill this brain-controlled but innocent person?

It is permissible, although unfortunate. The same is true of abortion, even if we assume the fetus is a person. The fetus is innocent, yet it poses a threat to the pregnant woman. Just as she is justified in defending herself from the brain-controlled killer, she is warranted in defending herself from the fetus.

Moral analogical arguments involve an implicit premise to the effect that "Similar cases should be treated in similar ways." This is a *formal* principle of justice or equality. The formal principle does not say what makes two cases similar or how they should be treated. "It is wrong to kill an innocent person, except in self-defense" is a material principle. What should count as a person, as innocent, and as self-defense must be spelled out and established by argument.

We can regard moral analogical arguments as enthymemes, in which the formal principle of equality is the implicit premise. When the principle is added, such arguments may become valid. But as we discuss below, this does not necessarily mean they are good arguments. (See Chapter 1 on enthymemes and Chapter 3 on validity in general.)

II. Models

Analogical reasoning in the natural and social sciences often takes the form of using models to reach conclusions. A **model** involves using a familiar and well-understood system to represent a system not as well understood. We assume that features of the model are similar to those of the unfamiliar system, and we extend conclusions about the model to it. Two important kinds of models in science are formal and material ones.

A. Formal Models

A **formal model** is a set of concepts and principles belonging to one system employed to develop an understanding of another system. The kinetic theory of gases may be modeled as a room filled with Ping-Pong balls. We assume that an ideal gas is made up of small spheres, represented by Ping-Pong balls, and the room represents its container. The room and balls are assigned certain characteristics—for example, the walls of the room are perfectly elastic and the diameter of the balls is negligible compared to the distance between them. Heating the gas is like making the balls bounce faster, and increasing the pressure is like moving the walls closer, which increases the number of balls within a unit of space. Thinking in these terms lets us apply concepts and laws that hold for a familiar type of physical system to an unfamiliar one.

Other examples of formal models are equally familiar. Galileo modeled free-falling bodies by rolling marbles down a slanted board, and Charles Darwin modeled his theory of natural selection on the behavior of animal breeders in making artificial selections. Aspects of Sigmund Freud's psychodynamical theory were developed in terms of analogies with hydraulic forces. Repressed rage, for instance, is like built-up pressure inside a pipe.

B. Material Models

No one believes that gas molecules are literally Ping-Pong balls or that rage flows through pipes in the body. In formal models, we consider only certain abstract properties of the model to hold for the system modeled. The case is different with **material models**, in which a physical system is taken to represent parts of another physical system. The representation rests on the assumption that the systems share enough features to allow us to extend discoveries about the model to the system it models.

The most familiar material models are laboratory animals. We use rats, mice, monkeys, dogs, cats, rabbits, and other organisms to study the causes and treatments of human diseases and the effects of drugs and other chemicals on human health. No scientist claims these animals and humans are biologically the same. However, sometimes we can assume animals and humans share enough relevant features to permit us to test hypotheses that, because of time or moral constraints, cannot be tested directly on people.

Rhesus monkeys, for example, are often used in nutrition experiments as biological models for humans. If monkeys fed a diet deficient in folic acid develop anemia, this finding may be extended to humans. The results are offered to support the conclusion that humans eating a diet lacking in folic acid will also develop anemia.

Animal models are essential to basic research in biology and medicine. Research into the causes of mental illness, most scientists agree, is severely hampered by the lack of animal models for disorders like sleep disturbances and schizophrenia.

Material models are also used in other areas of science. Tanks filled with a mixture of water and sand represent quicksand, and hydraulic presses represent the weight of a rock mass on top of a stratum. Archaeologists use modern garbage dumps to represent ancient middens and take construction techniques used in parts of contemporary Peru as models for ancient ones.

In all such cases, reasoning from a material model to the system modeled involves making a claim about this system on the basis of similarities between the model and it. Hence, reasoning from models is a kind of analogical argument.

III. Evaluating Analogical Reasoning

We have no rules that let us decide automatically whether an analogical argument is a good one. Yet two criteria are helpful in deciding whether a conclusion is worthy of belief.

A. The Degree of Analogy Must Be High

Common experience tells us that as the number of similarities between the two subjects in an analogy increases, so does the likelihood that if one has an additional feature, the other will have it also. If the number of resemblances is 100, it is more probable that an additional resemblance will be found than it would be if the number were only 10. However, the number of points of resemblance must be balanced against the number of points of dissimilarity between the two subjects. That two subjects share 100 features may mean little if the subjects differ in 1000 other ways.

The ways subjects resemble one another constitute the **positive analogy,** and the ways they differ constitute the **negative analogy.** If the points of resemblance and difference are taken together, then the degree of analogy is the ratio of the positive and negative analogies. When the positive analogy is proportionately larger than the negative analogy, then the degree of analogy is high.

The **limiting case** of a high degree of analogy occurs when two cases are virtually identical in every respect except for the space they occupy. Two hydrogen atoms or two water molecules are examples of limiting cases. Larger, more familiar objects begin to diverge from one another in specific ways. Glass marbles produced one after another from the same batch of glass and by the same machine come to resemble the limiting cases, but dogs, people, historical events, conversations, paintings, and political situations, even when they are of the same kind, may differ radically from one another. Biologists, psychologists, sociologists, anthropologists, and political scientists often point out that this lack of exact similarity among the objects they study makes getting reliable results more difficult than is the case in physics and chemistry.

We have no mechanical procedure to determine when the degree of analogy between two cases is adequate to justify a conclusion. Whether a conclusion should be accepted requires acquiring and weighing relevant facts. Ultimately, though, the decision is a matter of judgment.

For instance, without violating copyrights, can individuals use video recorders to copy television programs to watch later or to form a library for their personal use? A court decision held this was fair use. It decided that the degree of analogy between videotaping and audiotaping was sufficiently high that past rulings about the "fair use" doctrine and audiotaping applied to video. (Videotaping itself is sufficiently like copying onto a disc or hard drive that the court's resolution still stands.) Another court might have decided otherwise, for where degree of analogy is the issue, reasonable people can differ.

Criticism of moral analogical arguments often consists of pointing out that whereas similarities may exist between two individuals or groups, their dissimilarities are more important. A man previously convicted of child molesting, for example, can hardly claim he is being treated unfairly when a day-care center denies him employment and hires others who are otherwise comparable. In such cases, the number of similarities or dissimilarities does not count so much as their *relative importance*. We have no way, then, merely to count similarities and differences, get a numerical ratio, decide on a number at which we will accept a conclusion, then use the ratio to make the decision for us. We cannot avoid exercising judgment.

> Though analogy is often misleading, it is the least misleading thing we have.
>
> Samuel Butler

B. The Analogy Should Be Relevant to the Conclusion

Confidence in a conclusion is also increased when the characteristics the two subjects share are closely connected with the additional feature of the first that is attributed to the second. The connection may be statistical or causal.

Suppose we are concerned with whether the residents of a recently incorporated subdivision are likely to support a proposition to increase the school tax. They don't have a voting history, so we turn to analogy as a basis for prediction.

When we compare the new subdivision with an older one where we know the voting history, we find we get a good match for the distribution of income, occupation, age, and married couples. The degree of analogy between the two subdivisions appears to be high, and the older subdivision has always supported increasing school taxes.

Can we now conclude that the new subdivision will support the tax increase? Perhaps. But our confidence would be greater if we had evidence showing that those with school-age children in the older subdivision are likely to support this particular tax bill. Also, we could be more confident if we knew that the proportion of residents with school-age children in both subdivisions is roughly the same.

But our confidence will be severely shaken if we discover the new subdivision has a high proportion of families without school-age children. People without young children tend not to vote for school taxes. Thus, despite many similarities between the subdivisions, we may end up not feeling confident that we can predict the outcome of the voting. Arguments by analogy can be useful, but they can't always solve our problems.

For moral analogical arguments, the similarities between cases must be *relevant* similarities if they are to support a contention of unfairness or a demand for equality of treatment. To award an A to Gomez, who scores 90 on a calculus exam, and an F to Whitley, who scores 10, is prima facie fair. The numerical score on the exam is relevant to the letter grade a student deserves. If Whitley were to argue that the grades are unfair because she and Gomez studied the same amount for the exam and have similar overall grade-point averages, we would reject her claim. These similarities are not relevant to the grade she received on the calculus exam. By contrast, how she performed on the exam was relevant.

Models may also be criticized on the grounds of relevance. Critics who objected to the use of mice in research to determine the effects of saccharine, an artificial sweetner, on humans claimed that mice were bad models. The way mice metabolize the substance is different from the way humans do. Thus, the discovery that saccharine produces bladder cancer in mice cannot legitimately be extended to humans. The physiological process of metabolism is relevant to bladder cancer, so (critics claimed) the differences in physiology between mice and humans make the animal model an inappropriate one. (Other scientists disputed the relevance of the differences and defended the use of mice as the proper model.)

We have no rules for determining relevance. Even when facts are agreed to and principles are shared, disagreements about relevance may still divide people. This is particularly so in areas like criminal justice and moral and social decision making, where analogical arguments play a common and important role. Although we may hope for agreement about relevance, we sometimes must try to establish it by argument.

Exercises

A. *Consider the opposing analogical arguments presented in each of the following questions (after the introductory sections). Restate each argument in a brief and explicit form, then discuss its strengths and weaknesses.*

1. **Ethnic Profiling**

   Terrorist acts committed against the United States on September 11, 2001, prompted the country to introduce a variety of defensive measures. The preboarding screening of passengers at airports, in particular, was intensified. But should every passenger be given the same degree of scrutiny? Or should we engage in ethnic profiling?

   For. Suppose you are on a street corner and a man in a red hat walks up and punches you in the nose. A lot of men wearing green or yellow hats walk past you, as do several in red hats. Then another man in a red hat punches you. The next day another one does. The only people who punch you are men wearing red hats. So who are you going to be particularly suspicious of? Men in green hats? Women in yellow hats? That would be absurd. You're going to give men in red hats a close look so that you can protect yourself.

   That's why it makes perfect sense to engage in ethnic profiling in the war against terrorism. The terrorists who attacked the United States were all men with a Middle Eastern ethnic background. Screening every passenger to some degree before boarding is reasonable, but men who are ethnically Middle Eastern should be given closer attention.

   Against. This is a democratic country. Everybody has the same worth as everybody else. To single out men of a specific ethnic group for special suspicion—ethnic profiling—is simply wrong. It would be no different than making women pay more taxes than men or allowing people with red hair to go to the front of every line. When it comes to airport screening, or any other kind of security check, men who are ethnically Middle Eastern should be treated just like everybody else.

2. **Deep Throat**

   Carl Bernstein and Bob Woodward wrote the series of articles in the *Washington Post* exposing the connection between the burglary of the offices of the Democratic National Committee at the Watergate complex and the Republican Committee to Reelect the President. They also showed that President Nixon and his closest aides had used their positions to gain access to

FBI files about the investigation and attempted to cover up the burglary and pressure law enforcement agencies to drop the Watergate investigation.

The crucial information the reporters needed to conduct their investigation was provided by a highly placed government source they identified only as "Deep Throat." They refused to reveal the real identify of Deep Throat for decades, prompting endless speculation.

Then in 2005 W. Mark Felt, ninety-one years old and ailing, revealed to the public that he had been Woodward and Bernstein's anonymous source. Felt was second in command at the FBI and had been angry about the way the agency was being manipulated by the Nixon administration. The reporters confirmed Felt's claim.

Felt's revelation led some to praise his actions in feeding information to Woodward and Bernstein as courageous and patriotic, but critics condemned him as violating his duty as a law-enforcement official.

Should Mark Felt be considered a criminal?

For. If Felt possessed information about wrongdoing by President and his aides, it was his duty to have reported it to the Washington, D.C. police or to the FBI team responsible for investigating the Watergate burglary. Only criminals take the law into their own hands. In breaking FBI rules and talking to reporters, Felt turned himself into a criminal, in both a legal and moral sense.

Against. If you are in a burning building, you may have to break down the door of an apartment to save the child inside. What under ordinary circumstances would be a criminal act becomes an act of heroism when something of great importance is at stake. Felt needed to break the FBI rules to expose ongoing misconduct by high officials of the government. Had he never talked to the reporters but to FBI officers instead, he might have become a target of White House "dirty tricks," because Nixon's aides had access to FBI files.

3. **Driver's License**

   The State of Florida refused to issue a driver's license to Saltaana Freeman because she refused to be photographed without a veil. The veil completely covered her head and face, leaving only her eyes visible. Freeman, a Muslim woman, claimed that requiring that she remove her veil for the photograph violated her freedom of religion.

Should a Photograph Without a Veil Be Required?

For. This is a case in which state interest takes precedence over religious expression. We need to know people's identity. The police need to be sure the person driving is a person with a license, and a driver's license is also used as proof of identify at airport security and in a variety of commercial and public transactions. Maybe in the future fingerprints or a retina scan will become the mode of identification, but right now it is a photograph. Photographing someone wearing a veil would be like photographing someone wearing a skimask over his face. Yes, the license would show that person had passed the driving test, but it would be next to worthless for identification.

Against. The state is within its rights requiring a license to drive, because it testifies to the acquisition of the basic skills needed to avoid being a hazard to others. But requiring a photograph of the driver on the license in violation of her religious beliefs is going too far. The state doesn't require Hindu Sikhs to remove their turbans or Orthodox Jews to take off their hats. Nor does it require men to shave their beards and moustaches, Freeman should receive equal protection of the law for her religious beliefs.

B. *Identify the following arguments by analogy as factual or moral. Specify the points of comparison between the two different subjects in each case, then evaluate the argument.*

*1. People deserve pay for their labor. Whether you wash cars or transplant hearts, you ought to get paid. African Americans worked hard to build this country, and their sweat produced some of the nation's great fortunes. But because they were forced to work against their will as slaves, they were never paid. Now the bill is due, and it's time to give the workers the money they earned. The United States government owes reparations to every living African American—man, woman, and child.—Colby Brown (student, 2003)

2. I read with great interest the recent proposal by the American Medical Association to forbid doctors to conduct death-by-injection executions of convicted murders because "A physician [is] a member of a profession dedicated to preserving life." I find this view highly incongruous, considering the fact that hundreds and possibly thousands of doctors are involved in destroying human life at its very beginning by

their participation in and encouragement of abortions throughout this country.—Virginia Banner, *Dallas Morning News*, 1980

*3. Imagine someone placing your head in a stock. As you stare helplessly ahead, unable to defend yourself, your head is pulled back. Your lower eyelid is pulled away from your eyeball. Then chemicals are poured into the eye. There is pain. You scream and writhe hopelessly. There is no escape.

This is the Draize Test. The test which measures the harmfulness of chemicals by the damage inflicted on the unprotected eyes of conscious rabbits. The test that . . . cosmetic firms force on thousands of rabbits to test their products. . . . A healthy society does not inflict violence on the powerless; does not pursue "glamour" at the expense of innocent animals.—The Millennium Guild, *New York Times* advertisement, 2002

4. The issue of allowing military recruiters on campus . . . is not simply a problem of free speech and First Amendment rights. I doubt that anyone thinks that everyone has a right to come on campus and recruit. . . . It is unlikely that many of us would want to let the Mafia come and recruit, for example. That's because they have a reputation for killing. The military services have such a reputation as well. Essentially, when one signs a contract with the military, one signs oneself into bondage, pledged to kill on demand. . . . It may be said that the Mafia analogy is a spurious one, but certainly not to the many victims of the U.S. military since WW II.—Roger Haekins, *Daily Guardian*, University of California, San Diego, 1999

5. Users and sellers of heroin, cocaine, and other so-called dangerous drugs are treated unfairly by the laws of this country. Such drugs pose a health risk to individuals who use them, but so do such common drugs as nicotine and alcohol. We don't sentence smokers and drinkers to prison or throw grocery store owners into jail for selling dangerous drugs. We let people smoke and drink because we believe they have a right to do whatever they want so long as it affects no one but themselves. It's time we applied this principle consistently and threw out the laws that make it a serious crime to use or sell "dangerous" drugs.

6. High schools and colleges have added new courses and programs dealing with ethnic and gender studies. African American poetry, women's literature, Hispanic architecture, Native American music, Asian history, Islamic philosophy, and the like are now found in the curriculum. Such courses

are a welcome addition, because the more we understand the diverse cultures in our society, the more we appreciate the strengths of our society.

But an important area of study has been overlooked—the culture of people who are poor and white. It's the rich and powerful who dominate the history books, and the story of poor whites doesn't get told. Yet they also have their music and art, their literature, beliefs, and customs. They also have struggled against prejudice, and, despite their poverty and pain, they too have contributed to the richness of our heritage. Schools and colleges should introduce courses that focus on the culture of poor whites. Aren't they as entitled to be represented as any other group?

7. I reject the idea that parents alone, not states, should regulate the health needs of students by keeping junk food out of the public schools. The state already keeps students from smoking or carrying guns. Also, it requires that school cafeterias take steps to protect students from food allergies.

8. Mr. Hamad draws a parallel between Saudi Arabia and soccer. The country plays soccer according to the same rules as everybody else. So Saudis need to learn that their society, too, can afford the same kind of open debate and discussion allowed in other countries.—*New York Times,* 9 June 2005

9. The planet Mars possesses an atmosphere with clouds and mists resembling our own; it has seas distinguished from the land by a greenish color, and polar regions covered with snow. The red color of the planet seems to be due to the atmosphere, like the red color of our sunrises and sunsets. So much is similar in the surface of Mars and the surface of the Earth that we readily agree that there must be inhabitants there as here.—W. S. Jevons, *Elementary Lessons in Logic*

10. A full-grown cat is capable of much more than a human infant. The cat has a sense of its own interest and is capable of receiving and displaying affection. Further, it engages in play and activities like hunting that show that its level of intelligence is as great as, if not greater, than that of the infant. Hence, if we consider painful, destructive experiments performed on cats to be morally legitimate, we must also accept the legitimacy of similar experiments on human infants.

C. *Chief Justice of the U.S. Supreme Court John G. Roberts, when Deputy Solicitor General for the Department of Justice, presented arguments before the Supreme Court on October 6, 1992, supporting the legality of the antiabortion group Operation Rescue's practice of blocking access to clinics by women seeking an abortion. Operation Rescue was charged with interfering with women in the exercise of their rights, thus depriving them of the equal protection of the law. Roberts argued against this claim by using an analogy.*

Setting aside your own views on abortion and a woman's right to qain access to it without impediment, evaluate Roberts' analogical argument.

> Consider . . . an Indian tribe with exclusive fishing rights in a particular river. A group of ecologists get together who are opposed to fishing in the river, because they think it disturbs the ecology. They interfere with the Indians' rights. The impact of their conspiracy is on a particular Indian group, but it would be quite illogical to infer from that they have any animus against Indians. They are opposed to fishing in the river, not Indians, even though only Indians can fish in the river. Petitioners are opposed to abortion, not women, even though only women can exercise the right to an abortion.—Quoted in the *New York Times*, 21 July 2005

D. *In the cases below, (a) distinguish between the model and the subject modeled; and (b) discuss the ways in which the model may fail to serve as a reliable basis for conclusions about the subject modeled.*

   1. A major problem in the study of mental illness is that it is not clear that there can be animal models for the most serious of the psychiatric disorders. Schizophrenia, for example, one of the two major psychoses, does not have an animal model.

      Discuss some of the difficulties that stand in the way of getting appropriate animal models for studying mental illness.

   2. The atom can best be understood as a miniature solar system. The nucleus of the atom occupies the place of the sun, and the electrons move around the nucleus just as the planets move in orbits around the sun. The sun's gravitational attraction holds the planets in their places, and the nucleus's attraction keeps the electrons in their orbits.

   3. Here is a die-cast miniature model of the 1937 Ford pickup truck. The engineers and designers have been instructed to

create a pickup truck just like this one, except it should also include the latest in automotive technology.

4. Discuss whether spilling a bag of marbles would be a good abstract model for the behavior of people in a parking lot. Would it be a good model for the behavior of a crowd leaving an office building during a fire?

E. *Follow the instructions about developing, analyzing, or evaluating a predictive model in each of the following cases.*

1. One theory of aging holds that molecules called free radicals inflict such damage on cells that eventually the cells die or no longer function properly. Organs will then fail, and people will die of heart disease and cancer.

   Organisms contain genes that produce enzymes to combat free radicals in cells. The recombinant-DNA technology is available to provide fruit flies with an extra set of these genes. (See R. S. Sohal and W. C. Orr, *Science*, 25 February 1994.)

   Describe an experiment to test the free radical theory of aging by using two groups of fruit flies.

2. One of the difficulties standing in the way of using pig organs as transplants to save human lives is that pigs have a gene that encodes for a protein on cell surfaces that the human immune system recognizes as "not self," causing the body to reject the organ. Scientists have demonstrated with mice that it is possible to breed mice with certain genes "knocked out." Thus, some mice have the gene that produces insulin knocked out, and they become diabetic.

   Describe an experiment that might lead to the use of pigs to supply transplant organs.

3. Scientists and technologists in our society have the same uneasy status as the Jedi in the Galactic Republic. The masses and the deities claim to admire the Jedi, but they really fear and loathe them, because they have to depend on the Jedis' power. In our society, both the cultural left and the cultural right scorn scientists and technologists. Young people avoid science and mathematics classes, and we outsource the technical tasks to countries happy to sweat the details, so long as we can pay them. We like to think that, like the Jedi, we are the masters of advanced technology but live simple lives—that we have a geek standard of living and can spend copious leisure time vegging out.

The *Star Wars* movies are an exact parable for this state of affairs. Young people a century from now will watch them and ask, "Whatever became of that big rich country that used to buy the stuff we made?" The answer: It went the way of the old Republic.—Based on Neil Stephenson, "Turn on, Tune In, Veg Out," *New York Times*, 17 June 2005

What is the model? What is modeled? What is the prediction based on the model?

Chapter 8

ERRORS IN REASONING: FALLACIES

A **fallacy** is any error in reasoning. Traditionally, however, only errors that are common and that we have a strong temptation to commit are referred to as fallacies.

Most of the fallacies we'll discuss have Latin names. This is an indication that philosophers since antiquity have tried to identify and describe common failures in reasoning. Our aim, like theirs, is to make it less likely we'll be deceived by bad arguments. Knowing even a few ways in which reasoning can go wrong is useful in making us cautious in assessing arguments.

We divide fallacies into two groups. The first consists of errors in making a case for a claim. The second consists of errors in criticizing arguments or in responding to criticism. The groups and their subdivisions aren't exclusive, so some fallacies might be placed in more than one. A label, after all, can never be a substitute for a critical assessment. (Other fallacies are discussed in Chapters 4 and 11.)

I. Fallacies in Supporting a Claim

Some of the traditional fallacious arguments have premises that fail to be *relevant* to the conclusion. Others have premises that are relevant but fall far short of making an *adequate* case for the conclusion. A third subdivision consists of fallacies that depend on some *mistaken assumption*.

A. Five Fallacies of Relevance

Fallacies in this group involve premises that are not relevant to the conclusions they are meant to support.

1. Appeal to Ignorance (*Ad Ignorantiam*)

The **appeal to ignorance** consists in arguing that because a claim has not been demonstrated to be false, the claim is true. For instance:

> Of course I believe in ESP. No one has ever demonstrated that it doesn't exist.

Astrology has got to be right, because over the centuries no one has disproved it.

This case of legislative thinking has all the appearance of being reasonable, but it is fallacious:

The Speaker of the House summed up the thinking of the legislature in passing a law requiring public school teachers to swear an oath of loyalty to the United States. "There didn't seem to be any reason we shouldn't have such a law," he said. "No one showed us anything wrong with it, so we concluded it was all right."

To summarize, to establish a claim by argument, we must present reasons and evidence *for* it. The lack of a case *against* a claim is not the same as having reasons *for* it.

Good Reasoning That Looks Bad: Unstated Premise Sometimes good reasoning can resemble *ad ignorantiam* reasoning. For instance, we look in the living room, do not see an elephant, and conclude no elephant is there. Taken at face value, this looks like just another appeal to ignorance.

It has not been shown that there is an elephant in the living room.
___
There is not an elephant in the living room.

Really, though, the argument is entirely acceptable if we elaborate and add the commonsense unstated premise.

It has not been shown that there is an elephant in the living room; that is, I did not see one there.
If there were an elephant in the living room, I would have seen it there.
___
There is no elephant in the living room.

Sympathetically interpreted in this way, the argument is valid (an instance of *modus tollens*) and the premises are nearly certainly true. So, despite its superficial similarity to an appeal to ignorance, the argument gives strong ground for accepting its conclusion.

Good Reasoning That Looks Bad: Background Beliefs Some arguments may look like appeals to ignorance only because we are ignoring information we already have (on background beliefs, see Chapter 11) that relates to the argument. Suppose that you profess your odd beliefs about big cockroaches in jungles. I reply,

No one has given any good reason to think there are 10-foot-long cockroaches hiding out in the darkest jungles of the earth.
___
There are not any such giant cockroaches.

On the surface this looks like the *ad ignorantiam* fallacy. But in practice we are surely relying on our experience that insects do not get nearly that big. If we are sophisticated in biology, we also know that huge insects could not live because their lungs could not take in enough oxygen relative to body size. With the unstated premise that reflects this other knowledge, the argument is:

> Everyday experience and principles of biology tell us that insects are mostly under 6 inches in length.
> No one has given any good reason to think there are 10-foot-long cockroaches hiding out in the darkest jungles of the earth.
> ___
> There are not any such giant cockroaches.

The argument now gives good support for its conclusion.

In short, both the elephant and the cockroach arguments look like cases of appeals to ignorance, but both can be understood to assume unstated premises. Without the unstated premises, they really are fallacious appeals to ignorance. With the unstated premises, they are good arguments. We never want to be convinced by arguments that amount to nothing but appeals to ignorance. But we also want to be sensitive to interpretations that would show any underlying merit an argument may have.

Good Reasoning That Looks Bad: Not-Guilty Conclusions Court decisions of "not guilty" in the United States may look like cases of the *ad ignorantiam* fallacy:

> Prosecutors failed to prove Simpson killed his ex-wife.
> ___
> Simpson was not guilty of killing his ex-wife.

Issues of legal guilt are enormously complicated, but no fallacy is committed here. In the United States, a person is presumed innocent until proven guilty, so to be "not guilty" means only not to be found guilty in a court of law. The argument about guilt should be understood as:

> Prosecutors failed to prove in a court of law that Simpson killed his ex-wife.
> Anyone not proved to be guilty in a court of law is not legally guilty.
> ___
> Simpson was not legally guilty of killing his ex-wife.

This is faultless reasoning. (It is also reasoning that is compatible with Simpson's having killed his ex-wife.)

2. Appeal to Inappropriate Authority *(Ad Verecundiam)*

We base much of what we believe on the evidence of authority, and citing an authority is a legitimate way of justifying a belief. The rationale is that the authority is in a position to provide compelling evidence, even though we are not. A fallacy, however, is committed when the authority cited is not an authority in the proper area. The expertise of the authority is thus irrelevant to the claim and provides no support for it.

Aldous Huxley, the author of *Brave New World,* was convinced that nearsightedness could be corrected by eye exercises (the Bates method) and that glasses were unnecessary. He wrote a book advocating this position, and because of his eminence as a novelist, other writers frequently cited him to establish the claim that the Bates method could cure nearsightedness. Those who appealed to Huxley's authority in support of the claim were committing the fallacy of **appealing to inappropriate authority.**

The fallacy is one committed, usually implicitly, by those who base their political views on the claims of physicians, their economic views on the pronouncements of psychologists, or their nutritional views on the assertions of hairstylists.

3. Appeal to General Belief *(Ad Populum)*
This fallacy consists in asserting that a claim is correct just because people generally believe it is. Such an inference is in error because we have no reason to take what most people believe as a reliable indicator of what is true.

Probably the most common appeal to this fallacious argument type is this one: "People the world over have always believed God exists. It has to be true." (Notice that the premise is false as well as being irrelevant to the conclusion.)

Sometimes an appeal to popular belief is incorporated into a larger argument:

> We all know most people on welfare are just too lazy to work. So, we should start a program requiring those on welfare to provide community service to earn their money.

Here popular opinion is used as the authority for accepting an asserted claim, so this is a form of appealing to authority. But since it is difficult to think of any case in which popular opinion should be regarded as a genuine authority, it is a particular case of the fallacy of appeal to *inappropriate* authority.

4. Appeal to Popular Attitudes and Emotions (also called *Ad Populum*)
Popular attitudes and the emotions associated with them can be manipulated to incline people to accept claims that have not been demonstrated. Racial fears and prejudices, patriotic impulses, and the wish to be associated with a special social group are some sources of

such sentiments and attitudes. This fallacy is committed by appealing to these rather than to relevant reasons and evidence.

Here is an unsubtle appeal to patriotism:

> I'll tell you why I believe we were right to go to war with Iraq. It's because I love my country. If you love it, you'll agree.

In the following appeal, a presumed wish to be associated with a special social group is used:

> Now look, Hakim. You know that Marxism isn't right. What would your friends at the club think if they heard you talking this way?

Obviously such purely emotional appeals offer no relevant support for the issues in question.

5. Gambler's Fallacy

A classic case of the **gambler's fallacy** goes this way:

> According to the law of averages, if I flip a fair coin it should come up *heads* about 50 percent of the time and come up *tails* about 50 percent of the time. The last ten flips have been *tails*. So, it is well past time for *heads* to come up. We'd better bet all we have on *heads*.

This is tempting reasoning. Eventually there should be an equal number of *heads* and *tails*. So, we think, in this case it is time for *heads* to be catching up. *Expect the next flip to be heads.*

Tempting as it is, this reasoning is mistaken. Each flip of the coin is independent of the others. If the coin is fair, even 100 previous flips of either *heads* or *tails* have nothing to do with the likelihood that the next flip will or will not be *heads*. In the very long run, *heads* and *tails* can be expected to even out, but that has nothing to do with what we should expect on the next or any particular coin flip.

The idea that some things are "due" usually plays a role in the gambler's fallacy. Ten flips and no *heads*, so *heads* is due; fifty years and Miami has not had a major hurricane, so a hurricane is due; the best hitter in baseball has not had a hit in twenty times at bat, so he is due. All of these understandable and tempting claims are instances of the gambler's fallacy, and they all need to be resisted.

B. Two Fallacies of Inadequate Evidence

Fallacies in this group are arguments with premises that present relevant but inadequate evidence.

1. False Cause (Post Hoc)

The *post hoc* fallacy involves concluding that because one event occurred before another, the first was the cause of the second. Suppose, for example, that Templeton eats a candy bar, then commits a murder. It would be fallacious to conclude, on this ground alone, that eating the candy bar caused Templeton to commit the murder.

Legitimate causal explanations invoke a causal law that connects events of one type with those of another. Such laws must be based on data from a number of cases and established by an empirical investigation that rules out the possibility of a merely accidental correlation between the two types of events. (See "Testing Causal Claims" in Chapter 6.)

We have no law connecting candy bars and murder. (We don't even have laws connecting murder with physiological changes that occur when particular kinds of people eat candy bars.) That one event occurs before another is relevant to identifying the first as the cause of the second. We cannot, however, regard everything that happens before a particular event as causing it.

Post Hoc

In the nineteenth century, when train travel was a novelty, Joe and Maude Farmer, who had never been out of Silver City, Colorado, were taking the *Pacific Flyer* to San Francisco. When a vendor came down the aisle selling sandwiches and fruit, Joe bought a banana. Neither had tasted one before, and they gazed at it with curiosity.

"You go ahead and try it, Joe," Maude told him.

"If you say so," Joe said. He stripped back the peel and took a bite of banana. Just as he swallowed, the train roared into a tunnel, and everything went dark.

"Don't eat any, Maude," Joe cried out in alarm. "It will make you go blind."

---

2. Hasty Generalization

The fallacy of **hasty generalization** consists of generalizing on the basis of an inadequate set of cases. As a sample from a larger population, the cases are too few or too unrepresentative to constitute adequate evidence. Suppose you are a psychotherapist and your first two clients lie to you about crucial aspects of their lives. If you conclude from this experience, "All clients lie to their therapists" or even "Most clients lie to their therapists," then you are open to the charge of hasty generalization. Even if your generalization is true, your evidence is inadequate because your sample is very small, and we have no reason to think it is representative of the entire group.

C. Four Fallacies of Illegitimate Assumption

Fallacies in this group are tied together by the fact that each invokes some illegitimate assumption.

1. False Dilemma (False Alternatives)

A dilemma is a situation in which we are faced with choosing between alternatives. In the strictest case, the dilemma has exactly two alternatives that are both exhaustive and exclusive. "You must either stay or leave" offers exactly two possible choices. These alternatives exhaust all the possibilities, and they are exclusive in that it is not possible to both stay and leave.

We usually take a less strict view and think of a dilemma as involving two or more alternatives, and this view is the one we adopt here. Hence, "The government of Ruritania must either dissolve itself, replace its prime minister, or turn over power to the opposition leader" presents three alternatives facing the government.

Furthermore, we typically do not require the alternatives to be exhaustive and exclusive in a strict way (stay or not stay, for example), but only in a practical way. For instance, having fish or steak for dinner does not constitute an exhaustive and exclusive set of alternatives in the strict way. But in a practical context, they could be exhaustive and exclusive (if, for instance, they are both on the menu, nothing else is, and you can't have both).

The **false dilemma fallacy** consists of giving arguments that present alternatives as exhaustive and exclusive when they are not. The classic case of this is:

> Either you're for us or you're against us. It is obvious you aren't for us. So, you're against us.

The alternatives in the first premise pretend to be exhaustive, but they are neither strictly nor practically so. They leave out the possibility of a person's being carefully neutral or just having no knowledge of the issues.

"Either we cut spending or increase the deficit" is a false dilemma that ignores such possibilities as raising taxes. "Either we have much more capital punishment or keep putting murderers back out on the street" ignores possibilities like mandatory life imprisonment for murderers.

Such false dilemmas are aimed at convincing us to accept certain conclusions (cut spending; have a lot more capital punishment). Generally, false dilemmas are used to make us choose between given alternatives when other choices exist or we could accept both given alternatives.

2. Loaded Question (Complex Question)

The **loaded question fallacy** consists of attempting to get an answer to a question that assumes the truth of an unproved assumption. It "assumes a conclusion." The classic example is "Are you still beating your wife?" Whether someone answers yes or no to this question, he is committing himself to the truth of the implicit assumption that he has beaten his wife in the past.

The error is also called the fallacy of the **complex question** because we can analyze the question into a statement and a question: "You used to beat your wife. Do you still do so?"

A "question that assumes a conclusion" is not permitted in courts of law during the examination of witnesses—unless the conclusion at issue has already been established to lay the groundwork for the question that assumes its truth. The fallacy is an attempt to get the truth of the assumed conclusion tacitly acknowledged without presenting any reasons or evidence to support it.

Strictly speaking, loaded questions are not really arguments. But since they are attempts to get claims (the hidden assumptions) accepted without presenting any adequate or legitimate grounds for them, loaded questions resemble fallacious arguments. The important thing is that they are dangerous and misleading and should be recognized and guarded against.

3. Begging the Question *(Petitio Principii)*

The "question" is the issue at hand, and the question is "begged," not addressed, when some reason offered for some conclusion is not really different from the conclusion itself. The ways this may be done differ, but each involves stating as a conclusion something that also serves as a premise.

In one familiar way, the conclusion *restates* part or all of the meaning of a premise: "James is a murderer because he wrongfully killed someone." To call James a murderer is to say he killed someone wrongfully, so the argument is valid. The premise offered to justify the conclusion logically implies it, but no independent evidence for the premise is offered. Yet what we expect from the argument are reasons for believing James killed someone and was wrong to do so. We expect independent evidence for the claim made in both the conclusion and the premise. This evidence is just what is lacking in a question-begging argument.

A question is begged in a second way when a premise is used to support a conclusion while the conclusion is at least implicitly appealed to in support of the premise. This is known as **circular reasoning** or **arguing in a circle:** *A* because *B*, *B* because *C*, *C* because *A*. Such an argument is flawed because the premise purporting to provide independent support for the conclusion is itself taken to be supported by the conclusion.

Consider one interpretation of a famous argument by the seventeenth-century French philosopher René Descartes. Descartes considered the possibility that

> A. There is an evil demon deceiving him about any reasoning process that depends on memory.

Insofar as *A* is possible, Descartes cannot rely on any complex reasoning at all.

Descartes then constructs a fairly complicated proof that

> B. God exists, is himself no deceiver, and would not allow there to be a deceiver.

But how can Descartes know his proof of *B* is correct? To know it is, he must first know no demon is deceiving him about it. And to know that, he must know that God exists and would not allow deception. That is, he must know that *B* is true. So, the proof of *B* tacitly assumes *B*—treats *B* as a premise—which means the reasoning is circular and proves nothing. The more complex an argument, the easier it becomes not to notice that the argument amounts to nothing more than an unsupported assertion.

4. Slippery Slope

The mistaken idea behind the **slippery slope fallacy** is that when there is little or no significant difference between adjacent points on a continuum, then there is no important difference between even widely separated points on the continuum.

> A lot of people think a 70-mile-per-hour speed limit on interstate highways is too high. Actually it is too low. Everybody admits that 55 is a limit that is as safe as can be. But if 55 is safe, 56 or 57 must be also. For a mile or two can't matter. So 58 or 59 will also be safe. And you have to be crazy to think 60 would be a less safe limit than 59. Similarly, there can't be a significant difference between 60 and 62 . . . between 62 and 64 . . . 64 and 66 . . . 66 and 68. . . . Maybe there should be no speed limit at all on good roads!

Slippery slope arguments look plausible because it does seem arbitrary to draw a line between any particular adjacent points on the continuum.

Slippery Slope

The slippery slope fallacy often results in claiming that the most extreme and indefensible form of action is not significantly different from the simplest and most defensible form. Arguments about abortion, on both sides of the issue, are often like that.

> A newborn baby is obviously a person whom it would be wrong to kill. Since there is little difference between a newborn baby and a baby just prior to birth, the latter is also a person whom it would be wrong to kill. And there is little difference between the baby just prior to birth and the fetus at eight-and-a-half months, between the fetus at eight-and-a-half months and a few days before that. So, the fetus at any of these stages is also a person. But in the same way there is almost no difference between the fetus at eight months and just before that . . . and before that. . . . We must face the fact that there is no stopping place. So the newly fertilized ovum is a person whom it would be wrong to kill. Abortion is murder.

On the contrary:

> Not many people really think that a newly fertilized ovum is a person that it would be wrong to kill. It is nothing but a microscopic bit of protoplasm, and we can dispose of it without qualms. But there is hardly any difference between the just fertilized ovum and the ovum the next day. And not much of a difference to the next day nor to when the ovum is a week old. Similarly, progression to the following day or week doesn't make much difference in itself. We must face the fact that there is no stopping place. If the just fertilized ovum is not a person, there is no person prior to birth. It is very hard to see why there should be any objection to abortion at any stage. Or, for that matter, why killing a newborn would be wrong if there were good reason to do so. Abortion is not murder.

Whatever one's views on abortion, these are not good arguments. (Since they use the same "facts" for opposite conclusions, something must have gone very wrong.) It may be difficult to draw a line at any particular point between a newborn baby and a just-fertilized ovum, but this does not mean that they are exactly the same in all respects. Consequently, treatment that is morally legitimate in one case is not necessarily legitimate in the other.

Nonetheless, the arguments are clearly mistaken, since many small and "insignificant" differences can add up to a very large difference.

Related to slippery slope arguments are ones claiming that a particular practice should not be initiated because it would lead to a more extreme version of the practice. For example, some critics oppose giving extra time on exams to students with attention deficit/hyperactivity disorder on the ground that this encourages students who say they suffer from "test anxiety" or "social phobia" to demand additional time. Eventually, the critics say, anyone could get extra time by claiming any sort of disability, and this would be unfair to everyone not making such a claim.

To take another example, consider a law allowing physicians to administer a lethal injection to a terminally ill patient at the patient's request. This could be the first in a step-by-step progression toward a eugenics program involving killing without consent the old, the sick, the handicapped, or those who don't satisfy some social ideal.

Arguments like these tell us that we must be careful of "letting the camel get its nose under the tent," for, if we allow this much, soon we will find ourselves sleeping with the beast. "Camel's nose" arguments are not pure slippery slope arguments, since they have to do with similar practices *causing* one another. A camel's nose argument may or may not be a good argument, depending on whether it makes a persuasive case that one practice is likely to lead to another more extreme and undesirable one.

II. Fallacies of Criticism and Response

A number of errors in reasoning are commonly committed either in criticizing a supported claim or in responding to such criticisms. Hence, the errors we discuss here are most frequently found in the dialectical context of challenge and reply. We will limit our concern to this context, even though some of the fallacies also occur in nondialectical situations.

A. Five Fallacies of Criticism

1. Against the Person (Ad Hominem)
The *ad hominem* **fallacy** consists in rejecting a claim or an argument by offering as grounds some personal characteristic of the person supporting it. Suppose Barton has argued that Mozart was a more creative musician than Salieri. Someone who then argues "Barton is pretty much of a jerk, you know. I am sure he is wrong" is committing the *ad hominem* fallacy.

Strictly, the personal characteristics of individuals offering claims are irrelevant to the truth of those claims. Even if Barton is a jerk, he can still be correct. Similarly, some claims of bleeding-heart liberals, ultraconservatives, doctrinaire communists, and plain fools are right. If we wish to be fair and rational, we must recognize that even a claim presented by a fool can be true and that even the jerk's arguments could be good ones. We must not reject out of hand either claims or arguments because of their source.

However, personal characteristics can be relevant if we are trying to decide whether to accept a claim just on the word of the person making it. Although chronic liars, the demented, and practical jokers sometimes speak the truth, we should place little reliance on the word of such people. If a person is known to be a mentally unstable alcoholic who often has trouble distinguishing his fantasies from reality, something he tells us could be true, but we have no right to expect it to be true on the ground of his saying it.

Consider the Source

In 1999, Lanny Davis, a former advisor to and supporter of President Clinton, was asked about a statement critical of the president made by Linda Tripp, a key person in the events leading to the charges against the president. Davis dismissed the criticism, saying just to "consider the source."

"Consider the source" is a phrase that is often used. Sometimes it is used legitimately to mean something like "that is not a reliable source. Do not rely on her word for truth." (We assume that is what Lanny Davis meant.) But it might mean something more like "*she* said it so it *can't be true*." That is an *ad hominem* charge and is not legitimate. Of course, we should not rely on unreliable sources. But we should not assume that a claim must be false because its source is less than the best.

A special sort of argument against the person is called the **circumstantial *ad hominem.*** Here the charge is not against the general character of the person (she is a drunk, a paranoid, and so on); it is against the reliability of the person in a particular set of *circumstances.* The basically sound idea behind this sort of argument against the person is that those with reasons to lie may do so and those with a vested interest are likely to be biased so as not to acknowledge the truth even to themselves. Thus, a chemical company's representative may assure us his company's pesticide is harmless, a manufacturer may claim her product is safe to use, and a bureaucrat may assert his department is underfunded. All may be held suspect because even trustworthy and reasonable people can be affected by their circumstances. We should, then, suspect claims made by some sorts of people in some circumstances. But we commit a fallacy if we assume the claims presented must be false or that we have no need to examine the worth of any argument given.

2. You Too *(Tu Quoque)*
This is a special kind of *ad hominem* argument.

> Cook: Your argument for legalizing prostitution is ridiculous. You commit every fallacy in the book.
>
> Gordon: So? You're a fine one to talk. You can never open your mouth without committing a fallacy.

> Bledsoe: You are a cheat. You left half your income off your tax return last year.
>
> Manning: Big deal. You lied about deductions and had the nerve to claim your dog as a dependent.

The responses by Gordon and Manning—in effect, "you do it too"—are *ad hominem* and have no relevance to the truth or accuracy of the original claims. Cook and Bledsoe may be hypocritical in preaching what they do not practice, but that does not have any bearing on the truth of what they say.

3. Pooh-Pooh
To **pooh-pooh** an argument is to dismiss it with ridicule as not worthy of serious consideration.

> We don't have to waste time dealing with Ms. Thompson's claims about women not being promoted to executive positions. She's just giving us more of the usual feminist claptrap.

> Hong once again brings up that old liberal chestnut that minorities are being exploited by businesses out to keep their labor cost low, a view that's worth more of a groan than a laugh.

Pooh-poohing is a refusal to examine an argument seriously and evaluate it fairly. As such, the fallacy is an attempt to obtain by guile what should be earned by work. It is a case of misdirection.

4. Straw Man
A straw man is one that is easy to knock over. The **straw man fallacy** consists of misrepresenting an opponent's claim or argument so that it is easier to criticize or so obviously implausible that no criticism is needed. Although the misrepresented version is a caricature (a straw man), the critic treats it as equivalent to the original.

A classic historical example is James Kilpatrick's statement of former Supreme Court Justice William Brennan's and Professor Laurence Tribe's position on interpreting the Constitution. According to Brennan and Tribe, we cannot be sure of the intention of legislators who ratified a constitutional amendment, so the question of how an amendment should be interpreted cannot be answered by appealing to their intention. Kilpatrick represented the view in this way:

> In [Brennan's and Tribe's] view, original intention is often unfathomable and generally irrelevant. What counts is not what a word may have meant "then." It is what the word means "now." Theirs is the school of semantics that says words should mean exactly what they choose them to mean. —*St. Louis Post-Dispatch* (January 16, 1988)

Kilpatrick's version of the position suggested that Brennan and Tribe held that the meaning of a phrase like "equal protection under the law" could arbitrarily be assigned a meaning. This position is absurd and only a straw man version of the actual one.

One common way of creating a straw man is to reduce a complex argument to a caricatured, simplistic claim. For example, instead of presenting the fundamental concepts and principles that make up contemporary evolutionary theory, an opponent might represent the theory in this way:

> The theory of evolution boils down to the idea that human beings are descended from apes.

This statement presents no theory that any serious scientist holds. Yet the opponent who criticizes this position may convince some people that he has refuted evolutionary theory.

5. Loaded Words

Some years ago a newspaper columnist questioned the sexual and financial behavior of several senators who opposed a nominee to the Supreme Court. The columnist went on to ask us to consider, by way of contrast to the nominee's record, the records of "the four senatorial *sleazeballs* who are leading the Judiciary Committee's attack on him."

When we apply judgmental words like *sleazeball, incompetent, idiot, morally corrupt, venal, avaricious,* and *decadent* to people, policies, or practices, we must justify the application. (The same is also true of positive words like *competent, genius, intelligent,* and *generous.*) We must give reasons and evidence to demonstrate that, for example, an official or a government is morally corrupt. In effect, an argument has to be presented to establish the conclusion that the word may be legitimately applied.

The use of loaded language in arguments frequently results in begging the question.

> Medical research on animals simply must be stopped at once. This torture of innocent creatures is morally indecent. Those who

> perpetrate such crimes against feeling creatures are without feelings
> themselves. It is time to put a stop to these pointless atrocities.

Here it is *assumed* that medical research involves torture of innocents, crimes against feeling creatures, pointless atrocities, and more. With these loaded phrases built into the premises, it is just a short question-begging step to the conclusion that such research should be halted.

In short, to apply judgmental terms without providing reasons is another way of trying to get something for nothing. Such words are also called "loaded" because they assume the truth of a conclusion that has not been established.

B. Two Fallacies of Defense

A legitimate response to criticism requires addressing the criticism directly. If it cannot be answered, then we may have to withdraw or modify the position taken. **Fallacies of defense** are ways of skirting a criticism to avoid facing it and its consequences.

1. Definitional Dodge

The **definitional dodge** consists of redefining a crucial term in a claim to avoid acknowledging a counterexample that would falsify the claim.

Consider an example in which Smith claims "All pornography demeans women," and Hopkins responds by asking, "What about John Cleland's *Fanny Hill?* It's generally considered pornographic, but it doesn't demean women." Hopkins has offered a case apparently inconsistent with Smith's claim. Smith might respond legitimately by trying to show that *Fanny Hill* does demean women and so is not a counterexample at all.

However, if Smith responds by saying "Then *Fanny Hill* is not pornography, because pornography always involves demeaning women," Smith is pulling a definitional dodge. He is ruling out an apparent counterexample to his claim by altering the ordinary meaning of the word to make "demeans women" a necessary feature of pornography. Hence, it becomes logically impossible ever to mention a case of pornography that does not demean women.

If Smith wishes to make "demeans women" part of an arbitrary stipulative definition, he may. However, the claim is no longer about the character of what is generally considered pornography. The claim becomes nothing more than an implication of Smith's resolution about using the word *pornography*.

Words like *employment, crime, middle class, educated, patriotic, war,* and *peace* figure often in disputes in which an ordinary meaning is altered for the purpose of escaping from the crushing blows of counterexamples. Yet almost any key term in a claim can be redefined in a way that, in the context of a rational disagreement, is illicit.

Two Formal Fallacies

Two invalid argument forms are easily confused with similar valid ones. Because argument forms are involved, the mistakes are called *formal fallacies*.

1. Denying the Antecedent

If P, then Q

Not P
_____

Not Q

If Simpson is a Black South African, then she opposed apartheid.

Simpson is not a Black South African.
_____

Simpson did not oppose apartheid.

Opponents of apartheid were not limited to Black South Africans. Hence, that Simpson is not a Black South African does not allow us to conclude she did not oppose apartheid.

2. Affirming the Consequent

If P, then Q

Q
_____

P

If Ramirez is a member of the Animal Rights Society, then he opposes cock fighting.

Ramirez opposes cock fighting
_____

Ramirez is a member of the Animal Rights Society.

While it may be true that all members of the Society oppose cock fighting, others may oppose it as well. (Compare: All dimes are coins, but not all coins are dimes.)

The powerful appeal of these fallacies comes from their resemblance to the valid forms *modus ponens* and *modus tollens*. For further discussion, see Chapter 4.

2. Exception That Proves the Rule

The word *prove* may mean (1) establish as true or (2) test or try out. The sentence "The mathematician *proved* an important theorem, but he also *proved* to be a terrible teacher" illustrates both uses. In some contexts, the word is ambiguous, and this is dramatically the case in the traditional expression "the exception that proves the rule."

Fallacies

I. Fallacies in Supporting a Claim

   A. Fallacies of Relevance

      1. Appeal to Ignorance (*Ad Ignorantiam*)
      2. Appeal to Inappropriate Authority (*Ad Verecundiam*)
      3. Appeal to General Belief (*Ad Populum*)
      4. Appeal to Popular Attitudes and Emotions
      5. Gambler's Fallacy
      6. Equivocation (see Chapter 10)

   B. Fallacies of Inadequate Evidence

      1. False Cause (*Post Hoc*)
      2. Hasty Generalization

   C. Fallacies of Illegitimate Assumption

      1. False Dilemma
      2. Loaded Question
      3. Begging the Question
      4. Slippery Slope

II. Fallacies of Criticism and Response

   A. Fallacies of Criticism

      1. Against the Person (*Ad Hominem*)
      2. You Too (*Tu Quoque*)
      3. Pooh-Pooh
      4. Straw Man
      5. Loaded Words

   B. Fallacies of Defense

      1. Definitional Dodge
      2. Exception That Proves the Rule

The saying is often mistakenly taken to mean "an exception to a rule establishes its truth," whereas it actually means "an exception to a rule is a test of the rule."

This confusion allows someone defending a claim to commit a fallacy by dismissing apparent counterexamples as no challenge. Consider this exchange:

> Wexford: Women novelists have been nothing more than entertainers. None has been truly outstanding.
>
> Chang: Aren't you forgetting about Jane Austen and Mary Ann Evans?
>
> Wexford: They're just exceptions that prove the rule. We look to women writers for amusement, not literature.

If Wexford is prepared to admit that the cases mentioned by Chang are outstanding novelists, then Wexford's claim simply cannot be true. The counterexamples test it and prove it false.

Errors in reasoning are always difficult to avoid and often hard to detect. Knowing the names of a few prominent kinds of fallacies may be helpful, but it is no substitute for constant vigilance and ready skepticism.

Exercises

A. *Most of the passages below express arguments, but some do not. A few of the arguments are legitimate, but most are fallacies of relevance (appeal to ignorance, inappropriate authority, general belief, popular attitudes, gambler's fallacy) or inadequate evidence (post hoc, hasty generalization). Your job: (a) Identify each argument; (b) decide whether it a fallacy; (c) if it is, label it with the appropriate name. If you are uncertain about the name, explain what is wrong with the argument.*

* 1. After-death experiences are a reality. Despite years of attempts at debunking, no one has ever been able to show that reports from beyond the grave are all due to error, deception, or simply wishful thinking.

2. The birds were singing, and the trees were just coming into bloom. The sun bathed the meadows with a soft golden glow. The day was lovely, but I was miserable.

3. You don't have to be of noble birth to appreciate Cutty Sark Scotch Whiskey. All that is required is noble taste.

4. Americans reject gun control. A 2003 survey conducted at the National Hunting Association revealed that 71 percent of the fifty people interviewed are opposed to legal regulation, including the registration of assault rifles.

* 5. We are the richest nation in the history of the world, and we can afford to provide for the health care needs of our citizens in the same way that we provide them with police protection. It's time to recognize the needs of the uninsured and the underinsured and pass laws that extend federal health insurance coverage to everybody.

6. Nobody wants to say so in public, but we all know that immigrants don't have as strong a commitment to this country as those of us who were born here.

7. No one has ever demonstrated that Iraq didn't have WMDs, and in the absence of such evidence, it's reasonable to continue to cite them as a legitimate reason for the U.S. invasion.

8. As soon as the mercury preservative in vaccines was removed, the number of children with autism declined sharply. Parents of autistic children thus have a strong legal case against vaccine manufacturers.

9. Rape was extraordinarily rare in the American West in the nineteenth century. You can argue that it wasn't being reported, but I've never seen evidence of that.

10. We have a woman who works here, and her mother had cancer. She drank the Kabbalaha water, and her cancer disappeared.—Employee of London Kabbalaha Center, *20/20*, 17 June 2005

11. I've been feeding this slot machine for twenty minutes, and the person before me pumped in two hundred dollars with no payout. I'm going to keep going, because the machine is due to hit any minute now.

*12. Every society that has collapsed throughout the history of the world has done so because of rottenness within. The collapse has always been preceded and thus triggered by the slackening of shame typified by widespread public nudity.

B. *Identify the fallacies of illegitimate assumption (false dilemma, loaded question, begging the question, slippery slope) in the passages below.*

*1. Are women still discouraged from excelling in sports by a lack of financial or emotional support?—*Glamour*, May 1980

2. A person apparently hopelessly ill may be allowed to take his own life. Then he may be permitted to deputize others to do it for him should he no longer be able to act. The judgment of others then becomes the ruling factor. It is only a short step, then, from voluntary euthanasia (self-inflicted or authorized) to directed euthanasia administered to a patient who has given his authorization, to involuntary euthanasia conducted as part of a social policy.—J. Gay-Williams, "The Wrongfulness of Euthanasia," in Ronald Munson, *Intervention and Reflection* 7th ed., 2003, p. 709

*3. The Bible is inerrant—that is, infallible. That's how we know that God loves us, has a plan for our lives, and will one day reunite us with Him. The Bible also tells us that we can depend on God to tell us the truth about our world, our history, and our fate. That God tells us the truth means that we can rely on the Bible to be free of errors and fallacies.

4. You are either with us or you are with the terrorists.—President George W. Bush

*5. Pet dogs are said to be entitled to medical care because of their special place of dependency on people. But if we take this line of reasoning, then all pets—cats, goldfish, hamsters, or whatever—must also be given care. Indeed, so must domestic animals like horses, pigs, cattle, and chickens, for they are also dependent on people. Yet the amount of money it would take to provide care for chickens alone would virtually bankrupt the country. It's better to allow dogs to suffer without medical attention than ever to get started on a program that would soon lead to our financial ruin.

6. Adultery cannot be justified. The reason it can't is simply that it is never acceptable for a married person to have sex with someone who is not his or her spouse.

7. Why does *The New York Times* always show Muslims in a bad light?

8. We can achieve peace in the Middle East either by negotiations or by war. Negotiations have led nowhere, so what is there left to do but send in the troops?

9. If we recognize Cuba diplomatically, then we will have to grant the same status to every country run by an anti-American dictator.

10. Mr. Adrian, did you not enter the apartment of Tim O'Brian on the night of August 18th so you could catch him without a bodyguard and kill him without any risk to yourself?

11. Paying for drugs needed by people on Social Security is just the first step on a road that will end with our paying for old people to have face-lifts.

12. Senator Anson voted against the proposed constitutional amendment prohibiting burning the American flag as a form of protest. A legislator must either support the amendment or support flag burners. Senator Anson has made his choice, and next November the voters will make theirs.

C. *Identify the fallacies of criticism (ad hominem, tu quoque, pooh-pooh, straw man, loaded words) or defense (definitional dodge, exception that proves the rule) in the passages below.*

1. Gloria Grag's views on fighting terrorism are wrong. Is she an intelligence expert? No. Someone with police experience? No. I tell you what she is, she's a commercial baker. That's right, a cookie maker!

*2. If Ms. Harcan can't come up with something besides the feminist cliché that our policy demeans women, I don't see any reason to answer her charges.

3. A physician without a knowledge of astrology has no right to call himself a physician.—Hippocrates

4. You've never had a taste of beer, because beer can't be tasted in a sip.

*5. **Evanston:** The future of U.S. security requires that we establish close diplomatic ties with our European allies and take them into our confidence and solicit their advice before taking significant military actions.

   Chavez: Evanston wants us to go to the Europeans and get their approval before we take any actions to protect our nation.

6. **Mondino:** What I like about Robert Frost is the cleverness with which he makes all his poetry rhyme.

   Halah: But "Mending Wall" doesn't rhyme.

   Mondino: Ah, but that's the exception that exactly proves my point.

7. It's true that I don't want to see gays in the military, but you've got no room to object. You don't want to see women in combat positions.

8. **Monteel:** We need to extend basic health coverage to the 40 million Americans who cannot afford insurance. Basic care should be recognized as a right in our society.

   Brewster: Monteel wants us to forget about people paying their own way and let everybody go to the hospital and get whatever kind of treatment they want. I don't think our society is ready for Botox giveaways.

9. **Proposal:** Require businesses to defray the cost of health insurance for their employees.

   Response: Fining small business owners who can't afford health insurance certainly isn't going to make health insurance to workers more affordable.—Jess Brainton, lobbyist for National Federation of Independent Businesses

10. Dennett states that only someone with "professional knowledge" of the books' primary topic, geography, should review them. Yet Dennett himself, a professor of philosophy, has written widely on subjects about which he is not a specialist.—Greg Easterbrook, *New York Times,* 20 February 2005

D. *Most of the passages below express arguments, but some do not. A few of the arguments are legitimate, but most are fallacies. Your job: (a) Identify each argument; (b) decide whether it a fallacy; (c) if it is, label it with the appropriate name. If you are uncertain about the name, explain what is wrong with the argument.*

1. Is violence in the National Hockey League all that bad, or is it the main reason people come to the games?

2. The moon keeps one side turned toward the earth at all times. The earth turns on its axis, and the moon rotates around the earth.

3. Dr. Chance Tang told our class that a human embryo is a person just like me or you and entitled to the same treatment. Dr. Tang is an obstetrician, so I'm prepared to believe what he says and reject the destruction of embryos as equivalent to murder.

*4. Tax policies can favor either those who invest their money or those who spend everything they get. But those who invest create jobs for others, and that's why our tax laws should give them the biggest break.

5. The man's an idiot, and so everything he says is idiotic.

6. We decided, in the absence of any reason to the contrary, that we would eliminate recess as part of the school day.

*7. "Paul Goldberger is unqualified to judge my buildings," builder Donald Trump said of the architectural critic for *The New York Times*. "He wears cheap suits."—*Time*, 16 July 1989

8. Something about the clearing in the forest disturbed me. Perhaps it was the silence, the lack of insect or animal noises. Or perhaps it was the swampy odor of wetness and rotten-ness. And then I saw a reason for my fear. Man-sized and covered with green scales, its head was like that of a snake, with slitlike nostrils and round, lidless eyes. Fangs jutted from its upper jaw, and strings of thick saliva dripped from their needle-sharp tips.

9. A Texas rehabilitation hospital regularly brought in pets to cheer up patients. One day a German shepherd licked the face of a boy named Tom Lodge who, as the result of an accident, had been in a coma of three weeks. A week later, he regained consciousness. "It was the dog that brought Tom out of his coma," his mother said.

10. One proof for creationism is accessible to everyone. A 2003 poll by the Gallup Organization shows that 48 percent of Americans accept creationism, while only 28 percent accept

evolution. (The remainder are either unsure or tend toward creationism.) This means, according to Gallup, that more than twice as many people believe in the Devil (68 percent) as believe in evolution. This is some of the strongest nonreligious evidence favoring creationism science has produced.

11. We need stricter controls at airports to keep infectious diseases from entering the country. A passenger with SARS or even Ebola can get on a plane in Asia or Africa and get off in San Francisco or New York a few hours later. One person like that is enough to touch off an epidemic.

*12. Downloading music from the Internet is stealing. Period. End of story.

Chapter 9

DEFINITION

Definitions can be crucial to understanding. If the meaning of a key word is uncertain, it may be impossible to understand properly a claim, argument, rule, or explanation.

I. Definition of *Definition*

A **definition** is an explanation of the meaning of a word. The meaning of a word is the set of rules or conditions governing the word's use. Thus, to define a word is to state the rules or conditions for using the word. The rules may be ones followed in actual practice or ones adopted for some special purpose. Hence, we may say that to define a word is to explain how the word is actually used or is going to be used.

We define words, terms, expressions, symbols, and other linguistic entities. We also define the concepts and ideas that the linguistic entities represent or express. For convenience, we shall speak here of defining only words.

II. Two Types of Definition

Definitions can be divided into types on the basis of whether the account of meaning they give is a report or a stipulation about a word's use.

A. Reportive Definition

Definitions intended to explain how words are actually used are called **reportive definitions.** They are offered as factual reports to the effect that the word defined is used in accordance with the conditions mentioned.

For example, we may define "great-aunt" as "a sister of one's grandmother or grandfather." According to this definition, the expression "great-aunt" is properly used to refer to someone who is the sister of a grandparent. Anyone meeting this condition (satisfying this description) may be called "great-aunt."

Like other factual claims, reportive definitions may be true or false, accurate or inaccurate. A definition of "great-aunt" as "the brother of one's grandparent" is simply false. Similarly, defining "uncle" as "the brother of one's mother" is inaccurate. In our society, the word also refers to the brother of one's father, as well as to the husband of one's aunt. To be both correct and complete, we might define "uncle" as "the brother of one's parent or the husband of one's aunt."

Most words have several meanings that may be quite distinct. For example, the word *plate* has some twenty meanings. It is used in sports, printing, photography, metal manufacturing, geology, biology, electronics, and other fields. A definition is not defective if it fails to report on all distinct uses of the word. Although we might fault a dictionary for not informing us about the variety of meanings, a definition intended to explain only one of the meanings can be correct and complete. Thus, the definition of "plate" as "a shallow dish in which food is served or from which it is eaten" is a good explanation of one of the ways in which the word is properly used.

Reportive definitions are used to explain both ordinary and special meanings and on this basis may be divided into three types. The distinctions remind us that a report about a word's use in one area need not hold true for other areas.

1. Lexical Definition
A **lexical definition** is a report about the way a word is used in everyday life. The definition explains the word's ordinary or usual meaning. The previous definition of "uncle" as "the brother of one's parent or the husband of one's aunt" is a correct lexical definition.

2. Disciplinary Definition
A **disciplinary definition** is a report about the way a word is used in a particular discipline or special area. The definition is an explanation of the word's accepted meaning within that discipline.

Often a word has both ordinary meanings and disciplinary meanings. Consider the expression "acute pain." In ordinary usage, an acute pain is a sharp, stabbing pain, and the description "sharp and stabbing" must be met before we can properly call a pain an acute one. However, in medical terminology, an acute pain is one that occurs suddenly and without warning signs. Whether the pain is sharp, cramping, burning, or aching is irrelevant to whether it is acute.

"Acute" has still other meanings in other disciplines. In geometry, "acute" applies to angles of less than 90 degrees, and in poetics it designates a stressed sound in a metrical scheme. (Many of the twenty meanings of "plate" are special or technical ones.) Disciplines also have technical terms (*prion, afferent,* and so on) that have no ordinary uses.

3. Historical Definition

A **historical definition** is a report about how a word was used during a particular historical period. The definition may be lexical or disciplinary. If lexical, the explanation will be of the ordinary use of a word at a specific time. If disciplinary, the explanation will be of the use of a word in a specific discipline at a specific time.

Words, like other expressions of human culture, have a history. Some words come into being; others pass away. Some retain meanings for long periods; others shed old meanings and acquire new ones. Still others alter their meanings, acquiring new conditions without wholly losing the old ones. Without a grasp of the historical meanings of words, we cannot correctly interpret the literary, political, religious, scientific, and personal documents of the past.

Even when words are familiar to us, we must be certain their meanings have not significantly changed. For example, in the eighteenth century, to say someone was a "flasher" was to say he dressed in an ostentatious manner. Someone knowing only the current meaning might get a very wrong impression from an eighteenth-century letter.

The need for historical understanding also affects technical areas. The disease referred to as syphilis during the sixteenth through the nineteenth centuries included a variety of skin diseases, but now we limit the term to a particular disease caused by a certain spirochete.

A common error to avoid in connection with historical definitions is the assumption that an earlier or original meaning of a word is its "true" meaning. That the word *alternatives* was once properly used only in cases of just two options does not mean that it is now incorrect to speak of, say, "three alternatives." Current use and earlier use are merely different.

B. Stipulative Definition

To stipulate is to lay down a rule or condition. A **stipulative definition** is a statement of the rule that will be followed in using the word defined. A stipulative definition is a resolution to use a word in a certain way, to assign the word a particular meaning. Hence, stipulative definitions, unlike reportive definitions, cannot be true or false. Depending upon whether the meaning assigned is arbitrary or a modification of an accepted meaning, we can distinguish two types.

Types of Definition

1. **Reportive:** Explains how a word is actually used
   a. **Lexical:** How a word is used in ordinary life
   b. **Disciplinary:** How a word is used in some special area (technical use)
   c. **Historical:** How a word was used in a past time
2. **Stipulative:** Explains how a word is going to be used
   a. **Arbitrary:** How the writer or speaker has decided to use a word
   b. **Precising:** How the writer or speaker is going to restrict the meaning of an ordinary word to make it more exact (turn it into a technical term)

1. Arbitrary

A new word, abbreviation, or symbol is typically introduced simply by laying down a rule for its use. Since we are free to choose any rule we like, such stipulative definitions may be regarded as **arbitrary.** Here are typical examples:

> Let "D" stand for "disposable income minus savings."

> I shall use "!" written after a letter to mean "all letters in the Roman alphabet up to and including this letter." Thus, "C!" will mean "ABC."

> "BASIC" will stand for "Beginner's All-purpose Symbolic Instruction Code."

Words introduced by arbitrary stipulative definitions may later come to be accepted into the language and acquire a standard meaning. This happened with Thomas More's "utopia," Karel Čapek's "robot," and Francis Galton's "eugenics." In such cases, the conditions of the word's use may resemble those laid down by the inventor, but typically the meaning undergoes substantial change. "Utopia" is no longer just the name of More's ideal society, but has come to mean any ideal society.

2. Precising

Stipulative definitions that are **precising** restrict the ordinary meaning of a word to make the meaning more exact in a certain context. For example:

> For tax purposes, "head of household" will mean "the member of the household with the highest earned income."

"Savings," according to my theory, is money invested.

Herein, a "crash" should be understood as a total loss of computer programs and data.

Precising stipulative definitions are ways of turning ordinary words into technical terms. The more precise meaning assigned to a word is connected with the word's standard meaning, yet the assigned meaning is not a report on the word's standard use. A phrase like "head of household" has a common meaning broader than that required by the specialized needs of tax collectors.

Even though stipulative definitions cannot be true or false, they are not beyond criticism. A definition may be faulted for introducing a term that is unnecessary, misleading, awkward, or otherwise ill considered. For example, critics have suggested that the introduction of "adience" (liking) and "intense adience" (love) to describe human relationships was not needed. The social sciences, in particular, have often been accused of engaging in unnecessary naming.

Precising stipulative definitions also present the possibility of intentional or accidental deception. It is easy to assume when reading the text of a contract, solicitation, insurance policy, or law that crucial words have their ordinary meanings. So, when the words have restricted meanings, even if they are spelled out in the document's fine print, a naive, uneducated, or careless reader may be misled. To get a "free trip," an unwary consumer may have to sign a contract agreeing to pay expenses and "handling fees" in excess of normal costs. The free trip involves taking the consumer for a ride.

III. Methods of Definition

Any way the use of a word can be explained to someone counts as a method of definition. Accordingly, there is no set number of methods. The five traditional methods discussed here have met the test of experience and been found helpful. No single method is best for every word in every situation, and no one should hesitate to use new methods that might be equally effective.

A. Synonym

Definition by **synonym** requires providing a word or phrase equivalent (or approximately equivalent) in meaning to the word defined. This is perhaps the most common method of definition:

"Flat" means the same thing as "apartment."

"Heliocentric" means "sun-centered."

A "bicameral" legislature is one with two houses.

Probably no two words are exactly equivalent in meaning. In some contexts, one of the words cannot be substituted for the other without altering the meaning of the sentence. In practice, this possibility rarely presents a difficulty. We recognize that in offering a definition by synonym we must choose a word having roughly the same meaning in the same context. Thus, "flat" may be substituted for "apartment" when the reference is to dwellings, but "apartment" may not be substituted for "flat" when the reference is to tires.

B. Genus and Species

The method of **genus and species** consists in mentioning a feature of an object to which a word refers that places the object within a class, then mentioning another feature that places the object within a subclass. The general class is the genus, and the (proper) subclass is a species. In the definition of "democracy" as "a form of government in which people govern themselves," the genus is "a form of government" and the species is "people govern themselves."

The terms *genus* and *species* are relative ones. If "people govern themselves" is treated as a genus, then we can establish species consisting of "people govern themselves directly" and "people govern themselves through representatives." These subclasses correspond to the distinction between direct and representative democracy.

Sometimes we mention only the feature that places the object in a general class, saying nothing about the feature that would place it in a subclass. (Perhaps we are ignorant of such a feature or do not consider the species important.) For example, it may be enough in some situations to tell someone that "gorgonian" refers to "a kind of coral," that a "rondo" is "a musical form," or that "monetarianism" is "an economic policy."

C. Ostention

An **ostensive definition** consists in pointing to an object correctly designated by the defined word. If I gesture toward the proper sort of animal and say "jaguar," I give its meaning by demonstrating how the word is used in a paradigm case—that is, a noncontroversial and straightforward instance.

The demonstration might be helped by indicating that some animals that might be confused with the jaguar (cheetah, puma, and the like) are not correctly referred to by the word. The ostensive definition itself, however, consists in nothing more than pointing and naming.

Some words, such as color words like "red" and "yellow," can be defined only by means of ostensive definition. Although "red" may be identified with a certain wavelength in the electromagnetic spectrum, this identification is not a definition of the word *red*. Not only may we have the experience of seeing red when the wavelength is absent, but we must also be able to name the color red to identify the wavelength associated with it.

Words that function the way proper names do are the best candidates for definition by ostention. In the same way that we can point to a person and say "That's Richard Ford," we can point to the proper objects and define words that name colors, trees, animals, plants, chemicals, bridges, geological strata, and so on.

D. Example

When we cannot literally point to an example, we can define some words by mentioning examples of the sort of things they designate. For instance:

A "deficiency disease" is one like scurvy, pellagra, or beriberi.

"Even numbers" are ones like 2, 4, 6, and 8.

Methods of Definition

1. **Synonym:** Providing a word equivalent in meaning
2. **Genus and species:** Mentioning a feature that places the object the word refers to in a class (genus), then a second feature that places it in a subclass (species)
3. **Ostention:** Pointing to an object to which the word refers (a paradigm case)
4. **Example:** Mentioning an instance of the sort of thing the word designates
5. **Complete enumeration:** Listing all the items to which the word refers

---

Some words do not lend themselves to definition by ostention or example. This is true of words like "sad," "happy," and "pain" that are used to characterize subjective experience. Although such experiences cannot be pointed to in a direct way or examples of them cited, we can describe the circumstances that produce them. In this way, their correct use can be indicated by describing a paradigm case: Pain is what you feel when you are walking in your bare feet and you stub your toe on something.

We can use the same method to define words that do not necessarily refer to subjective experience. Again, a paradigm example is imagined or described:

> What is the "chilling effect" that censorship is likely to have on us? Imagine you are writing something and you pause to search for the right word, idea, or image. If while you are thinking it occurs to you, "Am I likely to be jailed or fined or humiliated by the choice I make?" that is a chilling effect. The thought itself is likely to interfere with the choice actually made.

Other ways of using examples to define words are familiar from ordinary life: pointing to pictures, inviting others to smell or taste something, describing modes of behavior, circumstances, situations, people, and so on.

E. Complete Enumeration

Some words can be easily defined merely by **enumerating (listing)** all the items to which the word refers. For example:

> Arabic numerals: 1, 2, 3, 4, 5, 6, 7, 8, 9, 0

> Baltic republics of the old Soviet Union: Estonia, Latvia, Lithuania

> The Axis powers: Germany, Italy, Japan

Defining by enumeration is useful in providing stipulative definitions. The potential vagueness of terms like "southwestern states" or "European Union" can be eliminated by naming exactly the items the phrase is supposed to refer to.

The way in which a definition is phrased is usually adequate to determine whether a list of items is a complete enumeration. A phrase like "for example" indicates an incomplete list.

Although reportive definitions can be given by this method, most words cannot be defined by complete enumeration because they refer to things that belong to a potentially unlimited class. For example, it is impossible to give a reportive definition of "tree" using this method, for it is not possible to provide an enumeration of every tree past, present, and future. Other sorts of words, such as "political power," do not clearly refer to anything in the direct fashion that words like "tree" do.

These five methods are useful and frequently employed, but any method at all that helps explain the meaning of a word is a legitimate method of definition.

IV. Standards of Definition

A definition appropriate for one purpose is not necessarily appropriate for another. The reader of a popular article on biology may need to know only that the "Hardy-Weinberg law" is "a law about the way genes in a population change in frequency," but a student of population genetics needs a definition that states both the law and the parameters of its application. However, the definition in the popular article is not defective even though it does not meet the needs in some other context.

No matter what our purposes are in offering a definition, certain errors should be avoided.

A. Avoid Complete Circularity

The definition of *arbitrageur* as "one who engages in arbitrage" is unhelpful because it is almost wholly uninformative. It is unlikely that someone would know the meaning of *arbitrage* and not know *arbitrageur*. Since the aim of definition is to explain the meaning of a word, a definition that assumes an understanding of a key part of the meaning is a failure.

B. Avoid Obscure, Metaphorical, or Ambiguous Language

The language in which a definition is expressed can frustrate the aim of explaining the meaning of a word.

The way in which **obscure language** may render a definition useless is well illustrated by Ambrose Bierce's satirical definition of the simple word *eat:* "to perform successively (and successfully) the functions of mastication, humectation, and deglutition."

Metaphors have their place in explanation, but defining a word solely by metaphor is of little help in understanding the word's meaning. A computer manual that defines "DOS" as "the policeman who directs the traffic inside the machine" does very little to explain the meaning of "disk operating system."

A definition fails when it is **ambiguous** because it is impossible to determine which interpretation of the definition is the right one. The definition of "minuscule" as "a form of writing developed during the Middle Ages" leaves unclear whether handwriting or literary composition is intended.

C. Avoid Accidental Features

A definition involves stating conditions that govern the use of a word. But in some cases words are associated with additional features that are not really part of the definition. These features are called "accidental" to contrast them with ones that are "essential" to determining the word's use.

Standards of Definition

Avoid:

1. Complete circularity
2. Obscure, metaphorical, or ambiguous language
3. Accidental features
4. Definitions that are too broad or too narrow

For example, the definition of "women" as "members of the more exploited sex" makes use of an accidental feature. As a matter of fact, the conditions mentioned happen to be satisfied by women at the present time. Yet we can imagine a social revolution that would reverse the situation and make men into the more exploited sex. If this happened, the meaning of "women" would not change. Hence, being exploited is an accidental feature, not a defining characteristic, of women.

D. Avoid Definitions That Are Too Broad or Too Narrow

The conditions governing a word's use establish a class of items to which the word correctly applies. The conditions governing the use of the word *cat* (a mammal with certain feline characteristics) establish the class of things referred to by "cat."

A definition may fail by being too broad—by making a class so large that it includes items not properly characterized by the word. A definition may also fail by being too narrow—by making a class so small that it excludes items properly characterized by the word. Thus, a definition of "apple" should establish a class that includes all and only apples. One that includes oranges is too broad; one that fails to include Golden Delicious apples is too narrow.

Even for words that cannot be defined with this sort of precision, it still makes sense to talk about the class established by a definition as being too inclusive (too broad) or too exclusive (too narrow). An accurate definition of "art" has eluded generations of thinkers, but we can still say with confidence that Tolstoy's famous definition of "art" as "that which communicates the religious sentiments of mankind" is too narrow. It excludes, for instance, most nonrepresentational art. We can also see that Tolstoy's definition simultaneously manages to be too broad. It could include such heartfelt expressions of sentiment as undertaking a pilgrimage, which none of us would be willing to think of as art.

Tolstoy's doubly defective definition can be used to illustrate a final point. Words and their meanings are important. Merely calling an object a work of art accords it a certain status. We come to look at it in a different way: We may put it in a museum or sell it for a much higher price at auction. Similarly, when we call someone a "hero," pronounce a defendant "guilty," describe a scientist as a "genius," or condemn abortion as "murder," we are making crucial judgments that turn partially on the meanings of "mere" words. Words do make a difference.

Exercises

A. *Using the method of definition indicated, define the words listed under each heading.*

1. By Synonym

*dozen	U.S.A.
attorney	*police officer
feline	improvised explosive device
gratuity	baker's dozen
DOS	3br/2b/ac

2. By Genus and Species

triangle	textbook
videotape	ballpoint
dog	shirt
art museum	symphony concert
sonnet	odd number

3. By Ostention

wall	floor
red	shirt
person	head

4. By Example

*beverage	reading material
*fruit	definition
armed services	rhymed couplet
pet	English sentence
malware	base metal

5. By Complete Enumeration

English vowel	primary color
*parent	armed service

Commander-in-Chief of the United States Armed Forces
Group of 8 (or G8) country   earth's natural satellite
U.S. military academy

B. *You no doubt know some words (or meanings) that aren't gener-
    ally familiar. They may be slang or specialized terms from music,
    movie production, acting, science, computer hacking, sports,
    cooking, or any number of other fields.*
    *Choose three unfamiliar words and provide definitions of
    them. Use any method you consider adequate.*

C. Reportive definitions *may be subdivided into* lexical, disciplinary,
    and historical; stipulative definitions *may be subdivided into*
    arbitrary *and* precising. *Use these categories to classify the
    following definitions.*

  *1. "To qualify as a writer (and hence for membership) a candi-
       date must have had at least one work of at least 5,000 words
       published by a newspaper, magazine, or professional journal
       (church or club sponsored publications are excluded)."
       —Serial Writers Guild

   2. "A set we shall define as any group or collection of entities."
       —G. W. Holton, *Basics of Statistical Inference*

   3. In poker, a full house is a hand consisting of a pair and three
       of a kind.

  *4. "Serendipity" means making a lucky discovery by accident.

   5. "I am bound by my own definition of criticism: a disinterested
       endeavour to learn and propagate the best that is known and
       thought in the world." —Matthew Arnold, *Essays in Criticism*

   6. Before the 1940s, a "computer" was a person hired to do
       lengthy computations, such as those involving the development
       of tables for determining the trajectories of cannon shells.

   7. "Phishing" means attempting to acquire a computer
       password or other private information by using an online
       deceptive practice.

   8. A "ghost detainee" is an inmate in a military prison who is
       not listed on the official roster.

   9. We use the expression hESC to refer to human embryonic
       stem cells.

  10. "Kill box: A three-dimensional area reference that enables
       timely, effective coordination and control and facilitates

rapid attacks."—Department of Defense, *Dictionary of Military and Associated Terms*

D. *Words may be defined by these methods:* synonym, genus and species, enumeration, ostention, *and* example. *Examine the definitions below and identify the method used.*

*1. If you imagine a line extending directly out from the dipper of the Big Dipper, then you will see that at the end of the line is Polaris, the North Star.

2. Old-world animals are those such as the horse, the water buffalo, the camel, the tiger, the pig, and the cow.

*3. "Back office space is nonexecutive space. It is the supply room, the broom closet, the computer installation, the library, the Kafkaesque desk grid of clerical and sales personnel." —C. B. Horsley, *The New York Times*, 18 June 1980

4. A perfect number is a number that is the sum of its divisors.

5. "Howitzer: a cannon with a barrel longer than a mortar that delivers shells with medium velocities against targets that cannot be reached by flat trajectories." —*American Heritage Dictionary*

*6. The letters *t.i.d.* on a medical prescription mean "take three times a day."

7. "The term 'mortgage,' when used herein, shall include deed of trust, trust deed, or other security instrument." —American Land Title Association Standard Form 3360

8. "By a *fallacy* is commonly understood any unsound mode of arguing, which appears to demand our conviction, and to be decisive of the question in hand, when in fairness it is not." —Richard Whately, *The Elements of Logic*

9. "For our purposes language may be defined as systematized combinations of sounds which have meanings for all persons in a given cultural community." —Thomas Pyles, *Origin and Development of the English Language*

10. If a guy who can meet the legal requirements goes into a gun store and buys a pistol for somebody with a criminal record who can't meet the requirements, that's called a straw purchase.

11. SCNT means the same as "somatic cell nuclear transfer."

*12. A "curette" is a spoon-shaped surgical instrument used to remove tissue from a body cavity.

E. *A definition may be defective by being too broad or too narrow, employing an accidental feature, using obscure, metaphorical, or ambiguous language, or being completely circular. Consider the definitions below and explain on what (if any) grounds they might be criticized.*

  *1. Chair: a four-legged piece of furniture

    2. Money: the root of all evil

    3. Triangle: a geometrical figure with equal sides and equal angles

    4. Triangle: a closed three-sided plane figure with equal angles

    5. Gouda: a cheese made in the Gouda district of Holland

    6. A neonatologist is someone who specializes in caring for neonates.

    7. "Truth is the shadow that existence casts across the realm of essences." —George Santayana, *Skepticism and Animal Faith*

    8. "Saw: dentated instrument, by the attrition of which wood or metal is cut." —Samuel Johnson, *Dictionary of the English Language*

    9. Cow: an animal sacred in India

   10. Parfait: a layered ice-cream sundae or pudding served in a tall glass

   11. A singletree is the same as a whiffletree.

  *12. Something is "harmful" if it is capable of causing harm.

   13. "Informal logic" is best defined as a travel guide to the world of correct reasoning.

   14. "Disaffected person: A person who is alienated or estranged from those in authority or lacks loyalty to the government."—Department of Defense, *Dictionary of Military and Associated Terms*

   15. Nylon is a product created by the Dupont Company that went on sale in 1940.

F. *Significant social issues can involve deciding how a crucial word should be defined. Consider the cases below and explain how different definitions might lead to different consequences.*

    1. Many states have laws shielding journalists from legal prosecution if they refuse to reveal the name of a confidential source, even when a crime might be involved. The idea

behind the laws is that journalists are likely to be more effective uncovering wrongdoing in government or industry if the people who provide them with information can be confident that the journalists cannot be compelled to reveal their names.

Should bloggers be considered journalists?

2. The Texas Board of Education refused to approve middle- and high-school health textbooks until publishers altered the wording when marriage is mentioned to reflect the definition of "marriage" in the state law. Holt, Rinehart and Winston agreed to add the definition of marriage as "a lifelong union between a husband and a wife." McGraw-Hill agreed to change expressions like "when two people marry" and "partners" to "when a man and woman marry" and "husbands and wives."

Texas does not recognize civil unions of same-sex couples, but Massachusetts does. Indeed, same-sex couples in a civil union, according to Justice Martha Sosman of the Massachusetts Supreme Court, "have literally every right, privilege, benefit, obligation of every sort that our law bestows on opposite-sex couples who are civilly 'married.'" However, same-sex couples joined in a civil union in Massachusetts are not considered married.—*New York Times,* 12 February 2004

Discuss what is at issue in any state's decision about who should (and who should not) be considered married.

Chapter 10

VAGUENESS AND AMBIGUITY

Vagueness and ambiguity are often confused with one another, but they are distinct concepts. In general, **vagueness** involves a term's lack of precision, whereas **ambiguity** involves different possible meanings, each of which may be quite precise.

I. Vagueness

We discuss *vagueness as fuzziness* and *vagueness of quantity and type*. We then consider reasons for deliberately employing vague expressions.

A. Vagueness as Fuzziness

This is the basic and probably the logically most important sense of vagueness. Terms are **vague** to the extent that they have blurry boundaries—are fuzzy at the edges—so there are borderline cases to which they may or may not apply. (Since 1965 a whole new field of "fuzzy logic" has been developed about the use of terms that are vague in this sense.)

A classic case of a quite vague term is *bald*. Clearly a person with a full head of hair is not bald, and a person with a head like an egg is bald. But what about someone with just fringes of hair around the sides? Or someone with a large bare spot on the top of the head? *Bald* is not precise enough to give any clear answers to such questions. The more such borderline cases, the more vague a term is. Vagueness, then, is a matter of degree.

It is often said that virtually all terms in ordinary language are somewhat vague, and that may be true. Still, some terms are much more vague than others. *Blue, vegetable,* and *can opener* are not nearly as vague as *tall, large, smart, democracy,* or *obscenity*. We are far more likely to be unsure whether something is obscene than whether something is blue.

Generally the use of vague terms does not cause problems. Saying that she is *smart* and *well educated* and a *hard worker* gives a picture that may be all that is needed for many purposes. But consider the following:

> Every player who comes to camp *overweight* will be fined $1000 a day until he makes his *proper weight.*

> I don't need so many *blond* actors. Fire all the *blond* extras.

> Anyone posting *child pornography* on the Internet is subject to arrest and a minimum of ten years in jail upon conviction.

Each of the italicized words has fuzzy edges, although in many cases their applications will be clear enough. A 500-pound human is surely over-weight, but how heavy can one be without being overweight? Just how blond is *blond?* What ages count as a *child?* When is something *pornography?* We just do not know how to apply the terms in some cases.

An easy way to solve the application problems is simply to stipulate some precising definitions of the vague terms.

> The *proper weight* for any player is the average weight of the starters at his position on other teams last year.

> A *blond* is someone whose hair is naturally a very light yellow throughout.

> *Child pornography* will be understood as any pictures or descriptions of any person under the age of 18 in any state of undress.

Such a procedure is much too simple because it decides important issues in arbitrary ways. Why, say, should a quarterback who is 3 inches taller than the average weigh the average? What difference could it make whether a movie extra is naturally blond or has skill-fully lightened hair? Any picture of a less than fully clothed baby becomes child pornography by this stipulation.

It is entirely appropriate to try to alleviate problems of vagueness by stipulating precising definitions. But the definitions should be care-fully considered and to the point. Suppose, for instance, that we must accomplish a task and are blocked from doing so because (1) we are uncertain about whether some term applies in a particular case, (2) we need to decide whether the term applies, and (3) we cannot resolve the doubt by acquiring additional facts. More particularly, suppose we must administer a law granting price-support payments to producers of what the law calls "agricultural products." Growers of wheat, corn, and rice apply for payments, and we have no doubt their crops make them eligible to receive the payments.

Then a grower of Christmas trees applies. Should Christmas trees be considered "agricultural products"? Christmas trees were not specifically included or excluded in the legislation; we cannot act until we decide whether they count as "agricultural products." Given the problem at hand, "agricultural products" is a vague phrase.

We easily recognize some cases to which the term *agricultural products* applies (rice, wheat, and watermelons) and some other cases to which it obviously does not apply (cars, coal, and computers). But does it apply to Christmas trees? How are we to decide?

Finding additional factual information does not seem promising. We already know that Christmas trees are trees planted and cultivated by "tree farmers" who harvest them to sell around Christmastime. Nothing else we can learn about Christmas trees is likely to help in determining whether they should count as "agricultural products." So, to perform our task in a reasonable and defensible way, we must find a way of resolving the vagueness of this phrase.

We may do this by devising a set of criteria for applying the term *agricultural product* to items offered as candidates for price supports. The criteria cannot be chosen arbitrarily or with prejudice. Rather, they must be developed and tested by considering how they handle the obvious and uncontroversial cases.

Consider how we might do this. The term *agricultural product* obviously applies to soybeans and squash, but not to petroleum and bricks. Thus, to be acceptable the criteria must include beans and squash and exclude petroleum and bricks. Criteria that excluded beans from the class of agricultural products would obviously be defective; they would be too narrow (too exclusive). Criteria that included bricks would be defective because they would be too broad (too inclusive). Ideally, the criteria should define a class that *includes* all undoubted agricultural products and *excludes* all undoubted nonagricultural products.

Suppose that through this process of examining the consequences of proposed criteria and revising them when needed, we arrive at the following criteria: To be correctly designated by the phrase *agricultural product*, something must be (1) a plant or part of a plant (leaf, root, nut, or berry) that is (2) cultivated (as distinct from wild-growing) and is (3) harvested (4) for use as food or as raw material in manufacturing a product.

The four criteria seem to reconstruct properly the differences between agricultural and nonagricultural products in cases about which there are no doubts. Ordinary vegetables are in the agricultural class. Timber for lumber is excluded, and so are flowers and ornamental shrubs. If the criteria are acceptable; we can now use them to resolve doubtful cases. They make it possible to decide in a *nonarbitrary* way whether to include or exclude disputed cases from the class of agricultural products.

Christmas trees, according to the criteria, are not agricultural products. Although they are plants that are cultivated and harvested, they are not used as food or as a raw material in making a product. In these respects, they are more like flowers than vegetables. Consequently, we must turn down Christmas tree growers who apply to us for subsidies under the agricultural products support plan.

Growers may disagree with our decision and claim it was the legislature's intent that the law cover their industry. However, unless they can demonstrate that our criteria are flawed by being too inclusive or exclusive in undoubted cases, our position is sound. Seeking a specific directive from the legislature to include Christmas trees in the class of agricultural products is their only recourse.

We can use similar sorts of procedures in contexts where we want or need to identify and rationally resolve vagueness involving terms such as *literature, conservative, rich, corrupt, incompetent,* and thousands of other useful but occasionally troublesome terms in ordinary language.

B. Vagueness of Quantity and Type

This sort of vagueness is resolved by supplying more specific factual information. Evans says to the clerk at the delicatessen counter, "I would like a pound or two of sliced meat." The clerk's questions are obvious: "Just *how much* do you want? *What kind* of meat would you like?" The clerk has to ask these questions because Evans has not been specific enough about the quantity or the kind of what it is that she wants. What she said is too vague in the sense of being too general in both respects.

In the strict sense, vagueness has to do with the fuzziness just discussed. But in ordinary life and language, we often accuse others of being too vague, meaning that they are being overgeneral. ("Don't just say that you will be here *in the afternoon.* Exactly when?") We do not know what really happened when a newspaper tells us vaguely that the robber had "a weapon." (A knife? A gun? A grenade? What?) Vague statements of this sort may tell us less than we want to know, but they are misleading only if we think they are telling us more than they are (if we wrongly assume that "in the afternoon" means before 3:00 P.M. or that the robber's "weapon" was a gun).

In fact, this sort of vagueness is often quite acceptable. We are not likely to reprimand someone who says "The Sahara Desert is a vast expanse of sand" for using a term like *vast* instead of providing exact quantitative information. In the context, the term is unobjectionable. Similarly, expressions like *big, tall, short, fat,* and *very high* might offer all the precision required. We may need to know only that a crowd was a *large* one, not that 80,000 people were present. Someone making a shopping list for another person may write down "small loaf of bread" rather than "1-pound loaf of bread." For practical purposes, numerically expressed measures, even when available, sometimes are not required, and to employ them might seem pedantic.

In some circumstances, though, we either need or want exact information. A cartographer drawing a world map could hardly be satisfied with the knowledge that the Sahara is vast. To do her job, she needs the answer to "How vast is it?" The answer can be provided in terms of some appropriate system of measurement—square miles, hectares, or whatever. In the context of mapping, then, the term *vast* is unacceptably vague. In the same way, a demographer may want to know how many people live in the Nile Valley. Because he wants a number, he would consider "quite a few" unacceptably vague.

In some cases, using comparative expressions is the best way to increase precision because we have no measuring systems to provide us with a numerically precise account. We have no metric for love, charm, or friendliness; we cannot assign a number to represent how bored we are or how tasty the ice cream is. Still, in most cases, we get by with little difficulty with expressions like "The lecture was terribly boring" and "I love you more than I can say."

In summary, a qualitative word may be considered unacceptably vague if we need or wish for a more exact description than the word provides. The vagueness may be resolved by replacing the word with a more precise description. The description may be a comparative one (not so heavy, rather heavy, very heavy) or a quantitative one expressed in the terms of some measuring system (118 pounds). A word considered unacceptably vague with respect to a particular aim or need may not be considered such with respect to some other.

Parallel considerations apply for vagueness of type. I may need to know only that the object in your pocket is a screwdriver (rather than, say, a knife). But in some cases *screwdriver* will be too general. According to the instructions, I will need a screwdriver to assemble the desk. Do I need a Phillips-head screwdriver or a flat-blade one? What size would be best, or will any do? As with vagueness of quantity, lack of specifics regarding type may or may not result in unacceptable vagueness in a given context. If the vagueness is unacceptable, we must get more specific information.

C. Deliberate Vagueness

Ordinarily, anyone who says or writes something wishes to be as clear as possible. Yet in special circumstances we consider it desirable or expedient to use language that is *deliberately vague*. The CEO of

Alpha Computers, being interviewed about the way her company has increased the speed of its new machine, probably won't want to say anything that would help her competitors. Hence, she'll limit herself to saying something about a "new way of masking chips during manufacturing," even though she could say exactly what new techniques her company is using. She chooses to be vague.

Someone wishing to be kind in refusing an invitation may do so by giving a vague response. The question "Would you like to go out to dinner tomorrow?" may be answered by "I'm sorry, but I have other plans." It would usually be considered rude to press for a more detailed answer.

Certain crucial words in agreements, treaties, laws, and resolutions are often deliberately vague. (Such words may also be described as *studiedly vague.*) These carefully chosen words are ones that avoid precision and are open to various interpretations. Thus, a congressional resolution directing federal agencies to provide "help and support" to refugees from "politically oppressive foreign governments" leaves open the crucial questions of how much and what kind of help and support should be provided and just which governments should be considered politically oppressive. Such language leaves room for much political maneuvering by federal agencies, members of Congress, and the executive branch.

Sometimes words are also chosen to permit the expression of an agreement-in-principle, leaving to later times the problems of interpreting the language. Suppose Xenoland commits itself to taking *substantial steps* toward *protecting the human rights* of its citizens so the United States will grant it a special trade status for a year. The United States has not ordered Xenoland to do anything in particular, leaving that country able to claim its sovereignty has not been infringed, but at the end of the year, the United States can review the changes that have occurred. Is allowing newspapers to publish articles critical of the government a *substantial step?* How about freeing political prisoners or allowing free elections? These are the sorts of questions the two countries must discuss before the special trade status can be extended for another year.

Vague language may usually cause puzzlement, misunderstanding, and aggravation. Yet in the right circumstances, vague language can be a valuable tool.

II. Ambiguity

To avoid both practical and intellectual confusion, three types of ambiguity are important to recognize. The types are not offered as exhaustive or exclusive.

A. Word Ambiguity

With the exception of a handful of technical terms, virtually every word in a language like English has more than one meaning, but this fact alone is not what leads us to say a word is ambiguous. A word is **ambiguous** when (1) it has more than one meaning and (2) it is not obvious which one is intended in a situation in which the word is used.

Ordinarily, the intended meaning of a word is so clear from the context that we may have to make a special effort to recall another possible meaning. It sometimes happens, though, that more than one meaning makes sense in the situation, and which one we are supposed to choose is not so obvious.

Suppose the head of a physics department tells a professor, "We cannot request an increase in research funds from the university until the end of the year." What does *year* mean here? Does it mean academic year, calendar year, or fiscal year? We have no way of knowing which is the intended meaning without knowledge of the university's budget-request procedure.

Ambiguity of this sort is most often easily resolved. In this case, all the professor has to do is ask which of the possible meanings is the proper one. However, the ability to ask this kind of question depends on being aware of possibilities. Someone who has never heard of a fiscal year obviously cannot ask whether this meaning is the appropriate one. Someone whose career has been in industry may not consider that a university might budget on an academic-year calendar. Consequently, someone may get the wrong idea about what is said without even being aware of the possibility of being wrong. When we are in doubt about what is meant, clearing away confusion is comparatively easy. Yet when we think we know what is meant and are mistaken, trouble may later arise in an unexpected way.

An error in reasoning that involves treating two distinct meanings of a word as though they were the same is traditionally called the **fallacy of equivocation.** Suppose someone argues:

> It is a well-founded constitutional principle that all men are entitled to due process of law. Ms. Walters, however, is not a man. Thus, the Constitution does not guarantee her this protection.

In the first sentence, *men* clearly refers to human beings; in the second, it is taken to refer exclusively to males. So, the argument is really this:

> It is a well-founded constitutional principle that all *human beings* are entitled to due process of law.
> Ms. Walters is not a *male*.
> _____
> The Constitution does not guarantee her this protection.

Properly spelled out in this way, without the equivocation, the argument is obviously worthless.

Political and moral terms like *free, able, obligation,* and *can* easily lend themselves to the error of equivocation in reasoning, as do terms like *personality, society, intelligence,* and *culture.*

B. Referential Ambiguity

We use words and descriptions to refer to particular people, objects, or states of affairs. We generally rely on context and shared information to make clear exactly what we intend to designate. Hence, we say such things as "Your car key is on the table," "The person who talks too much was fired for insubordination," and "Poor George has not been quite right since the war." We assume that the listener will know what table, what person who talks too much, and what war we are referring to.

Referential ambiguity occurs when this assumption fails and the referring expression can be interpreted as designating more than one thing. This may produce two possible results. First, the other person may be in doubt about what we are referring to. Your car key is on the table, but which table—the dining table, the kitchen table, or the coffee table? Second, the listener may wrongly believe we are referring to something that it is not our intention to refer to. Because it does not occur to him that we might be referring to the dining table, he assumes we mean the coffee table.

Once aware of ambiguity, we need only ask for clarification. Yet someone mistakenly believing he knows what is being referred to may fall into whatever sort of error such a mistake may lead to. The consequence may be as trivial as a few minutes' delay in finding a key or as profound as death.

C. Grammatical Ambiguity

We can read the mathematical expression $2 \times 3 + 4$ as $2 \times (3 + 4)$ or as $(2 \times 3) + 4$. Read the first way, the expression is equal to 14, and read the second way, 10. The expression is ambiguous, and parentheses are needed to make clear which possible reading is intended.

The grammars of languages like English permit similar sorts of ambiguity. A sentence is **grammatically ambiguous** when (1) it has a grammatical structure allowing it to be understood in more than one way and (2) it is not clear from the context which understanding is the intended one.

If someone in an ordinary context says, "So you like target shooting? I like to shoot myself," we can see the possibility of interpreting the second sentence as asserting that the speaker likes

Sentences of the "All Xs are not Ys" form always admit two possible meanings. Consider "All men are not sexist." Exactly what is being asserted here? The sentence can be understood in two quite different ways: (1) "*Every* man is *not* sexist"; that is, "*No* men are sexist." (2) "*Not all* men are sexist"; that is, "*Some* men are *not* sexist." The difference in meaning between these sentences is considerable, and how the original claim is interpreted may mark a major political or ideological difference. As important as the difference is, we have no way of telling from the sentence itself which of the two possible readings is the one intended.

to fire bullets into his body. However, this is so obviously not what is meant that we do not give the possibility a serious thought, if we notice it at all.

Sentences that are grammatically correct may still be grammatically ambiguous. (The example in the box is of that kind.) In some cases, though, it is grammatical error that introduces the possibility of ambiguity. Consider this example: "After returning from a long trip, the dog did not recognize him." Who took the trip? Who did not recognize whom? In this case, despite the error of a misplaced modifier, we have little doubt of the intended meaning of the sentence.

Yet is the meaning of this headline equally clear: "COURT UPHOLDS MAN'S RIGHT TO DIE IN CALIFORNIA"? It is possible that a court ruled that a certain man has the right to go to or stay in California to die. This interpretation seems unlikely, though. In defending euthanasia, many have argued that individuals have a right to die, but no one has argued they have a right to choose where to die. Presumably the headline should be interpreted as "COURT UPHOLDS CALIFORNIA MAN'S RIGHT TO DIE" or as "CALIFORNIA COURT UPHOLDS MAN'S RIGHT TO DIE." Yet without more information, we cannot say which possibility is intended.

We can usually resolve puzzles produced by the use of a vague word by substituting a precise expression or providing additional information. If this is not an appropriate solution and a matter of importance is at stake, we may have to face the task of developing a satisfactory set of criteria for applying the word in disputed or borderline cases.

A difficulty with ambiguity is that we may not notice it, and, as a result, we may fail to grasp the intended meaning of a sentence. The meanings of a word, the way a word is used to refer, and grammatical structure may each render a sentence ambiguous. Knowing how this may happen is a way to guard against becoming confused or misled by ambiguity.

Exercises

A. *Identify the words or phrases that might be considered vague and explain the sort of information that could be supplied to resolve the vagueness.*

   *1. American forces suffered limited casualties and captured a substantial number of Iraqi weapons.

   2. I'm very fond of Baroque music.

   3. We noticed something was wrong when we saw a number of people gathered in a crowd and looking down at something on the pavement. Then a handful of people ran out the door of a business establishment and started throwing things. We couldn't see what they were throwing at first, but each threw several. Then a few explosions made us think they were grenades.

   *4. Save as much as 50 percent on selected items during the sale period.

   5. The car-bomb exploded in the crowd gathered outside the police station, killing or injuring some civilians and others.

   6. Some military experts are saying that troop strength is inadequate to perform the mission.

   7. In the first year of his reign, the emperor Tiberius spent much time attempting to consolidate the empire by making peace with various warring factions.

   8. The last time I visited London, several new security measures had been put into place.

   9. Aquarius: You need to make a difference right now. Choose quick and easy tasks. Your state of mind is much improved when the results of your efforts are visible and immediate— Kelli Fox, Astrology.net

   10. A student must demonstrate proficiency in Spanish to register for a seminar in literature.

B. *In some of the cases below, the vagueness has been resolved, and in some cases it has not. Identify the problem involved in each case. When the problem has been resolved, evaluate the solution and identify the issues that had to be dealt with. When the problem is unresolved, propose and consider some criteria that might be used to solve the problem. The questions will serve as guides.*

   1. The U.S. Supreme Court, in a controversial decision, upheld in a 6–3 vote the constitutionality of the search of a motor home without a warrant. The motor home had beds, a sink, stove, closets, and other furnishings. Yet in *California v. Carney*, the

Court held that although the vehicle possessed "some if not many of the attributes of a home," it most closely resembled a car. Police can search cars without warrants, given probable cause, but searching a house requires a warrant.

Why might one object to the Court's decision?

Is it important to consider "the interest of the state" in deciding whether a motor home is a home? Or can the decision be made in an abstract fashion, without regard to its results?

2.   As the term *addiction* is used, people are described as addicted to (among other things) drugs, alcohol, coffee, cigarettes, food, exercise, sex, shopping, computer games, gambling, movies, music, and work.

Describe a situation in which it would be important to decide whether a person is addicted to something.

What criteria could you use to resolve the question of whether someone is addicted? ("A person A is addicted to X when A. . . .")

3.   The Mill School is a private, coeducational, college-preparatory school with tuition of $25,000 per academic year. Mill is committed to academic excellence, but it also promotes the development of special talents and athletic skills. It is also committed to diversity.

Suppose you are Mill's director of admissions. What do you tell prospective parents when they ask you what it means to be committed to diversity?

4.   Laws or rules restricting the liberty of individuals are sometimes justified by appealing to the offense principle. In its most general form, the principle holds that people ought not act in such a way that their actions cause offense to others. Hence, billboards depicting sexually explicit acts might be prohibited by the principle. Yet virtually everything is likely to offend at least some people to some extent—bad manners, eating in public, frowning, or not saying "Have a nice day."

Is it possible to apply the principle in a reasonable way?

C.   *Use language that is deliberately (or studiedly) vague to accomplish the aims described.*

1.   You are negotiating an international agreement on protecting biodiversity. You need to write a statement expressing a commitment to this goal that can be signed by nations that have taken no steps to protect the habitats of large carnivores.

*2. Write a statement expressing a commitment to diversity in all public sectors of society (business, medicine, law, education, government service) that will have a chance to be endorsed by representatives of racial groups, religious organizations, and gay and lesbian groups.

3. Write a sentence about the United States of America that you would be comfortable reading to a large crowd at a Fourth of July picnic in a small town.

D. *The resolution of legal and social issues often depends on how a crucial word or term considered vague should be understood. Consider the cases below and explain (1) what is at stake in each case and (2) what we commit ourselves to if we accept one way of resolving the vagueness instead of some other.*

Case 1. Abid M. Hanson, a physician, boarded an Olympic Airways flight from Athens to San Francisco and was seated near the smoking section. Dr. Hanson asked a flight attendant to change his seat, explaining that he was asthmatic and the cigarette smoke might trigger an attack. The flight attendant first said there were no empty seats, then later said she was too busy to find a passenger willing to switch seats. Hanson asked three times to be moved to the front and away from the smoke.

Two hours into the flight, Dr. Hanson walked to the front, then gestured to his wife to bring his syringe of epinephrine. He injected himself, then an allergist who happened to be on the flight, injected him with another dose. Even so, Dr. Hanson collapsed with an asthma attack. The allergist performed CPR and gave him oxygen, but Hanson died.

Hanson's widow sued Olympic Airways, alleging that the airline was liable for her husband's death. The trial evidence showed eleven empty seats at the front of the airplane.

Moreover, a large group of airline personnel were sitting at the front, so one of them could have been asked to change seats with Dr. Hanson.

The court hearing the case held that the flight attendant's failure to move Dr. Hanson constituted an accident under the Warsaw Convention regulating international airlines and that Olympic should pay Hanson's widow damages of $1.4 million. The airline appealed the case to the Supreme Court.

In deliberating about whether Dr. Hanson's death was accidental, the Court considered a 1985 airline-related court decision that defined "accident" as "an unexpected or unusual event or happening that is external to the passenger." Referring to this definition, Justice Clarence Thomas, writing for the majority, ruled that the flight attendant's failure to move Hanson was "external and unexpected" and thus was a link in the causal chain "resulting in a passenger's pre-existing medical condition being aggravated by exposure to a normal condition in the aircraft cabin."

Justice Anthony Scalia dissented. he pointed out in his opinion that courts in other countries that have signed the Warsaw Convention have consistently ruled that a failure to act cannot be called an "accident." The Warsaw Convention has no provision for penalizing an airline, except when it has been responsible for an accident, so Dr. Hanson's widow was not entitled to damages. "Whatever accident means," Scalia argued, "it certainly does not equate to outrageous conduct that causes grievous injury." Despite Scalia's argument, the Court (with one Justice not participating) ruled 6–2 in favor of Dr. Hanson's widow.

Is the definition of "accident" accepted by the majority of the Supreme Court reasonable? What is the ordinary view of what constitutes an accident?

Case 2. The Senator who employs you as an aide is considering sponsoring a piece of legislation that will make it illegal to desecrate the American flag. She asks you to furnish her with some guidelines as to what will count as desecration.

What difficulties do you foresee? What do you propose?

E. *Explain how the following sentences may be ambiguous, and classify the ambiguity as word, referential, or grammatical.*

1. Scientific Committee Defends Fat Report—*Dallas Morning News*, 27 June 1994

2. Steve scratched his chest badly while moving into his new apartment.

3. All pit pulls aren't vicious.

*4. It's ridiculous to deny that tooth decay is normal. Virtually every adult person in the world suffers from dental cavities.

5. Business managers who succeed have a good understanding of psychology.

*6. How Do Insects Smell?—*The New York Times*, 15 June 1987

7. The last volume of the *Worldbook Encyclopedia* was stolen from the library.

8. Lucky Man Sees Pals Die—*Baltimore News American*

9. Because of the flood, boil your water north of Interstate 10.

10. Conference on Reasoning at Flanders University

F. *Identify the fallacy of equivocation in each of the following arguments. Restate the arguments without the equivocation, then evaluate them.*

1. This textbook contains material on evolution. Evolution is a theory, not a fact, regarding the origins of living things.—Biology textbook sticker, Cobb County (Georgia) Board of Education

   [Hints: This may be regarded as an enthymeme. See Chapter 1 for an explanation.]

*2. Logic is traditionally regarded as a part of philosophy, but it should be reclassified as a part of psychology. The way people reason is, after all, an aspect of thinking, and it is psychology, not philosophy, that has the task of studying thought processes.

Chapter 11

REASONABLE BELIEFS

When we justify claims by giving arguments for them, we take some claims as premises and use them to argue for the truth of conclusions. Obviously, if *every* claim had to be justified by some preceding argument, we would have no place to begin and our reasoning could never get under way. Thus, we must have some starting points, some claims not based on prior arguments. What are the sources of these claims?

I. Granted Claims and Accepted Beliefs

We can interpret the question about the sources of claims in two ways. If we are wondering why some claims are taken as premises in a particular discussion, the answer is simple: Claims are taken as premises insofar as all parties in the discussion agree to them.

Imagine you and I agree to go to a movie together. As we discuss which one to see, we discover we agree we want a comedy. With this agreement as a premise, you might argue persuasively that the funniest comedy showing is the latest Steve Martin movie and that would settle the issue.

Now imagine that in the same situation I have murder on my mind and want to see something at a 1940s *film noir* festival. In this case, I do not accept the claim that we should choose a comedy, and so you cannot use that as a starting point in your arguments to me about what film we should see. Similarly, in 1955 a southern politician might have taken it as a premise in speeches to his white constituents that school integration ought to be resisted. By 1980 this viewpoint could no longer be assumed.

What claims one may take as premises in a particular discussion does not depend on what is true or even plausible. The southern politician's view was neither, yet he would not have had to argue for it in 1955. In practice, it is not necessary to give reasons for a point people already accept. We can call the premises agreed to in a particular argument **granted claims.**

Now consider the second way of understanding our question. Suppose that instead of looking at premises in particular discussions, we consider the set of claims a person accepts at any given time—the person's entire set of *beliefs*. We all think (or at least hope) our beliefs are reasonable ones. What makes them reasonable? Some are reasonable because they are supported by argument. But as we said, not all our beliefs can be based on arguments because we must have some beliefs as starting points for any chain of arguments. (We must justify eventually even granted claims for a particular argument, assuming we believe them to be true.) We can call our beliefs not based on arguments **accepted beliefs.**

We can identify at least three sorts of accepted beliefs: those that are *self-evident*; those *based on our own experiences*; and those *based on the authority of others*.

A. Self-Evident (Necessary) Truths

Most philosophers think some claims are self-evident. We do not need to support such claims by argument, testimony, or experience because their truth is simply obvious to anyone who thinks clearly about them. Just thinking about them makes it evident that they *must* be true, so claims of this sort are often called **necessary truths.**

The best examples of self-evident claims are **analytic statements.** Analytic statements are ones that are true or false because of their form or because of the meanings of the words that make them up. Those analytically true are **tautologies,** and those analytically false are **contradictions.**

These statements are analytically true because of their forms:

A rose is a rose.

If this is hemlock, then it is hemlock.

Either Jane is alive or she is not.

These are analytically true because of the meanings of the terms employed:

All squares have four sides.

A rose is a flower.

You never get a second chance to make a first impression.

$4 + 7 = 11$.

The following statements are analytically false:

That woman is male. (meaning)

It is both raining and not raining. (form)

Triangles have four angles. (meaning)

These statements *must* be false because either their forms or the meanings of their terms make them self-contradictory. A *male woman* and *four-sided triangles* are self-contradictory descriptions. And one contradicts oneself in both asserting and denying that it is raining. So, it is *not possible* for any of these statements to be true. They are *necessarily* false.

Besides telling us about analytically false statements, this provides a way of thinking about whether a statement is analytically *true*. If the denial of a statement is a contradiction, that denial cannot be true. Hence, the statement itself must be true. Thus, if we consider a statement and find that denying it produces a contradiction, we know the statement must be true. It is analytically true, a necessary truth.

Recognizing that some statements cannot be true—are analytically false—while others must be true—are analytically true—can prevent us from being uncertain about statements and from raising some foolish questions and inquiries. We do not need to search the world for a living corpse or measure one triangle after another to see if the sum of two right angles is ever less than 180 degrees. We do not need to take polls to determine that dissatisfied voters are not contented voters; there is no point in counting many things to be sure that $73 + 94 = 167$; and we don't even need legal research to know that in the United States a citizen cannot marry his widow's sister.

In short, then, a self-evident claim has a privileged status within our set of rational beliefs. Since it *must* be true, it is not subject to the possibility of doubt attached to even the best-founded of non-self-evident beliefs.

Finally, we must be careful about what we consider self-evident truths. Most of us find it obvious that fire is a source of warmth, humans are smarter than cows, killing other people for money is wrong, and the Atlantic Ocean contains more creatures than does a wading pool. Yet not one of these is a *self-evident* truth because any of them could conceivably be false. They are all true, but not *necessarily* true. ("Clover is a cow that is smarter than any human" can be conceived to be true, even though we know perfectly well it really isn't.) Failing to keep in mind the difference between "obvious" and self-evident truths could lead to thinking that everything from our

Some philosophers claim there are *necessary truths that are not analytic.* Here are some candidates:

> Red things take up space.
>
> Every event has a cause.
>
> Every meaningful claim is either true or false.

Perhaps (some have suggested) even truths of arithmetic and geometry, while necessary, are not really analytic.

Still, it is not obvious that any of the examples are actually necessary but nonanalytic. "Every event has a cause" does not appear to be necessary at all. "Red things take up space" seems necessary (how could it be false?), but it may be analytic because part of the meaning of *red* is having a color, and part of the meaning of *color* is being something in space. "Every meaningful claim is either true or false" and mathematical truths are even harder to be sure about. So, the debate goes on.

Fortunately, we do not have to decide about all of these issues. We need only say that a true claim is self-evident if anyone who understands it can see that it *must* be true. (A false claim is self-evident if anyone who understands it can see that it must be false.) We may include any self-evidently true claim in our set of rational beliefs and use it as a starting point for arguments.

well-founded convictions to our most firmly held prejudices deserves to be in the special category of self-evident truths.

B. Experience

Our senses can be important sources of beliefs:

> This is burgundy. I tasted it.
>
> I can tell by the odor that there is a gas leak.
>
> Judging by the feel, the fabric cannot be all wool.
>
> Don't tell me there isn't a horse nearby. I heard it whinny.

Usually we rely most on our sense of sight. We hold there are clouds in the sky because we look up and see them. We believe a mouse is in the house because we spied the creature running by. Many people are in prison because eyewitnesses identified them as perpetrators of crimes. Our reliance on our senses, particularly vision, is reflected in the common sayings "Seeing is believing" and "I'll believe it when I see it."

> **Self-Evident (Necessary) Truths:** Claims whose truth is obvious to anyone who thinks clearly about them; claims that evidently *must* be true.
>
> **Analytically True Statements:** Self-evident statements that are necessarily true because of their form or because of the meanings of the words that make them up. The denial of an analytically true statement is a contradiction and cannot be true.
>
> **Analytically False Statements:** Statements that must be false because either their forms or the meanings of their terms make them self-contradictory. These statements are *necessarily* false.
>
> **Tautologies:** Analytically true statements.

Not all our experiences are equally reliable. Dim light, nearsightedness, distance, and a multitude of other factors can make even vision unreliable. A cold can interfere with taste or smell, and an airplane ride can temporarily impair hearing. When conditions like these are present, we cannot completely rely on our senses. With a stuffy nose, we may mistake an onion for an apple.

A less obvious way of falling into error results from a lack of knowledge necessary to experience some things in a correct or useful way. Someone who believes all creatures living in the sea are fish can look at cavorting dolphins and not be aware of observing mammalian behavior. Similarly, someone who knows little about astronomy can gaze through a telescope and not realize he is looking at light that has been traveling for millions of years from distant galaxies.

Also, we typically do not take notice of everything we see, even when we possess the required knowledge to interpret it correctly. If we need a place to sit and read, we are likely to notice a comfortable chair in a room. Yet we are less likely to notice whether the chair has a high back or a low one. We tend to observe in terms of *categories* in which we have interests or needs: chair—good-for-reading; automobile—blocking-my-driveway. Beyond the categories, the details often escape our attention.

Thus, while our experiences are an indispensable source of rational beliefs, they are neither as simple nor as foolproof a source as we may think. We must be careful that conditions are right to enable us to see, hear, smell, taste, and touch accurately. We must have the knowledge that lets us experience certain things in an informed way, and we must be sure we were paying attention to the important features of what we experienced. Under these conditions, our experiences will generally be a reliable source of rational beliefs.

C. Reliance on Others

A great number of our rational beliefs are based on the words of others. We believe traffic is tied up on the thruway because we heard a radio rush-hour report; that tickets for *Othello* are sold out because a friend said she was turned away at the box office; that meteors were responsible for the extinction of the dinosaurs because a paleontologist announced it. If we try to trace the source of every belief we think is true, we soon find that many, probably most, are based in some way on the words of others.

The world is too vast and complex for us to attempt to ground all our beliefs on our own experiences or on arguments we have constructed personally or even on ones we are aware of. Nothing is wrong with this situation. If we are careful in our assessments, the words of others can be a reliable source of rational beliefs.

However, we should rely on the words of another only if we are sure that person is *in a position to know the truth* about the topic of discussion and is *not biased* on the issue. Together these conditions make it likely that the person (in fact) *knows the truth* about the topic. Also, someone may know the truth about something but lie about it. Hence, before we take someone's word as the basis for our own beliefs, we should be sure the person is not making a deliberate effort to deceive us.

1. Being in a Position to Know

We would not take the word of a child about how it feels to be elderly or the word of an illiterate about the use of images in James Joyce's *Ulysses*. Neither the child nor the illiterate is in a position to know the truth about those particular subjects. In general, we do not want to take the word of another about a claim unless that person can reasonably be expected to know the truth about the claim, and we do not expect a person to know the truth without being in a *position to know* about the claim. What is it to be in a position to know?

a. General Depending on the topic, many sorts of people are in a position to know. Eyewitnesses are in a position to know about the events they witness, and baseball fans are in a position to know what teams have won the World Series the past three years. We may get information directly from such people, but usually we must also rely on less direct information.

Newspapers, magazines, television reports, websites, encyclopedias, atlases, and books of all sorts (including fiction) are important sources of information. We trust such sources because we believe they are the work of researchers, writers, and editors who are collectively in a position to know about their subjects.

Not all sources are equally reliable, and we must exercise judgment as we read or listen. We accept *The New York Times* as more reliable than a supermarket tabloid and a new atlas as more accurate than one fifty years old. We trust the website of the National Library of Medicine more than the site of a company selling nutritional supplements. We must evaluate many factors to determine the reliability of a source. In most cases our experience with the nature of the source and its public reputation enables us to evaluate its reliability adequately.

b. Experts Some people are in a position to know because they have specialized knowledge of a given subject. They are **experts**. That they have this specialized knowledge usually makes it reasonable for others to rely on them in forming beliefs and making claims.

A person becomes an expert through a combination of education and experience. Years of advanced study in chemistry can turn someone into an expert on chemistry, and years of experience in business might make someone an expert on entrepreneurial matters. Extensive study and hospital experience may make a physician an expert diagnostician. Thus, when those of us who are not experts on a subject must decide who is, we should look for those having the relevant education and experience.

Reputation and position can also indicate expertise. Having a prestigious appointment at a major university or corporation and being known and respected by others in the same field add to the likelihood that an educated and experienced person really is a knowledgeable source.

In many cases it is clear that someone has the requisite education and experience to make her an expert on a given matter. A professor of English specializing in the eighteenth century should be an authority on the early novels *Pamela* and *Joseph Andrews*. A basketball writer of twenty years' experience with a major newspaper is correctly relied on as an expert on the recent history of the game.

By contrast, it would be an obvious mistake to take the word of the newspaper writer about *Pamela* and *Joseph Andrews* because of his experience in basketball or to presume that the person holding a Ph.D. in English is a reliable source about basketball.

Unfortunately, such obvious mistakes are common. Persons known and respected in one field are often treated as if they were experts in quite another one. Advertising actually encourages this error by frequently presenting athletes, actors, and other celebrities as if they were experts on toothpaste, electronics, or automobiles. If we give the matter any thought, we are not likely to take the word of an actor about cold medication or transportation.

c. Hard Cases and Soft Experts On some questions we find it hard to know who the experts are or even whether there are any. Consider the question of abortion. Some think whether abortion is morally acceptable depends on when human life begins, and it seems obvious to them that scientists such as biologists and medical doctors are the experts on this underlying issue.

What can these experts tell us about the beginning of human life? They can tell us that from the moment of conception the fertilized ovum is both alive and human. But the sperm and the ovum each by itself was alive, as is any individual cell of a moose, a mushroom, or

> General terms such as *scientists* and *experts* are often used to misrepresent expertise. "Scientists say evolution is impossible," but when we look carefully, we find the "scientists" are a few mechanical engineers, a physicist, and a medical anatomist. They are not biologists, not scientists that have specialized training in the field of evolution. If we are not careful, the term *scientists* may mislead us into thinking that relevant expert scientific opinion has it that evolution did not occur.
>
> In other cases, we find that the "*scientists*" and "*experts*" are just left anonymous. "Experts suspect we are being watched by intelligent beings in distant space." Who are these experts? What are their fields of expertise?
>
> There is no such thing as a "scientist" in general. There are physicists, biologists, chemists, and astronomers. Within these fields there are molecular physicists, cell biologists, organic chemists, theoretical astronomers, and many others. "Experts" encompasses even more, not just scientists but historians and sociologists, cooks and cab drivers and television technicians. We can rely on any of these in the appropriate situation. But we have to rely on the right ones in the right situations.

any other living creature. The scientific sense in which the fertilized ovum is *human* is just that it is the product of the species *Homo sapiens* and could, under just the right circumstances, become another member of the species. The fertilized ovum is not the product of, and could not grow into, a cat, a shark, or an oak tree.

Surely these scientific facts were not what we were uncertain about when we asked about the beginning of human life? We knew these facts all along; we didn't need to consult biologists or physicians to tell us such commonplace truths. Thus, when we are concerned about abortion and ask when human life begins, we must be wondering about something different.

What we really want to know is whether we should regard the fetus as a *person*, whether we should treat it in ways we must treat individuals we take to have rights and privileges. The scientific facts do not answer this question. Indeed, the real question is not a scientific one at all, and it cannot be answered from the perspective of the expertise of the biologist or physician.

Where should we look for expertise on whether we should consider a fetus a person? Or, more generally, on whether abortion is justifiable? Are there any experts on these issues? For that matter, are there experts on whether the god of Moses exists, life has a meaning, the *Mona Lisa*'s smile has any significance, or it is morally right to kill a person in self-defense? Can there *be* any experts on such matters?

Our first response may be to say no, and that would be partly right. Probably there can be no experts on these matters in the way there are experts on mathematics, physics, the history of sports, or television repair. The issues about god, art, and morality are, in some sense, less straightforward. As a result, we are not nearly so inclined, for instance, to defer without question to the word of the "expert" art critic about the meaning of Picasso's *Guernica* as we are to defer without question to the word of a physicist about the meaning of the Second Law of Thermodynamics. We all believe we are entitled to our own opinions in religion or politics in a way that we are not entitled to our own opinions about the square root of 225 or whether a bandicoot is a marsupial.

While this view is correct, it would be a serious mistake to conclude there are no experts in any sense on matters of art, morality, and religion. It would be an even more serious error to conclude that in such areas everything is "all a matter of opinion" or "one person's opinion is as good as another's." Art historians and critics are in a position to have better-informed views on the *Mona Lisa* or *Guernica* than the rest of us. Those trained in philosophy are unusually qualified to evaluate the validity and significance of arguments about the existence of God. Psychologists, philosophers, religious scholars, and those with knowledge and experience in other fields of study may be in a better position than most of us to think clearly about questions regarding the meaning of life.

These people are not "hard experts," authorities to whom those of us with less training must entirely defer in the way the nonphysicist must defer to the physicist. They are what we can call "soft experts," people whose views on certain matters are more informed and more carefully considered than the views of the rest of us.

We should not defer entirely to their views, however. We must finally think for ourselves about abortion, the existence of God, the meaning of life, whom to vote for as president, and so on. Yet if we try to think for ourselves without first learning from those who are most knowledgeable, we almost guarantee that our conclusions will be naive, ill informed, and quite possibly incorrect.

2. Bias

Being in a position to know is not enough to make someone a reliable source. We should distrust even experts and careful observers if they have a stake in a claim's truth or falsity. We wonder about the fairness of a judge in a diving contest who awards her son the highest number of points. We are suspicious of an expert on respiratory diseases who is a paid spokesman for a drug company and claims its asthma drug has not been shown to be a factor in developing emphysema. In such cases, we don't so much think the people are lying as suspect they are *biased*, that their interests prevent them from having objective views on the subjects.

Bias can affect anyone. The trained expert, the most thorough reporter, the most careful eyewitness may all turn out to be unreliable authorities if their interests interfere with their objectivity. Hence, we should be especially careful about accepting a claim from someone whose expertise may be compromised by a conflict of interest.

We should also stay aware of our own biases and not allow them to distort beliefs. Am I in favor of an airport bond issue because the community airport needs improvements or because the company I work for may get the contract? Do I reject the evidence showing a certain surgical procedure is pointless because I'm a surgeon who makes money from performing the procedure? Becoming aware of the possibility of bias in a particular case is the first step toward grounding beliefs on reasons and evidence.

3. Deliberate Deception

Our experience indicates that people most often tell the truth, so far as they know it. Yet in some situations we think it likely that a person would lie. We expect that someone accused of a serious crime will deny his guilt, regardless of whether he is the perpetrator. We think the first price quoted to us by car salesman will not be the price we must actually pay. And white lies told to hosts are a matter of simple politeness.

None of this means we can assume any particular person is lying in any particular situation. But it does suggest that whenever someone may have special reasons for not speaking the truth, we should be suspicious.

II. New Claims, Background Beliefs, and Rationality

Before we accept a new claim, we must do more than evaluate the nature of its support. We must also consider the extent to which it fits in with the reasonable beliefs we already hold.

Consider the following:

A neighbor tells you a dog is pulling your laundry from the line; or a neighbor says seven hippopotamuses have knocked down your clothesline poles.

You look out over a foggy bay and seem to see a sailboat tacking against a difficult wind; or you seem to see a boat sailing above the water as grinning skeleton passengers wave you closer.

You reason that since most automobiles cost less than $40,000, you can buy a Dodge minivan for less than that; or you conclude you can buy the Porsche convertible you like for less than that.

In each of these pairs, we are given exactly as much reason for believing the second claim as the first. Yet in each case, it is reasonable to believe the first claim but not the second, because the second of each pair of claims is contrary to our background beliefs.

At a given time, each of us holds a complex set of beliefs we take to be rational. Any *new* candidate for belief that comes from argument or observation, or is the claim of another, must be considered against this background of previous beliefs. Even a supposedly self-evident claim coming to our attention must be considered against this background.

Our background beliefs about natural habitats and the security of the local zoo make it incredibly unlikely that hippos should appear in our yard. These beliefs are so well grounded they make it much more likely that our neighbor is mistaken in his claim (he could be drunk or a practical joker) than that the hippopotamuses are there. What we know about physics and "living skeletons" makes it more likely that seeing a boat flying above the surface and inhabited by bony ghosts is a visual illusion. Our background knowledge is quite contrary to any notion that one can buy a Porsche convertible for less than $40,000.

If we fail to recognize that we must consider new candidates for belief in relation to background beliefs, we are likely to make serious mistakes. We will be too credulous and believe many things we should not believe. Consider some cases:

People at séances have often maintained they feel the table floating in the air, hear voices from beyond the grave, and see spirits of dead loved ones.

People have insisted that they have seen mentalists bend sturdy metal spoons by stroking them lightly.

Others claim to have witnessed "psychic surgery" in which the "surgeons" reach through the flesh of the patient and remove diseased tissue with their bare hands.

Those who think they have observed such occurrences, or who believe the accounts of others who claim to have observed them, often become indignant when faced with doubters. "All the witnesses there say the same thing. No witnesses deny it. You doubters are just being close-minded and dogmatic. And that is irrational."

But it is the believers who are irrational. They are credulous to the point of gullibility because they have not taken into account the importance of background beliefs. We do not need eyewitnesses who say, "I was there and I saw that what the 'psychic surgeon' said was diseased tissue from the patient was really a piece of chicken liver he had palmed." We have a very well grounded set of background beliefs that rules out the possibility of performing surgery with a bare hand without leaving so much as an external mark on the patient. Our background beliefs also give excellent reason to deny that spirits were present at the séance and that spoons were bent by psychic means.

A failure to recognize the importance of our background beliefs may also lead to the mistake of thinking that all claims coming from the same source must be equally believable. It is an error to hold that since I have known my friend for a long time and believed him when he told me of his service in the Army and his year as a law student, I must now believe him when he insists he was an astronaut and became a double agent for the CIA and Chinese State Security.

Similarly, we often hear that it is inconsistent to accept some parts of a basic religious document (the Hebrew Bible, the New Testament, the Koran) and not others. Both fundamentalist Christians and religious skeptics sometimes maintain that it is a mistake to accept the New Testament accounts that Jesus was born in Bethlehem, was trained as a carpenter, and threw the money-changers out of the temple, but not accept that he literally walked on water or turned water into wine. All of these, after all, are based on the authority of the same document, and so all must be accepted or rejected together. The fundamentalists' aim here is to support their view that everything in the New Testament should be accepted quite literally. The skeptics' aim is to discredit the entire document in the minds of anyone who would doubt the literal truth of stories about walking on water or changing a liquid of one chemical composition into one with a quite different composition.

Both sides are mistaken here, just as I would be if I thought that because I believed my friend was in the Army, I must believe he is a double agent. Our background beliefs indicate that the latter is simply less likely than the former, and so we need better reason to believe it. My friend's word is quite enough for me to accept the commonplace claim that he served in the Army. We have the background belief that many people have done so. The very same word is not enough for me to believe the extraordinary claim that he was a double agent. In the same way, we do not have to take an all-or-nothing approach to the Hebrew Bible, the Koran, or the New Testament. It may well be that we should accept their more usual claims while remaining skeptical about those that conflict sharply with our background beliefs. The failure to appreciate the importance of background beliefs leads to such common mistakes.

Finally, what about the charge of dogmatism? If no witnesses deny the accuracy of claims that tables floated or that spoons were bent by mental powers, is it just irrationally close-minded to refuse to believe these events happened? It *would* be dogmatic and entirely irrational to say that no new claim that conflicts with our background beliefs could ever be rationally accepted. But that is *not* what is being said.

The point is that the more a claim accords with our background beliefs, the less strong its own credentials must be. (The claim that it snowed in Minnesota in December does not need strong credentials to be accepted.) The less a new claim is in accordance with these background beliefs, the stronger its own credentials must be. (The claim that it snowed in Florida in July needs very strong credentials.) Any new claim, no matter how outlandish (that is, no matter how much it conflicts with our background beliefs), could conceivably turn out to be true. But some claims are so outlandish they must have extraordinarily strong credentials if they are to be taken seriously.

When we stand in the supermarket aisles and read the tabloid headlines I WAS KIDNAPPED AND OPERATED ON BY SPACEMEN and STATUES WEEP AFTER COUPLE DIVORCES, we should adopt a critical stance and consider each such claim in the light of both the reputation of the publication *and* our background beliefs. Lacking a mass of further evidence in favor of the claims, it is not dogmatic to reject any of them without further investigation.

That is exactly what a reasonable person will do.

Exercises

A. *Taking into account the information provided and generally accepted background beliefs, assess the extent to which the unusual events described below are worthy of belief. Consider in each case what additional information you might want to help you settle your belief.*

   1. A Death-Defying Fall

      Nicholas Alkemade was a crew member in a bomber flying over Germany during the Second World War. The plane was hit by antiaircraft fire and burst into flames, but Nicholas was squeezed into a space where there were no parachutes. Faced with the prospect of being burned alive, he bailed out anyway.

Rocketing through the atmosphere, he was sure he was going to die when he struck the ground. Yet, unknown to him, the plane was over a dense forest when it was shelled. Instead of hitting the ground, Nicholas struck the upper branches of a pine tree. The limbs broke his fall, and he landed in a deep snowbank at the foot of the tree. Although he was bruised and scraped, his only serious injury was a sprained ankle. The German soldiers who took him captive were puzzled by not finding his parachute.

Is Nicholas' story worthy of belief?

2. *Psychic Surgery*

Thousands of sick people in the 1970s traveled to the Philippines from all over the world to seek help from psychic surgeons who were reported to be performing medical miracles, despite the fact that they were all uneducated and untrained in even the most basic medical procedures.

Perhaps the most famous of the psychic surgeons was Tony Agpaoa in Manila. Observers claimed they had watched him many times as he plunged his hand inside a patient's body and plucked out a tumor, kidney stones, or part of a diseased liver or lung. When Agpaoa pulled out his hand, witnesses said, the diseased material would be covered with blood, but there would be no sign of an incision in the patient's skin. Dozens of patients said that Agpaoa had cured them of their diseases, and often these patients' own doctors had told them their diseases were incurable or inoperable.

Are you willing to accept psychic surgery as a genuine phenomenon, given your beliefs about disease, the human body, human nature, and surgery?

3. *Bermuda Triangle*

The Bermuda Triangle is a wedge-shaped area of the Atlantic Ocean, with Florida, Bermuda, and Puerto Rico lying at its three points. Hundreds of ships and airplanes and thousands of people have disappeared into this marine deathtrap, indicating that some unknown and perhaps as yet unrecognized forces are operating in this apparently quite ordinary area of the ocean.

Some of the most persuasive evidence for the presence of unusual phenomena is the unexpected loss of aircraft flown by military pilots. Perhaps the most dramatic of the cases is the one involving the Lost Patrol. On December 5, 1945, five Avenger torpedo bombers under the command of flight leader Lt. Charles Taylor disappeared during what should have been a routine patrol.

"We don't know which way is west," Lt. Taylor is supposed to have radioed to the control tower at the military base at Ft. Lauderdale. "Everything is wrong . . . strange . . . we can't be sure of any direction. Even the ocean doesn't look as it should."

At 4:45 P.M., the control tower is said to have received another radio call from another of the pilots. "We must be about 225 miles northeast of base. It looks like we are . . ." The transmission then abruptly ended.

The base immediately launched a thirteen-man Martin Mariner flying boat. The aircraft could land on the water and take on survivors, if necessary. Yet after a few routine radio transmissions, the Mariner fell silent, and the tower wasn't able to raise the aircraft.

Eventually, the area of the ocean where the Lost Patrol and the Mariner disappeared was searched. Yet no sign of the crew or the aircraft was discovered. Whatever mysterious forces in the Bermuda Triangle were at work had claimed eighteen more victims.

Are you prepared to believe that unusual factors are present in the Bermuda Triangle that are responsible for the inexplicable disappearances of aircraft, ships, and their crews? What questions might you want answered?

4. *Loch Ness Monster*

The first recorded sighting of the Loch Ness monster was in the year 565. Since then, hundreds, if not thousands, of sightings have been reported. Some have suggested that the lake is inhabited by a water-dwelling dinosaur—a plesiosaur, perhaps—that survived the catastrophic sequences of events that wiped out other dinosaurs. Or perhaps a remote ancestor of the whale may have been trapped in the glacial lake and not evolved. Theories abound.

Expeditions have been mounted in recent decades for the purpose of determining once and for all whether some creature or creatures that might correspond to the legendary monster actually live in the lake. Visual observation is rendered almost impossible by the billions of particles of peat dissolved in the water. The decaying vegetation pollutes the water, turning it into an inky blackness so dense that sunlight can penetrate only a few feet below the surface. Scuba divers and people in small submarines have descended into the lake, yet no visual observations have ever been made that scientists consider reliable. In 1968, however, a team of scientists made use of sonar equipment to survey the lake. The team got echoes suggesting that large objects of some kind were moving under the water. Yet no animals were directly observed, and sonar is notorious for producing ambiguous results.

Debate also continues over whether the famous photograph of "Nessie" from the 1950s actually portrays a creature in the lake. Skeptics have suggested that the photograph is a deliberate fake, yet some people accept it as genuine and claim it provides the best evidence available that some sort of animal lives in the murky depths of Loch Ness.

What can one reasonably believe about the Loch Ness monster?

B. *Decide whether each of the following claims is (a) analytically true; (b) analytically false; (c) not analytic; (d) impossible to classify (conceptually incoherent).*

  *1. Tuesday follows Monday.

   2. If this is a triangle, it has three sides.

   3. The past is present.

   4. $10 - 4 = 5$.

  *5. All three-sided figures are triangles.

   6. All rotten apples are rotten.

   7. All apples are red.

   8. All apples are grown in Colorado.

   9. She's awake, because I see a light in the window.

  10. My cat eats waffles.

  11. Humans are primates.

  12. The square root of four is dancing in the living room.

  13. Hydrogen has the atomic weight 1.

  14. The helium atom is wearing a funny hat.

  15. The dark night of the soul is between the hours of three and four in the morning.

C. *Using the same categories as in B, decide how to classify the following claims. Then are philosophically vexed however, and achieving agreement about their status, if possible, requires discussion and argument.*

1. Some machines can think.

2. Solitaire is not a game.

3. People are dead when their cerebral hemispheres are so damaged that they have lost the capacity for intelligent responses (e.g., recognizing faces, acting on commands, expressing emotions).

CHAPTER 12

RULES FOR WRITING

This chapter is not about writing in general but about writing an argumentative essay. Most professional papers in disciplines such as history, philosophy, political science, sociology, literary analysis, and even the natural sciences are argumentative essays. The papers assigned to students in these areas are also supposed to be written as such.

An argumentative essay is one that states a thesis and supports it by presenting relevant reasons and evidence. The essay or paper (as we'll call it) may involve reporting the results of research, but its major aim is to argue for a particular interpretation, attitude, or point of view. Thus, an argumentative paper can be regarded as an extended argument of the sort discussed in Chapter 2.

A paper, in the course of supporting a thesis, may also perform a variety of other tasks. The essay may provide essential definitions, explain the significance and implication of its thesis, examine alternative theses and give reasons against them, or consider and criticize counterarguments to its own thesis. The paper may do whatever seems needed to make its thesis clear and persuasive.

We will analyze the structure of a paper and present some rules of style to follow in writing one. The rules all concern writing, not conducting the research or doing the thinking necessary for the writing. Like all such rules, furthermore, they must be regarded as nothing more than bits of practical advice.

I. Structure

A writer must impose an order on the materials of a paper. Otherwise, they remain little more than a confusing jumble in which individual points may be interesting yet don't add up to anything. Structure is needed to provide coherence and demonstrate how the pieces fit together to form a picture.

The structure we'll describe here is typical of the one found in most academic papers. Other structures are possible, but understanding this one has definite advantages. First, it makes it easier to follow the arguments in professional articles. Second, it provides students assigned to write a paper with an acceptable model to follow. Any model is probably better than none.

The structure we advocate is as simple as one-two-three: Every paper should have a **beginning**, a **middle**, and an **end.** Each of these parts, furthermore, should play its proper role in the paper. A beginning ought to do what a beginning is supposed to do, and so on for the other parts.

A. Beginning

The beginning of a paper (the **introduction**) has the job of preparing the reader for the rest of the essay. The introduction is the place where the writer and the reader first come into contact. The writer hopes to engage the reader's attention, get her to keep reading, and persuade her to accept the thesis of the paper. The reader hopes the writer won't bore her, confuse her, or make foolish and unsubstantiated claims.

Quite apart from these aspects of engaging the reader's attention, the beginning of a paper has three specific tasks to perform.

1. Establish a Context

The beginning should set the scene within which the problems or issues discussed in the paper can be located. Seeing an issue from a wider perspective is a help to both a writer and a reader.

Indicating a context need not be done in an elaborate or detailed fashion. Sometimes a single sentence may be enough:

> Original studies with small children are the major source of information about the innateness of sex-role differences, but such studies are often flawed in their design or execution.

This sentence sets rough boundaries for the discussion to come. The reader knows that the paper is concerned, in some way or other, with sex-role differences. Furthermore, the writer is not just going to accept at face value the research on the topic. Thus, the sentence not only indicates the general subject of the paper; it expresses a definite attitude toward an aspect of it.

A second sentence can go a long way toward indicating just where the main concern of the paper will lie:

> So far, however, no one has done a systematic review of such studies and catalogued their errors.

> So far, however, no one has attempted to integrate the data from those studies that are not open to the charge of being flawed to the point of uselessness.

> So far, however, no one has attempted to compare the results of studies done with adults to data obtained from studies with children.

Any of these sentences restricts the context even more narrowly and calls attention to a problem in the field that has not been addressed. Thus, even two sentences can convey a great deal of information and be of great help to the reader.

2. State a Thesis

The introduction is the place to present a general sketch of what you intend to accomplish in the paper. In an argumentative essay, this means stating the argument of the paper—the major claim that you intend to establish:

> In this paper, I want to examine the alleged biological determinants of sex-role behavior. I shall argue that the evidence typically presented to show that particular patterns of behavior in humans are genetically predetermined is either open to direct challenge or does not show what proponents of biological determinism claim for it.

Beginning writers sometimes think that the best strategy to keep the reader reading is to avoid stating a thesis until the very end of the paper, on the theory that the reader will be pulled along by the suspense. Usually, though, this is not a good strategy. Rather than enjoying the suspense, a reader is more likely to feel puzzled about what the writer is getting at. The longer the writer delays revealing the secret, the more annoyed the reader becomes.

Stating the thesis of a paper in the introduction provides the reader with a reference point. He can discover at once whether you have an interesting claim to make, and he can then read with an eye to deciding whether what you say is relevant or persuasive with respect to your thesis.

3. Relate Your Work to Other Work

An introduction should indicate how your thesis stands with respect to the work of others:

> Stephen J. Gould has argued that the evidence for genetic determinism in humans consists of little more than arguments by analogy. I accept Gould's criticisms as correct, and I want to go on and show that the data drawn from anthropology that Wilson and others take as evidence of genetic determinism in humans will not support that interpretation. Along with Gould, I reject the general thesis of genetic determinism.

Remarks like these not only show your awareness of other work in the same area, they allow the reader to see how your work is supposed to supplement, support, or contradict that of others.

B. Middle

The middle of a paper should present the evidence and arguments that support its thesis. The middle is the place to attempt to demonstrate that the thesis is sufficiently well supported to be worthy of acceptance. Thus, the middle is the place where the actual work of the paper gets done. It's the meat in the structural sandwich of introduction, middle, and conclusion.

In the middle, you should do everything you said you would do in the introduction. If you said you would present data contrary to your claim and explain why they are not significant, then you must do so.

The middle section should also have some form of internal organization. One common form in academic papers is to begin by presenting a particular argument in favor of the thesis of the paper, then review and answer objections to the argument. Such a paper might have a structure like this:

Thesis:	Individuals in our society have a right to make their own decisions about euthanasia.
Argument 1:	The Constitution guarantees a right to privacy. This means that I have a right to make decisions that affect my life directly and the lives of others only indirectly. I am free, for example, to decide whether I want to adopt a child, spend my money on travel, get married, and so on. Euthanasia is a decision that affects me most directly. Thus, I have a constitutional right to decide, when my life seems beyond medical hope, whether I want to end it.
Objection 1:	The Constitution does not mention privacy. Thus, it is absurd to talk of a constitutional right to privacy.
Answer to Objection 1:	Although it is true that the word does not appear, the courts, including the Supreme Court, have repeatedly held that there is a scope of individual action that falls under the heading of "privacy" and that it has a basis in the Constitution.

This pattern can be repeated for other objections to Argument 1. It can also be repeated for other arguments for the thesis and other objections to it.

Another pattern common in academic papers is to review arguments against a thesis, give reasons for rejecting them, then provide arguments supporting the thesis. Thus, a writer might deal with the topic of euthanasia by considering three major objections to making its explicit practice legal. After doing this, positive arguments could then be presented.

A third pattern, also common, is to present the most persuasive and least controversial data and arguments supporting a thesis at the beginning of a paper. The writer may then hope that the reader will begin by giving assent and continue to do so later on.

More patterns are easily found, but these three are enough to suggest principles that can be used in deciding how to structure a paper. What is most important is that the middle of a paper should have some obvious form of organization.

C. End

The end of a paper, its **conclusion,** should bring to a focus all the major elements of the body of the work. If the paper is a long one, all the evidence and arguments for the paper's thesis ought to be summarized briefly. The main arguments of the paper should be mentioned in the same order as they were presented.

Most important, the reader should not be left in any doubt about what the thesis of the paper is. The thesis should be repeated at the end in terms similar to those used at the beginning:

> I have attempted to show that the anthropological evidence that has been taken as favoring a deterministic view of the heritability of behavioral patterns in humans will not stand up to scrutiny.

Such a restatement of the thesis may be the first sentence in the conclusion. The sentence, in this position, then serves to lead into a summary of the major lines of argument that support the paper's thesis.

* * *

This three-part division provides an obvious way to impose order on a diversity of materials. Indeed, some may think that the structure is so obvious that following it would make a paper uninteresting and inelegant. That's doubtful. The main interest of a paper isn't in its structure, but in its subject, thesis, and arguments. A good writer need not be held back by the three-part structure, and a poor writer can become better by following it.

II. Style

"Style" is used here to refer to those features of writing that are connected with clear and effective exposition. Following tradition, we present our advice about style in the form of rules or commandments.

Once again, though, keep in mind that rules of this sort are no more than rough guidelines.

A. Be Brief

One way to be brief is to leave out unnecessary words. Don't be long-winded. Expressions like "although it remains to be seen whether or not Boston will opt to play" can be replaced by ones like "Boston may not play." Phrases like "with respect to the aforementioned issue" and "it is hardly necessary to point out" are hardly ever necessary.

Another way to be brief is to leave out padding. Get to the point. Each sentence in a paper should have a function to serve, and any sentence without a function should be discarded.

The most direct style is usually the best in a paper. Long buildups like this are unnecessary:

> Since the time of antiquity, a great deal of attention has been paid by philosophers and, later, cognitive psychologists, neurologists, and computer scientists to the perplexing problems presented by what has traditionally been known as the mind-body problem. I have no wish to attempt to review the complicated history of the problem, but instead, I want to focus attention on the version of so-called reductive materialism as it has been defended by J. J. C. Smart.

Someone getting paid by the word or a student desperate to meet a required quota might write such a passage, but only the last clause of the last sentence does the real work. It should be salvaged and most of the rest of the passage junked.

B. Be Simple

A basic aim of writing is to promote understanding. When a reader fails to understand what you have written, other aims (such as persuasion, fascination, or amusement) are impossible to achieve. Simple writing helps bring about understanding, and various ways of being simple are worth pursuing.

1. Use Ordinary Words

Don't try to find words that are unusual, fancy, or technical only for the sake of decorating your prose with them. Don't use a word like "comestibles" when "food" will do. Technical terms (*genome, tort, legal right, gross domestic product*) have a legitimate place in writing, but they should not be used when they are not necessary.

2. Use Ordinary Sentences

The English language has grammatical forms that permit us to write long and complicated sentences. A single sentence may make an assertion about a subject, then qualify the assertion and also provide additional information about the subject. Not only are most people not good at keeping the grammar straight, but long sentences tend to be confusing.

Rather than pack too much information in a single long sentence, it is better to use two or more shorter sentences. Consider these passages and see if the second is not in some ways preferable:

> Zeno, a Greek philosopher who lived in the fifth century B.C. and was known to later times as Zeno the Eliatic, formulated logical paradoxes that, far from being anachronistic puzzles, are of enduring interest to logicians and mathematicians.

> The Greek philosopher Zeno lived in the fifth century B.C. and was known to later times as Zeno the Eliatic. The logical paradoxes he formulated are not mere anachronistic puzzles, but are of enduring interest to logicians and mathematicians.

C. Use the Active Voice

The passive voice contributes nothing to simplicity, directness, or brevity. The passive voice usually requires more words than the active, and the passive voice introduces vagueness into a sentence: Instead of:

> It is expected that the governor will approve the proposal that was made by the legislature to establish a committee to oversee the implementation of the guidelines on medical privacy that were made mandatory by Congress in its last session.

Write:

> I expect the governor to approve the legislature's proposal to establish a committee to implement the guidelines on medical privacy that Congress made mandatory in its last session.

Sometimes the passive voice is useful or necessary, but usually it should be avoided.

D. Consider Using the First Person

We all have a great deal of experience telling other people what we did or what happened to us: "I caught a bus from the airport to the hotel, then called the airline to see if they had been able to trace my luggage." This experience may be turned to advantage in writing papers by using the first person. Instead of writing:

> This paper will be devoted to showing that the governmental mechanisms introduced by the invading forces were successful only because they made use of existing social structures.

write:

> I will show that the governmental mechanisms introduced by the invading forces were successful only because they made use of existing social structures.

The first person is often avoided in academic papers, although rarely for good reasons. Even if you're writing a paper as part of a research team, you should consider using first person, plural—*we*. Avoiding the first person only because papers written in the third person sound more "authoritative" or "scientific" is foolish. "We assigned each person to either an experimental group or a control group" is not less scientific than "Each person was assigned to either an experimental group or a control group."

E. Use Examples

Principles, rules, descriptions of procedures, and other abstractions are difficult to grasp if the explanation isn't accompanied by an example.

Imagine how hard it would be to understand multiplication without an example. It's perhaps even more difficult to understand *representative democracy, just war, market economy, legal tort,* or *use-mention distinction* without at least one example.

F. Write for an Audience

Writing is a way of conducting a one-sided conversation. You have something you want to say to the reader, and although the reader is prepared to listen, she can't ask you any questions. This means that you have to put yourself in the reader's place and try to imagine what she knows already, what she needs to be told, where she is going to be hardest to convince, and where she is likely to get confused and need extra help.

Keep in mind that what you write will be read by someone much like yourself. If you think something you've written is confusing or difficult to understand, you can be sure that another reader will have the same experience. If you think something might be confusing, then the chances are good that for someone else it will be confusing. Change it.

Decide who you want your audience to be. Do you want to write something appropriate for readers of *Cosmopolitan* or for readers of the *Journal of Social Psychology?* Is it to be read by others in your Social Psychology class or published in the campus newspaper? Your thesis may be the same for all audiences, but the way you present the arguments and evidence for it surely must be different.

G. Revise

No one gets everything right the first time.

Everyone must revise, but not everyone must do it the same way. Some people work best by writing a quick draft, then going back and correcting it. Such people may go through several complete drafts before finishing the paper. Others labor over one paragraph at a time, writing it and revising it as often as needed before going on to the next.

Revise in whatever way works best for you, but do it.

H. Check Spelling and Grammar

Misspelled words and incorrect grammar distract the reader from the aims of the paper. What's more, the reader is likely to distrust the intellectual qualifications of a writer who is unable to use even the basic tools properly.

Few people spell well, so get accustomed to looking up words in dictionaries. The spelling checkers of word-processing programs have a limited vocabulary and aren't context sensitive, so be careful in choosing among the options they offer. (If you don't know the difference between *it's* and *its, they're* and *their,* you need to learn it.)

Also, computers aren't so good at parsing sentences that you can rely on grammar-checking programs to determine that your paper is grammatically correct and punctuated properly. The program may raise questions, but you have to be able to answer them. This means you must learn the rules of English grammar and punctuation (or at least be prepared to look them up in a reference work).

* * *

Advice about writing is worthless unless you make an effort to put it into practice. Writing well, like rock climbing and surfing, is a skill that can be acquired, but no one can acquire it who is not willing to work at it.

Working directly with a reader can be a major help. When you've completed a draft of a paper you think is good, ask someone else to read it. Then talk to the person and try to find out if parts of the paper were unclear, dull, confusing, or irrelevant. Ask if the thesis was clear and the arguments for it clearly stated. Finally, ask the person to suggest ways the paper could be made more effective.

"Easy writing," the poet Byron said, "makes damned hard reading." The rule, then, is work hard to make the reading easy.

EXERCISES:
SOME ANSWERS, HINTS,
AND COMMENTS

Some exercises have straightforward answers, but others may depend on interpretations of meanings, intentions, or situations. The answers here are based on reasonable interpretations, but other reasonable interpretations may be possible and may yield different answers. More important than getting the "right" answer in such cases is being aware of the possibilities and approaching them with a questioning and analytical attitude.

As the title above indicates, sometimes we give not so much an answer as a hint or comment on the exercise.

Chapter 1

A. *(p. 15)*

1. Not an argument. No claim here is intended to provide support for any other.

3. A complex argument. In the first sentence, the word *so* indicates that what follows is a conclusion drawn from the previous claim. This conclusion in turn is a premise for "the job will go to Herbert," as indicated by the conclusion indicator word *thus*.

5. A simple argument. Although there are no indicator words, the first three claims are each independent evidence for the last claim.

7. Not an argument.

9. Not an argument.

11. A simple argument. The first two sentences are claims intended to provide support for the last sentence.

13. A simple argument. The quoted passage constitutes the man's support for the conclusion that his wife had the right to commit suicide.

15. A simple argument. The conclusion is "we should not have a constitutional amendment banning flag burning." The following claims are all in support of this conclusion.

17. A simple argument. We should regard "ritual or habitual cannibalism is either rare or non-existent" as the conclusion. What follows this claim is the support for it.

19. There appear to be two distinct arguments here, one complex and one simple. The conclusion is the same in each case: there should be copyright laws. The complex argument goes like this: compensating people encourages more creative works and our society benefits from these works; *therefore* people have a right to compensation for their creative work; *therefore* there should be copyright laws. The simple argument is a little harder to see, but try this: if there were no copyright laws then the only creative works would be those arising from the support of government and rich patrons; but there should be creative work arising other than from the support of government and rich patrons; *therefore* there should be copyright laws.

B. *(p. 17)*

1. Unstated premise: anything that deliberately leads us to see an ordinary object in a new and interesting way is a genuine work of art.

3. Unstated conclusion: Lopez ought to resign as governor.

5. Unstated conclusion: there is no justification for allowing Hovey to compete.

7. Unstated premise: any case of killing a living human being is murder.

9. Unstated conclusion: I should not completely trust my senses.

11. Unstated conclusion: There is no god.

13. Unstated premise: anything that is offensive to a lot of us should be outlawed.

15. Unstated premise: if at one time there was nothing in existence, then now there would be nothing in existence.

17. Unstated premise: the table itself does not change as I change my perspective.

19. Unstated conclusion: the killer was Colonel Sebastian Moran.

Chapter 2

A. *(p. 31)*

1. An explanation.
3. An explanation.
5. An explanation.
7. Neither.
9. Neither.
11. An argument.
13. Neither.

15. An explanation.
17. Neither.
19. An explanation.

B. *(p. 33)*

1. Higher speed limits will result in more needless deaths on the highway.

   The speed limits should not be raised.

3. 1. Without a tax increase there will soon be runaway inflation.
   2. Congress refuses to raise taxes.
   3. There will soon be runaway inflation. 1, 2
   4. You should borrow all the money you can right now. 3

5. 1. Studying history makes a person less likely to repeat the mistakes of the past.
   2. Not repeating past mistakes is a sign of wisdom.
   3. People who study history are wiser than those who do not. 1, 2
   4. The primary aim of education is producing wisdom.
   5. All universities should require the study of history. 3, 4

7. 1. Anything worth recording has been entered in the ship's log.
   2. A mermaid would be worth recording.
   3. If I had seen a mermaid it would have been entered in the ship's log. 1, 2
   4. There is nothing about a mermaid in the ship's log.
   5. I have never seen a mermaid. 3, 4

9. 1. Higher education should increase our ability to think critically and appreciate a greater variety of experiences.
   2. It is good to take courses in the humanities, sciences, and social science. 1
   3. Students who take the advanced-level course in twentieth-century American poetry have made a wise choice. 2

11. 1. The only people we have seen in the last three hours have been toting big backpacks.
    2. We must be pretty far from civilization. 1
    3. We had better turn around before we get lost in the middle of nowhere. 2

13. 1. The butler was passionately in love with the victim.
    2. The butler did not commit the murder. 1
    3. Either the butler or the judge committed the murder.
    4. The judge committed the murder. 2, 3

15. 1. White racists are especially unreliable witnesses when the accused is a person of color.
     2. If the detective is really a racist he should not have been allowed to testify. 1
     3. The detective is a racist.
     4. The detective should not have been allowed to testify. 2, 3

17. 1. If Angelina is wise, she will enter the singing contest.
     2. Angelina is wise.
     3. Angelina will enter the singing contest. 1, 2
     4. If Angelina enters the singing contest, she will have a great career in show business.
     5. Angelina will have a great career in show business. 3, 4

19. 1. The liquid is either acidic or alkaline.
     2. If the liquid is acidic the paper will turn red.
     3. If the liquid is alkaline the paper will turn blue.
     4. The paper will either turn red or blue. 1, 2, 3
     5. I am color blind.
     6. I will not be able to tell if the liquid is acidic or alkaline. 4, 5

21. 1. Either this is the bottom of the market or it is a bad time for investors.
     2. If this is the bottom of the market, then the Fed will not lower rates.
     3. The Fed will lower rates.
     4. This is not the bottom of the market 2, 3
     5. This is a bad time for investors 1, 4

Chapter 3

A. *(p. 42)*

1. Invalid. Genevieve might deserve punishment for some other infraction.
3. Valid.
5. Invalid. Obviously, this argument has two true premises and a false conclusion.
7. Valid.
9. Valid.
11. Valid. If the premises *were* true, the conclusion would have to be true too.
13. Valid.

15. Valid.

17. Invalid. It is possible that you might not take the medicine according to the directions.

19. Valid.

B. *(p. 52)*

1. Valid.

3. Non-deductively successful, though there are many ways she might fail to do very well.

5. Non-deductively successful. Again, although this is not a particularly strong argument, the premise does make the conclusion somewhat likely.

7. Unsuccessful.

9. Non-deductively successful. Although the premise does not guarantee the conclusion, if the statistical claim in the premise is true then the conclusion is quite likely.

11. Perhaps non-deductively successful. However, since the sample is limited and biased towards zoo-dwelling animals, it's hard to see that the premise makes the general conclusion more than barely likely.

13. Unsuccessful.

15. Non-deductively successful.

17. Unsuccessful. In order to be successful, this argument needs a premise linking the factual claims in the premises to the value claim in the conclusion.

19. Non-deductively successful. Most of the inferences in this complex argument are deductively valid. However, the last inference is non-deductively successful, and this characterizes the whole argument.

C. *(p. 57)*

1. The premise about the nature of good literature seems questionably true.

3. A case of relevant information not being taken into account. A calculus professor is much more likely than other intellectuals to know about a mathematical proposition.

5. The premise is irrelevant. The best debater may not be the best manager.

7. Again, a problem of relevance.

9. The premise is almost certainly false.

11. An odd argument in which the premise is entirely irrelevant to the conclusion.

13. Unless Bailey's Gym is the only option, the premises do not lead to the conclusion that it is this particular gym you should attend.

15. The premise is debatable at best.

17. The most obvious problem with this argument is that the premise appears to be false. It suggests that only these two options are possible. Yet, it may be the case that the administration had good reason to believe that there were weapons of mass destruction even though it wasn't true, in which case it would not have been lying. The mistake in this argument sometimes goes by the name of the fallacy of false dilemma.

19. You don't have to know anything about soccer to recognize the flaw in this argument. The conclusion is based only on evidence about the US team and makes no mention of the qualities of the opposition. Without knowing how good the opposition are, the premises give us no good reason to believe that "the US has as good a chance as anyone."

Chapter 4

A. *(p. 63)*

1. $(Q \bullet R) \to (W \vee F)$

3. $E \to (A \to B)$

   $$\frac{A \bullet E}{B}$$

5. $(M \bullet C) \to B$

   $$\frac{\sim B}{\sim M \vee \sim C}$$

B. *(p. 69)*

1. *Modus ponens.* Valid.

3. Denying the antecedent. Invalid.

5. Affirming the consequent. Invalid.

7. *Modus tollens.* Valid.

9. *Modus ponens.* Valid.

11. Affirming the consequent. Invalid.

13. Hypothetical syllogism. Valid.

15. *Modus ponens.* Valid.

17. Hypothetical syllogism. Valid.

19. Addition. Valid.

21. Conjunction. Valid.

23. Constructive dilemma. Valid.

25. Affirming the consequent. Invalid.

C. *(p. 70)*

1. $\sim F \to \sim G$

   $\dfrac{G}{F}$

   Modus tollens. Valid.

3. S

   $\overline{S \lor P}$

   Addition. Valid.

5. $G \lor C$

   $\dfrac{\sim G}{C}$

   Disjunctive syllogism. Valid.

7. $A \to \sim P$

   $\dfrac{A}{\sim P}$

   Modus ponens. Valid.

9. $S \lor D$

   $\dfrac{\sim D}{S}$

   DS. Valid.

D. *(p. 74)*

1.
   1. $\sim H \to (B \lor L)$
   2. $\sim H$
   3. $B \lor L$ 1, 2   MP
   4. $\sim L$
   5. B 3, 4   DS

E. *(p. 74)*

1.
   1. $E \to (A \to B)$
   2. $A \cdot E$
   3. A 2   Simp
   4. E 2   Simp
   5. $A \to B$ 1, 4   MP
   6. B 3, 5   MP

3.
   1. $S \to P$
   2. $P \to L$
   3. S

	4.	P	1, 3	MP
	5.	L	2, 4	MP
5.	1.	$K \rightarrow W$		
	2.	$W \rightarrow H$		
	3.	$\sim H$		
	4.	$\sim W$	2, 3	MT
	5.	$\sim K$	1, 4	MT
7.	1.	$V \vee E$		
	2.	$M \rightarrow \sim V$		
	3.	M		
	4.	$\sim V$	2, 3	MP
	5.	E	1, 4	DS
	6.	$E \rightarrow \sim P$		
	7.	$\sim P$	5, 6	MP
9.	1.	$P \rightarrow Q$		
	2.	$P \vee R$		
	3.	S		
	4.	$S \rightarrow \sim Q$		
	5.	$\sim Q$	3, 4	MP
	6.	$\sim P$	1, 5	MT
	7.	R	2, 6	DS

F. *(p. 80)*

   2. b and d.

G. *(p. 80)*

2.	1.	$\sim E \rightarrow L$		
	2.	$\sim L \rightarrow E$	1	Contra
4.	1.	$\sim(A \cdot D)$		
	2.	$\sim A \vee \sim D$	1	DM
6.	1.	$\sim S \rightarrow O$		
	2.	$S \vee O$	1	Imp
8.	1.	$C \rightarrow \sim H$		
	2.	$\sim\sim H$		
	3.	$\sim C$	1, 2	MT
10.	1.	$\sim G \vee \sim P$		
	2.	$\sim(G \cdot P)$	1	DM

H. *(p. 83)*

1. 1. $B \rightarrow L$
    2. $L \rightarrow P$
    3. $B \rightarrow P$ 1, 2   HS
    4. $\sim P$
    5. $\sim B$ 3, 4   MT
    6. $\sim B \rightarrow I$
    7. I 5, 6   MP

3. 1. $F \rightarrow (T \rightarrow \sim L)$
    2. L
    3. $(F \bullet T) \rightarrow \sim L$ 1   Exp
    4. $\sim (F \bullet T)$ 2, 3   MT
    5. $\sim F \vee \sim T$ 4   DM

5. 1. $L \rightarrow (\sim P \rightarrow \sim B)$
    2. $L \bullet \sim P$
    3. L 2   Simp
    4. $\sim P \rightarrow \sim B$ 1, 3   MP
    5. $\sim P$ 2   Simp
    6. $\sim B$ 4, 5   MP

7. 1. $G \rightarrow (L \rightarrow F)$
    2. $G \bullet \sim F$
    3. G 2   Simp
    4. $L \rightarrow F$ 1, 3   MP
    5. $\sim F$ 2   Simp
    6. $\sim L$ 4, 5   MT

9. 1. $(\sim P \vee Q) \rightarrow \sim (R \bullet \sim S)$
    2. R
    3. $\sim P$
    4. $\sim P \vee Q$ 3   Add
    5. $\sim (R \bullet \sim S)$ 1, 4   MP
    6. $\sim R \vee S$ 5   DM
    7. S 2, 6   DS

11. 1. $Q \vee (R \bullet S)$
    2. $\sim Q$
    3. $S \rightarrow (T \vee U)$
    4. $R \bullet S$ 1, 2   DS
    5. S 4   Simp

6.	$T \vee U$		3, 5	MP
7.	$\sim T \rightarrow U$		6	Imp
13. 1.	$\sim(\sim P \bullet \sim Q) \rightarrow R$			
2.	P			
3.	$\sim\sim P$		2	DN
4.	$\sim\sim P \vee \sim\sim Q$		3	Add
5.	$\sim(\sim P \bullet \sim Q)$		4	DM
6.	R		1, 5	MP

Chapter 5

A. *(p. 91)*

1.

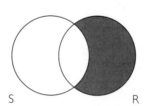

3.

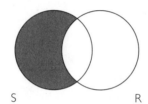

5.

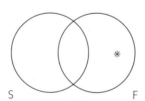

7.

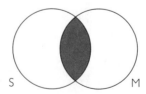

9.

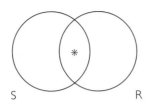

11.

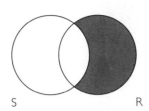

13.

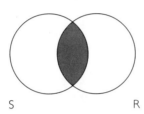

15.

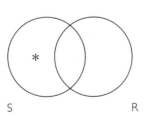

B.   *(p. 98)*

1.

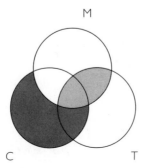

Regions 3 and 4 are shaded, so there is nothing in the intersection between machines and thinkers. The argument is valid.

3.

Dangerous things

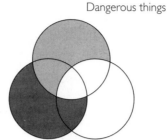

Fallacies   Things to be avoided

Regions 2 and 5 are shaded, thus nothing in the set of fallacies is outside the set of things to be avoided. The syllogism is valid.

5. Valid

7. Valid

9. Invalid

11. Valid

13. Invalid

15. Valid

17. Invalid

19. Valid

Chapter 6

A. *(p. 116)*

1. b, d (When hair loss is due to vitamin deficiency it can be restored by taking vitamins, so 4 may be appropriate.)

3. h

5. e

B. *(p. 116)*

1. d

3. a (The claim may be false, unless "freedom" is understood in some special way.)

5. e (The icing may have been the proximate cause.)

7. b ("One of the causes" is usually understood as sufficient condition [one of several]. Viral infection is also "one of the causes" of fever.

[Strictly, either infection is only one of the factors that combines with others to constitute a set of factors sufficient for fever.])

9.   e and f (It was a factor Hitler controlled; from the historian's standpoint, it was a standing condition for some events.)

11.   b (Earthquakes may also result from volcanic activity and land subsidence, so plate activity is not a necessary condition.)

13.   e

15.   c

Chapter 7

B.   *(p. 132)*

1.   Moral. Points of resemblance: Paying workers for work done. Points of difference: People paid by reparations are not the people who did the work.

3.   Moral. Points of resemblance are the test conditions and that creatures able to experience pain are being caused pain and eye damage. A point to debate is whether it matters that the creature in the test is a rabbit and the one in comparison ("you") is a human. Also to discuss: Does it matter that the aim of the test is to produce a safe cosmetic, rather than (say) a safe drug that would benefit humans to some extent? Does the extent of the benefit matter (e.g., clearing up nasal congestion vs. saving life)?

9.   Factual. Earth and Mars are said to be alike in that both have an atmosphere with clouds and mists, seas, land, and snowy polar regions. Earth has inhabitants. Thus, Mars must have them as well.

   We now know that some of the claimed resemblances either do not exist or are not as close as once thought. Mars has no seas and no (free) atmosphere. Even when this was not known, and even granting the resemblances asserted, the conclusion ("Mars must have inhabitants") is much too strong for the premises to establish as likely, much less as virtually certain.

D.   *(p. 135)*

1.   Mental illness is still diagnosed in terms of the behavior and subjective reports of afflicted people. This is true of the two major psychoses: bipolar (manic-depressive) disorder and schizophrenia. Schizophrenia, for example, may involve visual or auditory hallucinations, flattened affect (little or no emotional response), inappropriate affect (laughing upon hearing a friend has died, for example), or paranoid delusions (thinking people are talking about you or plotting against you).

   With animals, we have no way of knowing whether they are hallucinating; we may judge some animal behavior as indicating depression, and for some animals (such as the primates), we may judge inappropriate affect. However, we have no way to determine whether animals are subject to delusions. In general, the range of traits we identify as manifestations of mental illness have not been identified in animals. Consequently, we are in no position to test most causal hypotheses.

Compare this situation with the study of somatic diseases. We can identify diabetes (for example) in rats and investigate the mechanisms involved in producing changes that distinguish normal sugar metabolism from abnormal. We can breed the rats and track the genes involved, and we can feed the rats special diets and observe the outcomes. We cannot identify schizophrenia in animals and so are stopped from additional direct inquiry.

Chapter 8

A.   *(p. 155)*

   1.   Appeal to ignorance (*Ad ignorantiam*)
   5.   Legitimate argument
   12.   *Post hoc*

B.   *(p. 156)*

   1.   False dilemma
   3.   Begging the question/circular argument
   5.   Slippery slope

C.   *(p. 157)*

   2.   Pooh-pooh
   4.   Definitional dodge
   5.   Straw man

D.   *(p. 159)*

   4.   False dilemma
   7.   *Ad hominem*
   12.   Loaded words

Chapter 9

A.   *(p. 171)*

   1.   12 = dozen
        cop = police officer

   2.   Sonnet = a poetic form consisting of 14 lines
        shirt = an article of clothing for the upper body

3. [by pointing appropriately]

4. beverage: tea
   fruit: orange

5. parent: mother, father

B. *(p. 172) Use your experience.*

C. *(p. 172)*

1. Stipulative precising

4. Reportive lexical

D. *(p. 173)*

1. Ostention

3. Genus (space) and species (nonexecutive). Also by example: "supply room" and so on.

6. Synonym

12. Genus (surgical instrument) and species (spoon-shaped and used to remove tissue from a body cavity)

E. *(p. 174)*

1. Too broad: includes stools, tables, etc.

7. Metaphorical language

9. Accidental feature. Being sacred in India is true of cows but not a feature governing the use of the word "cow."

12. Circular

Chapter 10

A. *(p. 185)*

1. "American forces" (name services or even units involved); "limited casualties" (how many and of what sort, injuries or fatalities); "substantial number" (how many); "weapons" (what kind).

4. The advertising phrases "as much as" and "selected items" are deliberately vague. The first tells us is that we can't expect to save more than 50 percent on anything. Although the "selected items" could be specified, advertisers like to generate hope and excitement.

10. How is "proficiency" to be determined?

C. *(p. 186)*

2. Something like this should do: We are a nation of people who come, directly or by heritage, from many lands; we are a nation of many races, many religions, many beliefs. We prize both diversity

and individuality and reject prejudice and conformity. In our country, people are permitted to be themselves, making their own choices and shaping their own lives."

E.   *(p. 188)*

4. Word. "Normal" may mean "most frequent statistically" or "nondiseased."

6. Grammatical. "What do insects smell like?" or "By what means do insects smell?"

Chapter 11

A.   *(p. 202)*

1. The event seems unlikely, but reliable witnesses suggest that it did happen. Also, we know of numerous cases in which people have lived after falling considerable distances.

B.   *(p. 205)*

1. Analytically true (given our convention for naming the days of the week)

5. Analytically false. All triangles are three-sided figures, but not all three-sided figures are triangles—for example, those that are unclosed and shaped like a ⊔ or a *.

C.   *(p. 206)*

1. Philosophically vexed. We can imagined advanced computers (or androids like C3-P0) that we might be willing to call persons because of their behavior, yet they feel no pain (or don't report feeling pain).

INDEX

THE AUTHORS

Ronald Munson, a nationally acclaimed bioethicist, teaches at the University of Missouri–St. Louis. He was educated at Columbia University (Ph.D. in Philosophy) and Harvard University (Postdoctoral Fellow in Biology). A medical ethicist for the National Institutes of Health, he is the author of *Intervention and Reflection: Basic Issues in Medical Ethics,* 7th ed., the nation's best-selling bioethics text, and *Raising the Dead: Organ Transplants, Ethics, and Society,* named a Best Book in Science and Medicine in 2002 by the American Library Association. Known for his clear, accurate, and vivid writing, Munson is also the author of the novels *Nothing Human, Fan Mail,* and *Night Vision.*

Andrew Black was educated at University College, London, and University of Massachusetts, Amherst, from which he received his Ph.D. He taught at Dartmouth College and Southern Illinois University, Carbondale, and is currently Affiliate Assistant Professor at University of Missouri–St. Louis. He has published in the areas of history of philosophy and epistemology and is the writer and presenter of the educational television series *Great Philosophers.*